THE AUSTRALIAN EMBASSY IN TOKYO AND AUSTRALIA–JAPAN RELATIONS

THE AUSTRALIAN EMBASSY IN TOKYO AND AUSTRALIA–JAPAN RELATIONS

EDITED BY KATE DARIAN-SMITH
AND DAVID LOWE

Australian
National
University

ANU PRESS

Australian
National
University

ANU PRESS

Published by ANU Press
The Australian National University
Canberra ACT 2600, Australia
Email: anupress@anu.edu.au

Available to download for free at press.anu.edu.au

ISBN (print): 9781760465391
ISBN (online): 9781760465407

WorldCat (print): 1348276014
WorldCat (online): 1348275797

DOI: 10.22459/AETAJR.2022

Cover design and layout by ANU Press

Cover photograph: Night view of entry. Australian embassy, Tokyo, Japan, c. 1990.
Architects: Denton Corker Marshall Pty Ltd. Photograph by John Gollings.

This book is published under the aegis of the Social Sciences editorial board
of ANU Press.

Contents

Abbreviations

A£	Australian pound (pre-1966 currency)
ABC	Australian Broadcasting Corporation
ACTU	Australian Council of Trade Unions
ADF	Australian Defence Force
AJBCC	Australia Japan Business Co-operation Committee
AJF	Australia–Japan Foundation
ANU	The Australian National University
ANZLSJ	Australia and New Zealand Literary Society of Japan
ANZUS	Australia, New Zealand and United States (Security Treaty)
AOST	Australian–Overseas Student Travel
APEC	Asia-Pacific Economic Cooperation
ARPANSA	Australian Radiation Protection and Nuclear Safety Agency
ASAJ	Australian Studies Association of Japan
ASEAN	Association of Southeast Asian Nations
BCOF	British Commonwealth Occupation Force
CCRJ	Consultative Committee on Relations with Japan
CITES	Convention on International Trade in Endangered Species
CPAS	Center for Pacific and American Studies (Tokyo University)
CSR	Commonwealth Sugar Refinery
DCM	Denton Corker Marshall
DFAT	Department of Foreign Affairs and Trade (Australia)
FCN	treaty of friendship, commerce and navigation
FTA	free trade agreement

GATT	General Agreement on Tariffs and Trade
GNP	gross national product
ICJ	International Court of Justice
INTERFET	International Force East Timor
JAEPA	Japan–Australia Economic Partnership Agreement
JDSC	Joint Declaration on Security Cooperation
LES	locally engaged staff
MFP	multifunction polis
MITI	Ministry of International Trade and Industry (Japan)
MOFA	Ministry of Foreign Affairs (Japan)
NAA	National Archives of Australia
NALSAS	National Asian Languages and Studies in Australian Schools
NLA	National Library of Australia
OECD	Organisation for Economic Co-operation and Development
OPG	Overseas Property Group
PAFTAD	Pacific Trade and Development (Conference)
RAAF	Royal Australian Air Force
SCAP	supreme commander for the Allied powers
SCJ	Standing Committee on Japan
TEPCO	Tokyo Electric Power Company
TPP	Trans-Pacific Partnership
UNTAET	UN Transitional Administration in East Timor
WTO	World Trade Organization
YWCA	Young Women's Christian Association

List of Illustrations

Figures

Tables

Australian Diplomatic Representation in Japan

Trade Commissioner/Commissioner
Eric Edwin Longfield Lloyd, 7 June 1935–17 August 1940.

Ministers to Japan
John Latham, 17 August 1940–8 December 1941.
Suspension of relations, 8 December 1941–30 March 1947.
William Macmahon Ball, 30 March 1947–17 August 1947.
Patrick Shaw (acting), 27 August 1947–12 September 1949.
William Roy Hodgson, 12 September 1949–18 April 1952.

Ambassadors to Japan
Edward Ronald Walker, 18 April 1952–17 December 1955.
Alan Watt, 22 February 1956–8 November 1959.
Laurence McIntyre, 1960–1965.
Allen Brown, February 1965–April 1970.
Gordon Freeth, April 1970–December 1973.
Mick Shann, December 1973–February 1977.
John Menadue, 2 March 1977–August 1980.
James Plimsoll, January 1981–September 1982.
Neil Currie, October 1982–August 1986.
Geoff Miller, August 1986–1989.
Rawdon Dalrymple, 1989–December 1993.
Ashton Calvert, December 1993–1998.
Peter Grey, March 1998–June 2001.

John McCarthy, June 2001–2004.
Murray McLean, 24 November 2004–July 2011.
Bruce Miller, August 2011–January 2017.
Richard Court, February 2017–October 2020.
Jan Adams, November 2020–June 2022.

Key Treaties and Events

1927   Japan–Australia Association formed by business firms and bankers.

1932   The Ottawa Agreement upheld the principle of preferential trade and confirmed Britain as Australia's most important customer and central to its trading interests. Countries such as Japan, while important to Australia, had to take second place behind the trading concerns of the United Kingdom.

1934   The 1934 Australian Eastern Mission—Australia's first diplomatic mission outside of Britain and its empire—sent Attorney-General John Latham to the countries of East and Southeast Asia. Popularly known as the 'Goodwill Mission', this included Latham's goodwill visit to Tokyo.

1936   22 May: the Australian government further entrenched the principle of preferential trade with the implementation of a new Australian trade policy—a 'trade diversion policy'. Tariff rates were to be raised substantially and a special licensing system introduced which would discriminate against imports from countries such as Japan and the United States while favouring British imports. Before May 1936, Japan and Australia had been negotiating a treaty of friendship, commerce and navigation. This was abandoned. The bitter trade dispute in 1936, together with the Australian iron ore embargo, left a disagreeable aftertaste in commercial relations, and trade between the two countries did not fully recover for many years.

1936–37   Australian exports to Japan more than halved and continued to fall. Japanese imports of Australian wool and wheat declined noticeably in the late 1930s.

1940   17 August: Sir John Latham appointed first Australian minister to Japan.

1941   8 December: Australian prime minister John Curtin declared war on Japan.

1945   6 and 9 August: Atomic bombs dropped on Japan.

15 August: Japanese emperor Hirohito announces surrender, which is officially accepted on 2 September.

1947   Australian embassy established in Tokyo.

1947–48   The Sterling Payments Agreement settled the mode of payment between Australia and Japan and overcame one of the main practical obstacles to trade, setting trade between the two countries on a firm footing.

1952   28 April: the San Francisco Peace Treaty with Japan, signed by Australia, entered into force.

Land and residence for Australian embassy in Tokyo purchased by the Australian government.

1953   Japanese embassy established in Australia.

1955   Late October: Japan requested that Australia consider a new commerce treaty.

1957   First visit to Japan by an Australian prime minister (Robert Menzies). First visit to Australia by a Japanese prime minister (Nobusuke Kishi).

6 July: Agreement on Commerce between Japan and the Commonwealth of Australia signed; a major Australia–Japan trading relationship formalised and sustained.

1963   5 August: After incorporating amendments, the revised Agreement on Commerce between Australia and Japan was provisionally agreed to and signed in Tokyo. Japanese prime minister Hayato Ikeda visited Australia in September–October 1963. Japan and Australia suggested making concerted efforts towards regional economic stability.

1964   April–June: Protocol amending the Agreement on Commerce between Australia and Japan came into force on 27 May 1964.

27 May: Agreement on Commerce between Australia and Japan ratified and came into force, Canberra.

1966   19 December: The Asian Development Bank, of which Australia and Japan were founding members, opened in Manila with Japan's Takeshi Watanabe as the bank's first president.

1966–67   After years of gradually narrowing the gap, Japan finally supplanted the United Kingdom as Australia's largest export market. It held that position until 2007, when it was overtaken by China.

1968–69   27 November 1968: Agreement on Fisheries between the Commonwealth of Australia and Japan signed in Canberra. Ratified in Tokyo on 25 July 1969, it entered into force on 24 August 1969.

Organization for Pacific Trade and Development was first advocated by Kiyoshi Kojima and Peter Drysdale at the 1968 Pacific Trade and Development (PAFTAD) Conference.

1970   Agreement between Japan and the Commonwealth of Australia for the Avoidance of Double Taxation and the Prevention of Fiscal Evasion with respect to Taxes on Income entered into force.

1972   Australia and Japan established the Australia–Japan Ministerial Committee, first meeting in Canberra.

1973   Prime Minister Whitlam visited Japan and proposed the idea of a general treaty: Japan accepted immediately. The second meeting of the Australia–Japan Ministerial Committee was held in Tokyo.

The Australia–Japan Research Centre (AJRC) was initiated as the Australia, Japan and Western Pacific Economic Relations Research Committee, which, in 1980, became the Australia–Japan Research Centre when it was endowed by the Japanese government, Australian government, and Japanese and Australian business communities. The founding director was Professor Peter Drysdale.

1974   1 November: Cultural Agreement between the Government of Japan and the Government of Australia signed. Gordon Freeth formed the Australia Japan Society of WA.

1975   Third meeting of the Australia–Japan Ministerial Committee was held in Canberra. March: the Australia–Japan Relations Symposium was held in the Australian Academy of Science, Canberra.

1976   16 June: Prime Minister Fraser visited Tokyo and signed the Basic Treaty of Friendship and Cooperation between Japan and Australia, with Japanese prime minister Takeo Miki.

The Crawford–Ōkita Report delivered.

Australia–Japan Foundation (AJF) established, with headquarters in Canberra, supported by an office at the Australian embassy in Tokyo.

1977   Fourth meeting of the Australia–Japan Ministerial Committee held, Tokyo. 21 August: Basic Treaty of Friendship and Cooperation came into force.

1978   26–27 June: fifth meeting of the Australia–Japan Ministerial Committee held.

1980   15–17 January: Japanese prime minister Masayoshi Ōhira visited Australia.

9–10 June: sixth meeting of the Australia–Japan Ministerial Committee held.

September: Pacific Community Seminar held in Canberra, considered to be the first meeting of the Pacific Economic Cooperation Council (PECC).

Australia–Japan Research Centre (AJRC) established at The Australian National University.

1982   Australia–Japan Relations Symposium held in Melbourne. The Australia–Japan Relations Essay Contest established.

1983   *Continuum '83*: the first exhibition of Australian contemporary art in Japan is held.

1988   Australian embassy in Tokyo was redeveloped—as part of the redevelopment, the old residence in Mita district of Tokyo was demolished to make way for the new embassy.

1989   January: Asia-Pacific Economic Cooperation (APEC) forum established.

The Garnaut Report was published: Ross Garnaut, *Australia and the Northeast Asian Ascendancy*.

1990	Ambassador's residence and staff apartments at the Australian embassy in Tokyo were completed.
1995	May: Joint Declaration on the Australia–Japan Partnership was made by Prime Ministers Paul Keating and Tomiichi Murayama.
1997	August: Australia–Japan Partnership Agenda formalised.
1997–98	Asian financial crisis.
1998	Japan Australia Friendship Association established: a social and cultural non-profit volunteer organisation to promote friendship between Australia and Japan.
2000	17 August: *Japan's Economy Implications for Australia* is published by the Australian Senate Standing Committee on Foreign Affairs, Defence and Trade.
2002	'Australia–Japan Creative Partnership' Prime Ministerial Joint Statement made by Prime Ministers John Howard and Junichiro Koizumi.
2003	16 July: Australia–Japan Trade and Economic Framework signed in Tokyo.
	16 July: Australia–Japan Joint Statement on Cooperation to Combat International Terrorism made in Tokyo.
	Memorandum of Defence Exchange signed.
2006	Australia–Japan Year of Exchange.
	Australia–Japan Joint Ministerial Statement on Building a Comprehensive Strategic Partnership.
2007	27 February: Agreement between Australia and Japan on Social Security signed in Canberra.
	12 March: Memorandum on Cooperation in Education between the Ministry of Education, Culture, Sports, Science and Technology of Japan and the Department of Education, Science and Training of Australia signed in Tokyo.
	13 March: Australia–Japan Joint Declaration on Security Cooperation signed in Tokyo.
	Australia–Japan Free Trade Agreement talks launched.
	Inaugural Australia–Japan 2+2 Foreign and Defence Ministerial Consultations held.

2008   31 January: Australia–Japan Convention for the Avoidance of Double Taxation and the Prevention of Fiscal Evasion with Respect to Taxes on Income signed in Tokyo.

12 June: Australia–Japan Joint Ministerial Statement on Comprehensive Strategic, Security and Economic Partnership made by Prime Ministers Kevin Rudd and Yasuo Fukuda.

2010   Australia–Japan Acquisition and Cross-Servicing Agreement signed.

2012   Japan–Australia Information Security Agreement signed.

2015   15 January: Australia–Japan Economic Partnership Agreement signed and in effect.

2016   March: the Australian embassy in Tokyo held an afternoon tea to commemorate the fifth anniversary of the 2011 Tohoku earthquake and tsunami.

25 July: sixth ministerial meeting of the Trilateral Strategic Dialogue held, in Laos.

2017   20 April: the seventh Australia–Japan 2+2 Foreign and Defence Ministerial Consultations are held.

2018   2 July: First Japan–Australia Economic Dialogue held in Tokyo.

4 August: Australia–Japan–United States Trilateral Strategic Dialogue held in Singapore.

2020   January: Second Ministerial Economic Dialogue.

July: Australia's and Japan's prime ministers held the first-ever virtual summit.

November: the Reciprocal Access Agreement between Australia and Japan was signed, enabling increased defence cooperation.

2021   11 March: Representatives from the Australian embassy in Tokyo attended the tenth memorial service for the Tohoku earthquake and tsunami, in Minamisanriku, Miyagi Prefecture.

Acknowledgements

This collection has been several years in the making. We are indebted to all its contributors, who have generously shared their expertise and experiences relating to the Australian embassy in Tokyo and the Australian–Japanese relationship.

The initial work in framing and developing this book benefited from a one-day seminar hosted by the Contemporary Histories Research Group at Deakin University in December 2017, and we thank all attendees for a stimulating gathering. Research was supported by a grant from the Australia–Japan Foundation in 2016–17, and this assisted us to undertake several oral histories with former Australian ambassadors to Japan, which are held by the National Library of Australia and are a resource for future research. We acknowledge the important role of the Australia–Japan Foundation in fostering rich bilateral ties and thank those we interviewed for their time and insights. A very special thank-you is extended to the Australian and locally engaged staff at the Australian embassy in Tokyo who were interviewed in both countries during the research.

Many colleagues in Australia and Japan, including those at the Center for American and Pacific Studies, University of Tokyo, have provided support and advice, as have members of the Australian Department of Foreign Affairs and Trade, both in Canberra and from the Australian embassy in Tokyo. Broader support for scholarly work has been provided by our own institutions: Deakin University and the University of Tasmania.

The comments of two anonymous peer reviewers, and those of the Social Sciences editorial board of ANU Press, have been invaluable in the preparation of the final manuscript. We are grateful for the support of Dr Claire McCarthy, Dr Kirstie Close and Ellen Gray in assisting with background research and other organisational tasks, and in particular thank Dr Jackie Dickenson for detailed research on some key issues and assistance with details large and small in bringing the book into fruition.

Foreword

Jan Adams AO PSM

As I sit down to write this foreword, Tokyo's cherry blossom trees are in full bloom. There are few better places to admire the fleeting beauty of Japan's favourite flower than the garden of the Australian embassy in Tokyo. The spectacle of the cherry blossoms in full bloom is truly breathtaking, making invitations to view the garden at this time of year much coveted in Tokyo.

When I took up my post as Australian ambassador to Japan, during the pandemic in 2020, there were very few high-level Australian visits to Japan and I was not able to travel much outside of Tokyo. Despite this, the embassy continued to be a hive of activity facilitating close linkages between Australia and Japan, both online and face to face in the embassy garden and residence.

Having worked extensively on Australia's trade relationship with Japan throughout my career, I had visited the embassy many times over the years before I commenced as ambassador. I have fond memories of first visiting in 1994 as part of the delegation for a senior ministerial meeting, and I visited regularly between 2005 and 2009 as Australia's ambassador for the environment and climate change.

When I came back for regular visits as chief negotiator for the Japan–Australia Economic Partnership Agreement, I always enjoyed the support of the embassy teams as well as a good briefing from the ambassador on the political context in Japan.

The gorgeous dining room at the ambassador's residence has hosted many lunches and dinners with Diet members, business partners and cultural figures. These occasions are of course important for transacting business but they also provide an opportunity to build trust with key contacts in a social setting.

I am privileged at the moment to be displaying some remarkable works of Australian art, including stunning pieces by Emily Kame Kngwarreye and Angelina Pwerle, on loan from Janet Holmes à Court AC (initially to my predecessor Richard Court AC and then generously extended to me).

The embassy property itself is holding up well in its middle age. In addition to the ambassador's residence and the chancery, the embassy is home to the diplomatic families who live on the compound. There is a strong community feel that reminds me of a small town in Australia. This shone through during the pandemic, when families confined to their apartments in isolation would receive food deliveries at the door from their neighbours and colleagues.

There are more than 30 children currently living on the compound and they are a central part of the embassy community. It is not uncommon for me to be taking a senior Japanese visitor on a tour of the garden and have a group of kids excitedly tear past on the way to the playground.

I would like to pay tribute to the Australian ambassadors who have served the bilateral relationship before me. Ambassadors from Ashton Calvert onward have all been mentors to me, and the chapters in this book contributed by Murray McLean AO and Bruce Miller AO reflect the great work that was taken on during their times and beyond. Together, they cover important times in the Australia–Japan relationship, and their reflections highlight the importance of our bilateral relationship.

It is an extraordinary honour to be following in their footsteps. We all bring different backgrounds to the role but we build on the work of our predecessors. As others have done before me, it is my objective to maintain momentum and leave an even more vibrant relationship to my successor.

The bilateral relationship continues to grow in profile and substance. With a similar vision for the Indo-Pacific region and a like-minded approach to the challenges facing us, Australia and Japan have become more intimate and more strategic as partners.

I am very pleased to see this slice of Australian diplomatic history so well accounted for in this book. I commend Professor Kate Darian-Smith and Professor David Lowe for editing the book, and each of the contributors for sharing their fascinating insights.

April 2022

1

The Australian Embassy in Tokyo and Australia–Japan Relations

Kate Darian-Smith and David Lowe

On 24 January 2017, the Australian embassy in Tokyo hosted an informal afternoon tea for three former Japanese ambassadors to Australia. We were fortunate to be present as Ambassador Yoshio Okawara (1976–80), Ambassador Masaji Takahashi (1998–2001) and Ambassador Hideaki Ueda (2005–7) generously reflected on their time in Australia and their interactions with Australia's leaders and ambassadorial representatives in Japan. These reminiscences were framed by broadbrush historical interpretations, situating the 1970s and early 1980s as crucial to the development of the Australia–Japan relationship, with Australia required to consider its regional relationship with Japan more seriously in the wake of Britain's joining the European Community. The Basic Treaty of Friendship and Cooperation (known as the NARA Treaty, from 'Nippon Australia Relations Agreement') signed in 1976 was recalled as important in this process, although the bargaining over some of its terms was hard. The Japanese ambassadors also acknowledged the rich people-to-people interactions they experienced with Australians, both at official levels and in more vernacular terms. The deepening cultural ties between the two nations, such as the spread of 'sister city' agreements between municipal authorities, and exchanges of school students and tourists in both directions, were enthusiastically noted. The ambassadors also recalled key individuals who contributed to the bilateral relationship, such as the transformative efforts of Japanese-speaking Ashton Calvert during the 1990s and early 2000s, first as Australia's ambassador in Tokyo and then as secretary of the Department of Foreign Affairs and Trade; and key moments when the social and diplomatic worlds merged to good effect, such as the friendly Australia–Japan competition at the Royal Canberra Golf Club.[1]

One week earlier, the Japanese press had reported on the visit to Australia by Prime Minister Shinzō Abe, welcoming what appeared to be a close relationship developing between Abe and Prime Minister Malcolm Turnbull. A signed revision to the Australia–Japan Acquisition and Cross-Servicing Agreement between the Australian Defence Force and Japan's Self-Defense Forces, enabling more sharing of supplies, led one Japanese government official to describe the two countries as 'quasi-allies'.[2] Both leaders looked forward to closer security cooperation, and while avoiding mention of China, also looked to the United States to continue playing a strong role in regional security throughout the Asia-Pacific. Although not all aspects of the Australia–Japan relationship were sailing smoothly—the Abe government was still smarting from being overlooked for the contract to build Australia's next generation of submarines, and anti-whaling activists reported the Japanese killing of whales in the Southern Ocean— the two prime ministers were keen to convey a relationship of breadth and deep historic roots. At a press conference, Turnbull reminded reporters of the looming 60th anniversary of the 1957 Australia–Japan Agreement on Commerce, signed when Abe's grandfather Nobusuke Kishi was prime minister of Japan, thus highlighting the role that 'Shinzo's' family had played in strengthening Australia–Japan relations.[3]

These two episodes at the beginning of 2017 suggested that relations between Australia and Japan had blossomed after the end of World War II in ways that defied early expectations, not only in the economic sphere but also through broader cultural and educational exchanges. Indeed, the 60th anniversary of the bilateral Commerce Agreement provided a time for reflection on more than just trading relationships. This book takes this general proposition as a starting point for examining the history of Australia's diplomatic representation in Tokyo, and how it has evolved over

---

1   Authors' notes from the meeting, 24 January 2017. It was also noted that both Calvert and Ueda had served respectively in Tokyo and Canberra as junior diplomats earlier in their careers.

2   Summary of the Japanese Press, Interpreting and Translation Unit, Public Diplomacy Section, Australian embassy, Tokyo, 23 January 2017.

3   Ibid.

time. These changes have occurred in response to the shifting political and economic pressures and objectives of both nations, which have unfolded across decades within wider regional and global contexts and alliances. However, the representative activities undertaken by Australia's embassy in Tokyo have also evolved through the extraordinary changes to technology, communications and security that have determined day-to-day practices, and opened fresh opportunities for interactions between the nations and their peoples.

The timing of this volume on aspects of the role of the Australian embassy in Tokyo and the Australia–Japan relationship also coincides with recent developments in what is often designated as 'new diplomatic history'. This approach has encouraged scholars to focus more directly on the sociability of diplomacy, thus recognising that the complexities of 'diplomatic sites' and influence extend well beyond the public roles and actions of national leaders and their appointed representatives abroad.[4] Such a lens takes into account, for instance, how businesses and international educational providers can be examined as diplomatic actors, and how 'soft power' can be advanced through channels of cultural diplomacy, sports diplomacy or science diplomacy. It seeks to uncover the experiences of those individuals and groups who have often been overlooked in the history of international relations, including senior diplomats. The role of the ambassador, writes Bruce Miller, a recent Australian ambassador to Japan, is both strategic and future-looking and akin to the role of a foreman on a building site.[5] How was this unusual and diverse skill set wielded by successive Australian ambassadors in Tokyo? New diplomatic history also includes the crucial work in cross-national translation and negotiations undertaken by locally engaged staff (LES) at overseas missions, another feature of this book.

Fresh perspectives on diplomatic history have also evaluated embassies as places of architectural and social intent, as influential settings for the representational qualities of staged events and for particular modes of human interaction, ranging from dress codes to social encounters and elaborate

---

4   Iver Neumann, *Diplomatic Sites: A Critical Enquiry* (Oxford: Oxford University Press, 2013), doi.org/10.1093/acprof:oso/9780199327966.001.0001; Pauline Kerr and Geoffrey Wiseman, eds, *Diplomacy in a Globalizing World: Theories and Practices*, 2nd ed. (New York: Oxford University Press, 2017); Michele Acuto, *Global Cities, Governance and Diplomacy* (London: Routledge, 2013), doi.org/10.4324/9780203073810; see also articles in *Diplomatica: A Journal of Diplomacy and Society* nos. 1, 2 (2019 and 2020).
5   See Bruce Miller, 'The Tokyo Embassy, Past, Present and Future: Reflections', in this volume.

meals.[6] In the case of Australian representation in Tokyo, this is not to ignore the substantive diplomatic work on such matters as trade, security, investment and cultural exchange but to enrich it by viewing the relationship more expansively and holistically, situating the activities of diplomats within their wider historical, social and political milieux. It is to acknowledge that official diplomacy might well be construed as the working of the state, in this instance either Australia or Japan, but that the boundary between state and society is necessarily porous: peoples of diverse backgrounds, and a broad range of material objects, exist outside of state-defined roles but then connect in particular ways when involved in diplomacy.[7]

Over time, too, social movements and demographic change have led to increasing diversity among the diplomatic workforce. Indicative of these shifts, and the entry of more women into higher education and professional and government roles, is that by 2019 a clear majority—61 per cent—of employees in Australia's Department of Foreign Affairs and Trade (DFAT) were women. Until 1966, Australian women in the foreign service were subject to a 'marriage bar', which usually required resignation upon marriage or, if ongoing employment was allowed, forbade an overseas posting. Australia had its first female head of mission in 1971, when Dame Annabelle Rankin took a political appointment as Australian high commissioner to New Zealand. The first female career diplomat to serve as an ambassador was Ruth Dobson, who headed Australia's embassy in Denmark in 1974. While women have subsequently taken more senior and ambassadorial roles within DFAT, gender equality has yet to be achieved at the highest echelons of Australia's international representation.[8] In this context, the appointment in 2020 of distinguished career diplomat Jan Adams as Australia's first female ambassador to Japan is an important milestone in the history of the Australian embassy in Tokyo.[9]

---

6   For instance, see Louis Clerc, 'Global Trends in Local Contexts: The Finnish Embassy in Paris, 1956–1990', *New Global Studies* 11, no. 2 (2017): 101–15, doi.org/10.1515/ngs-2017-0017; Pascal Lottuz, 'Violent Conflicts and Neutral Legations: A Case Study of the Spanish and Swiss Legations in Wartime Japan', *New Global Studies* 11, no. 2 (2017): 85–100, doi.org/10.1515/ngs-2017-0018.

7   See, among others, J. Dittmer, *Diplomatic Material: Affect, Assemblage and Foreign Policy* (Durham NC: Duke University Press, 2017), doi.org/10.1515/9780822372745; Costas M. Costantinou and James Derian, eds, *Sustainable Diplomacies* (London: Palgrave Macmillan, 2010), doi.org/10.1057/9780230297159.

8   Moreen Dee and Felicity Volk, eds, *Women with a Mission: Personal Perspectives* (Canberra: Commonwealth of Australia, 2007); Department of Foreign Affairs and Trade, *WIL (Women in Leadership) Refresh* (Canberra, Commonwealth of Australia, 2020).

9   Adams previously served as Australia's ambassador to China (2016–19) and held overseas postings in Washington and the OECD Secretariat, Paris.

A further dynamic affecting the loosening and broadening of the field of diplomatic history is increasingly relevant, and concerns the questioning of the future need for ambassadors and sizeable overseas missions in a globalised and highly connected world. While the focus in this book is on the history, the legacies and the current state of Australia's diplomatic representation, and therefore contributors do not directly engage with the future of embassies, two features prominent in the scholarly literature and emerging discussion are important to note. Firstly, there is some degree of consensus among historians and other commentators that while embassies and consulates are likely to survive as important to diplomatic relations, the forms that these may take—including levels of staffing, and the need for prominent embassy buildings—will continue to be evaluated. Secondly, such debates have led to a greater interest in the past, prompting methodological innovation in understanding the role of embassies and overseas representation, including in the arenas of culture, education and sports, as these have developed and adapted to new circumstances.[10]

The chapters in *The Australian Embassy in Tokyo and Australia–Japan Relations* derive, in part, from a conference we convened at Deakin University in 2017, and are written by historians and others in academia and by observer-participants, including former ambassadors. This study has also been accompanied by the collection of oral histories conducted during 2017–18, and we are grateful for the generosity of those who agreed to share their memories. Interviews with several former Australian ambassadors to Japan were undertaken and are now held in a designated oral history collection at the National Library of Australia, where they constitute an important archive for future scholarship on Australia's diplomatic mission in Japan and the Australia–Japan relationship more broadly.[11] We also conducted interviews in Australia and Japan with past and present staff at the Australian embassy in Tokyo during 2017–19.

---

10   See Giles Scott-Smith, 'Introduction', *New Global Studies* 11, no. 2 (2017): 77–84, doi.org/ 10.1515/ngs-2017-0013; Alex Oliver, 'The Irrelevant Diplomat: Do We Need Embassies Anymore?', *Foreign Affairs*, 14 March 2016, www.foreignaffairs.com/articles/world/2016-03-14/irrelevant-diplomat; Geoffrey Wiseman, 'Contemporary Challenges for Foreign Ministries: At Home and Abroad', *Diplomacy and Statecraft* 30, no. 4 (2019): 786–98, doi.org/10.1080/09592296.2019.1673 554; Philip Seib, *The Future of Diplomacy* (Cambridge: Polity Press, 2016); Paul Sharp, 'Who Needs Diplomats? The Problem of Diplomatic Representation', *International Journal* 52 (1997): 609–34, doi.org/10.1177/002070209705200407.
11   Australian Ambassadors to Japan Oral History Project, National Library of Australia, Bib ID: 7384765, see catalogue.nla.gov.au/Record/7384765, accessed 1 November 2020. We acknowledge the support of the Australia–Japan Foundation, Department of Foreign Affairs and Trade, in compiling the interviews.

This has ensured that the voices of those LES members who worked at the embassy have been considered, and indeed their long tenure and insider/outsider status provide distinctive perspectives on the breadth of external-facing activities and inner complexities of the embassy.

Making the Modern Relationship

While this volume is concerned with the post–World War II decades, diplomacy between Australia and Japan and personal and commercial interactions between the two countries date back to the nineteenth century. In the interwar period, a Japanese merchant class concentrated in Sydney participated in global trading networks, while small Japanese communities were located in the pearl shell industries of the remote north, including at Thursday Island, Darwin and Broome.[12] Relations between the two nations were strained by Australia's anxiety about Japan's military aggression in East Asia, and its emphasis on the maintenance of the racially restrictive White Australia immigration policy.[13]

During the interwar years, Australian trade missions were sent to Japan, and a trade commissioner in Tokyo was established in 1935. An Australian legation, led by judge and politician Sir John Latham, was in place in August 1940. Accompanying Latham to Tokyo as his secretary was Bernice Campbell, who was, according to the *Women's Weekly*, the first Australian woman to be appointed by the Commonwealth to work in a foreign country (noting that appointments to London were not considered foreign).[14] Following Japan's entry into World War II on 8 December 1941, the legation staff were confined to the grounds of Hachisuka House before being repatriated to Australia in August 1942.[15]

---

12   See Paul Jones and Vera Mackie, eds, *Relationships: Australia and Japan: 1880s to 1950*, University of Melbourne History Monograph 28 (Melbourne: University of Melbourne, 2001); Masayo Tada and Leigh Dale eds, *On the Western Edge: A Colloquium on Comparisons of Australia and Japan* (Perth: Network Books, 2007); and for a photographic history of the relationship see Melissa Miles and Robin Gerster, *Pacific Exposures: Photography and the Australia–Japan Relationship* (Canberra: ANU Press, 2018), doi.org/10.22459/PE.2018.

13   David Walker, *Anxious Nation: Australia and the Rise of Asia 1850–1939* (St Lucia: University of Queensland Press, 1999); see also David Walker and Agnieszka Sobocinska, eds, *Australia's Asia: From Yellow Peril to Asia Century* (Perth: University of Western Australia Publishing, 2012); and for a political perspective, Warren G. Osmond, *Frederic Eggleston: An Intellectual in Australian Politics* (Sydney: Allen & Unwin, 1985).

14   *Australian Women's Weekly*, 19 July 1941, 19.

15   Alan Fewster, *Trusty and Well Beloved: A Life of Keith Officer, Australia's First Diplomat* (Carlton: Miegunyah Press, 2009), 211–26.

Prime Minister John Curtin famously declared that with Japan's entry into the Pacific War, Australia faced 'its darkest hour'. The nation quickly shifted to a total war economy, introducing rationing and civil defence, and providing a base for the US troops serving under the Allied command of US general Douglas MacArthur. In February 1942, the British naval bastion at Singapore fell to the Japanese, and Darwin was bombed, with more than 250 people killed; over the next 18 months, Japan was to attack Australia's northern towns around 100 times, and shells were launched on Sydney's harbourside suburbs. Australian forces played a key military role in Papua, New Guinea and across the Asia-Pacific; the fighting was intense, and more than 22,000 Australians were taken prisoner by the Japanese. The US dropping of atomic bombs on the Japanese cities of Hiroshima and Nagasaki in early August 1945 precipitated Japan's surrender, which took place formally on 2 September 1945. In Australia, the impact of World War II was profound, accelerating the move to a modern industrial nation and transforming the nation's approach to regional security, notably through an alliance with the US.[16]

Reflecting on the modern history of Australia–Japan relations, Neville Meaney suggests the period from 1945 to 1952 was to be the last phase of what was, from an Australian perspective, 'A Half-Century of Menace'.[17] This immediate post–World War II period, and the transition whereby Australia came to regard Japan as a valued regional partner, has attracted considerable scholarly attention. This is especially so in relation to Australia's military involvement in the British Commonwealth Occupation Force (BCOF), headquartered in the southern port city of Kure, in Hiroshima Prefecture. Between 1945 and 1952, more than 16,000 Australians spent time in Japan as part of the BCOF, and while their encounters with Japanese people were complex, they did encompass many examples of cross-cultural friendship and compassion. Two other aspects of the occupation period have also been analysed by historians: the trial of Japanese war criminals and the administration of Japan

---

16   See Kate Darian-Smith, 'World War 2 and Post-war Reconstruction, 1939–49', in *The Cambridge History of Australia*, ed. Alison Bashford and Stuart Macintyre, vol. 2 (Cambridge: Cambridge University Press, 2013), 88–111, doi.org/10.1017/CHO9781107445758.035; Kate Darian-Smith, 'Pearl Harbor and Australia's War in the Pacific', in *Beyond Pearl Harbor: A Pacific History*, ed. Beth Bailey and David Farber (Lawrence, Kansas: University Press of Kansas, 2019), 173–93, doi.org/10.2307/j.ctvqmp3br.13; Hank Nelson, *P.O.W. Prisoners of War: Australians under Nippon* (Sydney, ABC Books, 1985).

17   Neville Meaney, 'Australia and Japan: The Historical Perspective', in *The Japanese Connection: A Survey of Australian Leaders' Attitudes towards Japan and the Australia–Japan Relationship*, ed. Neville Meaney, Trevor Matthews and Sol Encel (Melbourne: Longman Cheshire, 1988), 18–20.

under Supreme Commander General Douglas MacArthur.[18] Australia's contribution to the diplomatic work that laid the basis of the Peace Treaty with Japan signed in San Francisco in 1951 has also been examined by Australian scholars, largely as important context to the conclusion of the Australia, New Zealand and United States (ANZUS) security pact signed in the same year.[19]

One of the key features of the historical literature on Australia–Japan relations has been a focus on the 1957 Agreement on Commerce, the first step in extending the bilateral relationship beyond mere diplomatic recognition to one where trade and politics were paramount. Indeed, Australia was the first country to give Japan the trade status of 'most favoured nation' after the war. Few would disagree with the comment by economist Peter Drysdale that the agreement 'was a remarkable watershed in the relationship, little more than a decade after the bitterness of the war'. Drysdale is one of Australia's foremost experts on the economic dimensions of the relationship, having been part of Sir John Crawford's research team on Australia and Japan created at The Australian National University (ANU) in the 1960s. In 2004 he wrote that the Australia–

---

18   On Australians in the British Commonwealth Occupation Force, see Robin Gerster, *Travels in Atomic Sunshine: Australia and the Occupation of Japan* (Melbourne: Scribe, 2019); Christine de Matos, *Imposing Peace and Prosperity: Australia, Social Justice and Labour Reform in Occupied Japan* (Melbourne: Australian Scholarly Press, 2008); Basil Archer, *Interpreting Occupied Japan: The Diary of an Australian Soldier, 1945–1956*, ed. Sandra Wilson (Carlisle, WA: Hesperian Press, 2009); Walter Hamilton, *Children of the Occupation: Japan's Untold Story* (Sydney: NewSouth, 2012); George Davies, *The Occupation of Japan: The Rhetoric and Reality of Anglo-Australasian Relations, 1939–1952* (Brisbane: University of Queensland Press, 2001). On the prosecution of war criminals, see Dean Aszkielowicz, *The Australian Pursuit of Japanese War Criminals, 1943–1957: From Foe to Friend* (Hong Kong: Hong Kong University Press, 2018), doi.org/10.5790/hongkong/9789888390724.001.0001; Sandra Wilson, Robert Cribb, Beatrice Trefalt and Dean Aszkielowicz, *Japanese War Criminals: The Politics of Justice after the Second World War* (New York: Columbia University Press, 2017); Georgina Fitzpatrick, Tim McCormack and Narrelle Morris, eds, *Australia's War Crimes Trials, 1945–1951* (Leiden, Boston: Brill, 2016), doi.org/10.1163/9789004292055. On the administration of occupied Japan, see Alan Rix, ed., *Intermittent Diplomat: The Japan and Batavia Diaries of W. Macmahon Ball* (Carlton: Melbourne University Publishing, 1988); Alan Rix, 'W. Macmahon Ball and the Allied Council for Japan: The Limits of an Australian Diplomacy under Evatt', *Australian Outlook* 42, no. 1 (1998): 21–28, doi.org/10.1080/10357718808444957; Ai Kobayashi, *W. Macmahon Ball: Politics for People* (North Melbourne: Australian Scholarly Publishing, 2013).

19   See Andrew Kelly, *ANZUS and the Early Cold War: Strategy and Diplomacy between Australia, New Zealand and the United States, 1945–1956* (Cambridge: Open Book Publishers, 2018); W. David McIntyre, *Background to the ANZUS Pact: Policy-making, Strategy and Diplomacy, 1945–55* (New York: St Martin's Press, 1995), doi.org/10.1057/9780230380073; David Maclean, 'ANZUS Origins: A Reassessment', *Australian Historical Studies* 24, no. 94 (1990): 64–82, doi.org/10.1080/10314619008595832; and Neville Meaney, 'Look Back in Fear: Percy Spender, the Japanese Peace Treaty and the ANZUS Pact', *Japan Forum* 15, no. 3 (1990): 399–410, doi.org/10.1080/095558003 2000124790.

Japan relationship that had grown since the 1950s was 'one of the most remarkable diplomatic and political achievements in the past half century', and that getting the relationship right with Japan had been key to Australia's getting relationships right with East Asia more generally.[20] The chapters in this volume do not take issue with these broadbrush observations. They do, however, address much that lies in between a string of notable bilateral agreements, situating the work of the Australian embassy in relation to these developments, and examining some dimensions of the relationship that have not received sufficient scholarly attention.

Nuclear power has been a significant factor at key moments in Australia–Japan relations. The beginnings of the modern relationship were forged in the aftermath of World War II, when anti-Japanese sentiment was high in Australia. The Australian military personnel and a small number of civilians who were stationed in Japan during the Allied occupation were shocked by the destruction caused by nuclear warfare, and many were prompted to offer practical assistance to Japanese people, particularly women, children and the elderly. This included the establishment of orphanages, visits to children's homes and, to give one example, the rebuilding of classrooms burnt by the atomic bomb at a primary school in the Senda area of Hiroshima city.[21] Person-to-person interactions extended beyond everyday cooperation and the ban on fraternisation, to incorporate instances of friendship and respect between individuals. Some of these exchanges were romantic, and more than 650 Japanese women bravely migrated to Australia as the wives and fiancées of Australian servicemen.[22]

Many decades later, and in a different context, Australia's cooperation with and support of Japan and its people during a natural and nuclear disaster indicate the depth of the current relationship. On 11 March 2011, a massive earthquake unleashed a tsunami that inundated the Tohoku coast, in north-east Honshu, resulting in a death toll of around 20,000, damage to 800,000 buildings and a system failure at the Fukushima Daiichi Nuclear Power Plant. We open this volume with a chapter by Murray McLean, ambassador to Japan from 2004 to 2011, explaining how he led the Australian embassy's on-the-ground response, and offering

20   Peter Drysdale, 'Reflections on the Relationship with Japan', *Japanese Studies* 24, no. 2 (2004): 160, doi.org/10.1080/1037139042000302465.
21   Gerster, *Travels in Atomic Sunshine*, 238–40.
22   See Keiko Tamura, *Michi's Memories: The Story of a Japanese War Bride* (Canberra: ANU Press, 2011), doi.org/10.22459/MM.09.2011.

a lesson in crisis management. Although embassies of other nations closed in Tokyo, the Australian embassy sat tight, with additional DFAT staff flying in from Australia to help. Embassy staff kept the Australian government informed of developments, locating Australians who were in disaster zones, and preparing for a potential evacuation. They often risked their own safety to provide consular assistance, and facilitated Australia's aid and rescue efforts.[23] The swift arrival in Japan of then prime minister Julia Gillard, and her much-photographed emotional response as she toured the obliterated fishing village of Minamisanriku, demonstrated the strength of the bilateral relationship.[24] Later, embassy staff held a charity dinner in Tokyo to raise money for the people of Tohoku, and, with Australian expatriates, organised a sausage sizzle in Minamisanriku, selling lamingtons and Australian wines to raise funds for the local community.[25]

Ambassadors and Embassy

Australia's ambassadors to Japan loom large in this study, but with the exceptions of two contributions by recent incumbents—Murray McLean (ambassador from 2004 to 2011) and Bruce Miller (ambassador from 2011 to 2017)—the chapters here do not pivot on the terms and experiences of individual ambassadors. Instead, in Chapter 3, David Lee and David Lowe provide a guide to those appointees who have served since 1952, with an eye for the changing status of the diplomatic post and the key issues demanding the attention of each head. This overview of Australian ambassadors to Japan matches this book's intention to capture, as best as is possible, the growth of the distinctive relationship between Australia and Japan as it occurred in diverse ways, and to highlight the presence of multiple forms of agency.

23   Liam Walsh and Angus Grigg, 'After the Wave: Untold Stories of Australia's Response to Fukushima', *Australian Financial Review*, 6 March 2021, www.afr.com/policy/foreign-affairs/after-the-wave-untold-stories-of-australia-s-response-to-fukushima-20210227-p576dq, accessed 31 May 2021.

24   'Gillard Tours Tsunami-Devastated Minami Sanriku', *Sydney Morning Herald*, 23 April 2011, www.smh.com.au/world/gillard-tours-tsunamidevastated-minami-sanriku-20110423-1ds1j.html, accessed 6 November 2020.

25   'Australia Stands with Tohoku', Australian embassy in Tokyo, japan.embassy.gov.au/tkyo/tohoku.html, accessed 13 March 2021; Australia–Japan Foundation and Department of Foreign Affairs and Trade, *The Reconstruction Initiative: Australia–Japan Foundation's Response to Japan's 2011 Earthquake and Tsunami* (Canberra: Australian Government Department of Foreign Affairs and Trade, November 2015), 5, 10–12, 17.

World War II was a formidable legacy for those Australians working in the embassy in Tokyo during the 1950s and 1960s. Even the purchase of the embassy mansion and property in Mita was leveraged from the value of disposed Australian equipment from BCOF. Fortunately, the Australian government appointed senior and skilled diplomats to this difficult task from the beginning, with initial appointments of E. Ronald Walker (ambassador 1952–55) and Alan Watt (ambassador 1956–59). As David Walton shows in Chapter 4, this enabled adroit responses to Japan's re-emergence in the international community, and mutually beneficial exchanges in the United Nations and with reference to the Afro-Asian bloc and growing turbulence in Indonesia.

Other Australian individuals stand out for their contributions to the relationship. David Lee describes in Chapter 5 the lead role played by Sir John Crawford, over nearly three decades, as the architect of major policy development in the Australia–Japan relationship. This chapter also highlights the importance of looking beyond the Australian Department of External Affairs (now Foreign Affairs) for developments that shaped the work of the Australian embassy in Tokyo. As secretary of Trade, Crawford played a crucial role in the negotiation of the watershed commerce treaty of 1957, arriving at a formula that extended most-favoured-nation treatment by Australia towards Japan while preserving tariff preferences for British imports. Afterwards, at ANU, Crawford collaborated with Saburō Ōkita, who became Japan's foreign minister in 1979, to set up a research program to further explore economic growth and complementarity for Australia, Japan and the Western Pacific. These efforts led to Crawford's strong push, eventually winning Prime Minister Gough Whitlam's support, for a more comprehensive Australian treaty with Japan. The 1976 Friendship and Cooperation Treaty (NARA Treaty) was the result, with Crawford continuing his advocacy afterwards to help establish the Australia–Japan Foundation (AJF), the first of Australia's cultural councils.

The Australian embassy's grounds and buildings, located in Mita, in the Minato district of Tokyo, are a prominent feature in the rich narrative of Australia's official representation in Japan. As Alison Broinowski and Rachel Miller show in Chapter 6, the site and its buildings are a symbolic and material microcosm of the last 450 years of Tokyo's history. In post-Meiji Japan, the Hachisuka family established a large estate in Mita, which incorporated the current site of the embassy. By the twentieth century, much of the estate had been sold, but during the interwar period there was major work in the building and gardens in the section occupied as Australia's official diplomatic base. This boasted a special mixture of architectural and garden styles, with historical references straddling several centuries. In outlining the significance of this earlier history, Broinowski and Miller argue that the redevelopment of the Australian embassy site in the late 1980s, including the demolition of the historic residence, needs to be understood as part of the impermanence of Tokyo's built environment more generally.

The diplomatic symbolism of the 'new' Australian embassy is explored in detail by leading architectural historian Philip Goad in Chapter 7. He focuses on the implications of the destruction of the old Hachisuka mansion and sale of part of the land in 1987 for an extraordinary sum at the height of a recession, and the construction of the current embassy and residential accommodation for staff. Opened in 1990, the Australian embassy in Tokyo was designed by the Australian firm Denton Corker Marshall, who were also responsible for the Australian embassy in Beijing. As Goad points out, the Tokyo building invited comparisons not only with its immediate urban environment but also with the other major Asian posts for Australian diplomats. He describes how the architects drew upon an appropriate and assured internationalism and urban typology, with a building that was restrained rather than overtly defined by 'Australianness'. Embassy buildings are risky assertions of national identity, and to date there is has been little research on either the functionality or the symbolism and multiple identities of the built form of Australia's overseas missions; these chapters go some way, at least in the Tokyo case, in redressing this gap.

In Chapter 8, Kate Darian-Smith and David Lowe probe the inner life of the embassy, turning to the building itself as a place of work and cross-cultural friendships for local staff. In ways that are often invisible to the public eye, and indeed to the queries of historians, overseas missions are indebted to the skills and hard work of local employees who labour as translators, administrators, liaison officers with government and industry, policy advisers, and, more mundanely, drivers, cleaners, and caterers. Predominantly female, this group of Japanese nationals are instrumental to the continuity of diplomatic work, especially as, contrary to the fixed terms of Australian staff, they can remain in their embassy position for decades. Drawing upon oral histories with LES, this chapter adds further insight to the history of the Australian embassy in Tokyo.

Exchanges and Cultural Diplomacy

The NARA Treaty of 1976 heralded a new stage in Australia–Japan relations, enshrining both symbolically and formally the depth of friendship, combined interest and interdependence of purpose between the two nations. It provided a framework for strengthening investment and economic and political ties, and indeed over the next decade trade between Australian and Japan grew fourfold. Through this emphasis on cooperation, the founding of the Working Holiday Program, and unprecedented person-to-person relations between Australians and Japanese, the ghosts of White Australia and World War II were put to rest. New alignments were formed in the 1980s and 1990s, including through the formation of the Asia-Pacific Economic Cooperation (APEC) ministerial dialogues in 1989 and the Joint Declaration on the Australia–Japanese Partnership in 1995. In Chapter 9, Kate Darian-Smith explores how broad-reaching cultural connections between the two nations matured from the 1980s through a myriad of personal, institutional and government contacts and initiatives. These two-way flows have spanned tourism; cultural and educational exchanges; artistic residencies, performances and exhibitions; and sporting demonstrations and competitions. In Tokyo, staff at the Australian embassy led, supported and encouraged these activities and played a vital role in ensuring their success.

Crucial to these maturing bilateral connections was the Australia–Japan Foundation, which from 1976 was to fund educational and cultural programs that increased awareness between the two nations. As David Carter investigates in Chapter 10, the AJF was to fund important educational programs about Australia for Japanese schools, and in the tertiary sector to foster collaborative Australian–Japanese academic research across the sciences, social sciences and humanities. The growth of these scholarly networks led to the formation of the Australian Studies Association of Japan in 1989 and to the mobility of university staff and students between Australia and Japan. Carter examines the key role of the annual Visiting (Associate) Professor in Australian Studies, based at the University of Tokyo since the late 1970s, a role more recently supported by the AJF. In examining the connection between scholarly activity and cultural diplomacy in Australia–Japan relations, he finds that it was this relationship that was both the subject of and the inspiration for much of the pioneering thinking behind Australian cultural diplomacy.

By the mid-1980s the so-called 'Japanese miracle' of spectacular economic growth had attracted world attention, and the Australia–Japan relationship had expanded to a point that was, as Richard Broinowski says in Chapter 11, almost too good to be true. He describes, from the perspective of one at the heart of policy formation in Canberra, the urgent creation of committees in the late 1970s to better educate Australians about all aspects of Japan, and to coordinate the interests of Commonwealth and state governments, business, the public service departments and academia. This type of education and coordination became all the more important after Japan's revaluation of the yen in 1985, prompting their need to curb imports or bargain for lower prices. Broinowski's study of these events and policies from the late 1970s to mid-1990s reveals the importance for the Australia–Japan relationship of the steady building of networks, and institutional stability and guidance. Within APEC and the ASEAN (Association of Southeast Asian Nations) Regional Forum, some of the important architecture underpinning the relationship was also regional in scope.

Looking Back and Looking Forward

Two perspectives from Australian ambassadors to Japan serve to underline the scale of changes that are explored throughout this collection, from the end of World War II to today. In recalling his experiences as ambassador in Tokyo in 1957, Sir Alan Watt said that he went to Japan (arriving in 1956) with many reservations, partly on account of his previous posting to Singapore, where memories of the war were raw. 'No Australian who served in Singapore and Malaya can forget Changi prison', he said, '[or] what happened to Australian prisoners of war, and so I went … not prepared to believe everything that I found in Japan.'[26] Watt found Tokyo both fascinating and challenging. It took him some time, he said, to understand Japanese motivations. Slowly, by reading Japanese history, building his social network (including as president of the Tokyo Lawn Tennis Club) and shedding certain assumptions, he began, in his words, to 'untie some of the knots I had in my mind when I went in'.[27] Watt left Japan more optimistic about the country and about Australia–Japan

---

26   Transcript of Bruce Miller's interview with Sir Alan Watt, 11 December 1974, TRC 306, 2:2/12, National Library of Australia (NLA).
27   Ibid., 2:2/13.

relations, but still puzzling over Japanese behaviours in ways that reflected both his intellectual curiosity and a residual, orientalist 'othering' of Japan.[28]

By contrast, Ambassador Bruce Miller, who concluded his term in Tokyo at the beginning of 2017, reflects in Chapter 12 of this book on how his interest in Japan and its people shaped his learning and career. Miller's first encounter with Japan was a Japan Foundation–sponsored study visit in his last year of high school, which sparked his study of Japanese language, history and literature, and led to further study in Japan and his subsequent joining the Australian Department of Foreign Affairs. He enjoyed three different postings to the embassy in Tokyo, the last as ambassador. Miller also found great satisfaction in watching, and being directly involved in, the maturing and broadening of the Australia–Japan relationship, including a free trade agreement signed in 2014. Not all the changes he witnessed should be interpreted in bilateral terms. A changing region, shifts in power and alliance dynamics, and the overarching features of globalisation drove some of the changes in the relationship. But Miller highlights how strategic and defence cooperation enjoys equal prominence with economic aspects of the relationship; he also points to the significant movement of people annually between the two countries, a mobility underpinned by education, tourism, and science and research connections.[29]

This book testifies to the breadth of the modern Australia–Japan relationship by showcasing multiple perspectives not often gathered in the one place. While the relationship has undergone testing times as well as celebrated ones, it has grown in ways that were not anticipated when ambassadorial-level representation began in 1952. In 2016, the recently retired former secretary of the Australian Department of Foreign Affairs and Trade, Peter Varghese, wished that Australian relations with India, another relationship in Asia he suggested was of great importance for Australians, might broaden and deepen in ways similar to what we had observed with Japan.[30] Most recently, a detailed report from the Australia–Japan Research Centre at ANU argues that it is time for an urgent 'Reimagining the Japan Relationship', given the formidable security,

28   Ibid., 2:2/14–15.
29   See Miller, 'The Tokyo Embassy' in this volume.
30   Peter Varghese, 'Reflections on Australia–India Relations Since the 1990s', October 2016, as reported by David Lowe in David Lowe and Eric Meadows, eds, *Rising Power and Changing People: The Australian High Commission in India* (Canberra: ANU Press, 2022), doi.org/10.22459/RPCP.2022.

energy and economic challenges facing both countries. But the report is also upbeat about the foundations upon which such a reimagining can occur:

> Australia's economic, geographic and strategic interests are overwhelmingly in Asia and no partner is more important to those interests than Japan. Japan is Australia's benchmark relationship and strategic anchor in Asia and that is an enduring strategic reality.[31]

This volume, we hope, goes some way to explaining how the Australia–Japan relationship acquired benchmark status, and how the Australian embassy in Tokyo was involved.

---

31   Shiro Armstrong, *Reimagining the Japan Relationship: An Agenda for Australia's Benchmark Partnership in Asia* (Canberra: Australia–Japan Research Centre, The Australian National University, 2021), i.

2

The Australian Embassy in Tokyo and the Tohoku Earthquake and Tsunami of March 2011

Murray McLean AO

On 11 March 2011, a massive earthquake struck the north-eastern coast of Japan—the biggest experienced on record. The fault line unleashed a tsunami that inundated the Tohoku coast, in north-east Honshu, leading to the deaths of approximately 20,000 people and damaging more than 800,000 buildings. It also triggered a cooling system failure at the Fukushima Daiichi Nuclear Power Plant, a level-seven nuclear meltdown and the widespread release of radioactive materials, with continuing consequences. Murray McLean AO served as Australia's ambassador to Japan from 2004 to 2011 and led the Australian response to the disaster.

* * *

When the earthquake and tsunamis occurred on 11 March 2011, the Australian embassy team and their families in Tokyo had long shared a commitment to living and working together cooperatively in the large-scale Australian residential and office compound, while meaningfully integrating in diverse ways within the broader local host community. This close-knit spirit and workstyle were critical to the effectiveness of our shared rapid response to the challenges of the unfolding disasters.

Everyone posted to Japan, even relative newcomers, had frequently experienced regular local tremors of distant or weak earthquakes occurring along the Japanese archipelago. Elaborate crisis contingency plans were well in place, including regular earthquake drills, emergency assembly posts, and initial first task responsibilities in the aftermath of any major shock. Stronger tremors had been experienced in preceding months. The instinctive response—to shelter *in situ* under tables, evacuating the building only after any shaking had stopped, then to gather in groups on the embassy's back lawn—always kicked in quickly. The shaking caused by the first main earthquake shock of 11 March 2011, for all those who experienced it around Tokyo, was unbelievably longer in duration and severity than usually expected. A second major shock 20 minutes later confirmed our worst fears and concerns for others less safe than ourselves at that moment. Our anxiety rose to learn what was going on and where.

That day, that time—2.46 pm, 11 March 2011—would never be forgotten as the first severe shaking continued for five minutes, increasing in strength. We were keenly aware of its unusual pattern. We understood from the length of time and from the limited extent to which fixtures around us moved but without excessive damage, that despite the horrendous shaking, the earthquake epicentre must be massive, but likely some distance from Tokyo. None of us had ever experienced what would turn out to be a 9.0 magnitude earthquake or in any way were able to comprehend the scale of the event immediately.

As the Tohoku earthquake struck, a group of us in a small meeting in my office, as if on cue, automatically sheltered under shaking furniture, listening to the ominous rattling of venetian blinds and swaying light fittings and the thud of objects falling from desks and shelves. When the seemingly eternal minutes of severe shaking ceased, we evacuated the building quickly with others, gathering in our pre-planned groups on the embassy's back lawn. We were greatly relieved for our immediate safety but were starting to realise the enormity of what must have occurred for others across Tokyo and elsewhere in Japan, while still unsure of where.

We all followed our usual cues, confident in our preparedness as an immediate strength. Standing on the lawn we carefully checked for those present and accounted for the whereabouts of others. The need to locate everyone safely was now of utmost and frightening urgency. Some of us had family members, including young children, elsewhere in the city that day experiencing terrifying events in other districts. It would be long, distressing hours before all the children were safely home. There were several high-level visiting delegations and others that it would be our responsibility to locate and bring to safety.

The post's dedicated emergency committee convened on the lawn immediately, activating the embassy's consular contingency and crisis response plans. Buildings would immediately be checked thoroughly and as evening approached, we had the confidence of possibly returning to shelter in the embassy buildings constructed to superior earthquake tolerance standards. It was imperative that consular services commence for the possibly 12,000 Australians with Japanese resident visas located throughout Japan at that time. Only 2,000 Australians were registered at the embassy, 45 known to be located in the devastated areas. Many Australians would seek assistance for their family members with Japanese citizenship to evacuate together to Australia. Other casual visitors, like tourists, would need to be assisted where possible.

We promptly communicated briefly from outdoors with Canberra (the Australian Department of Foreign Affairs and Trade, or DFAT) via a satellite telephone from our emergency kit, advising on the immediate status of staff and families, and that we would begin efforts to contact and locate Australian citizens in the earthquake zone as soon as possible. Ironically, Canberra knew more about some details of the quake from global coverage than we did at the embassy in Tokyo. DFAT advised us that the crisis centre was already operational in Canberra and would activate an interdepartmental emergency task force (IDETF). Special consular operations support (ConOps) had been set up to handle the expected high volume of concerned enquiries in Australia, and extra staff would be sent immediately to support the post's consular team in Tokyo in the task of locating and caring for Australian citizens across Japan. ConOps received over 11,000 calls and more than 5,500 Australians were confirmed safe. DFAT, through ConOps and the augmented consular team at the embassy, accounted for all Australians about whom the public enquired.

In Tokyo, our crisis contingency plans were well-prepared and practised, but no manual predicts exactly the scale or character of any critical event, while individual fears and concerns in response to crises vary. Ongoing, the IDETF held daily videoconference calls between the embassy in

Tokyo and senior representatives of all relevant government departments and agencies, enabling well-coordinated, effective and timely responses to the crisis.

The Australian embassy in Tokyo is one of the largest and most comprehensive of Australia's bilateral representative posts. Alongside staff from DFAT carrying out the broad-ranging traditional consular and representational roles of a diplomatic mission, senior advisory staff from Australia's major federal government agencies, including the Australian Defence Force (ADF) are accredited. In facing this critical new situation beyond any expectations, we could draw on the experience of skilled personnel from diverse backgrounds. In particular, senior military officers who had served in war zones like the Middle East and Afghanistan, and who had strong Japanese counterpart networks and knowledge, including Japanese language, strengthened our capabilities and skills base as we faced rapidly escalating 'unknowns'. Their preparedness to deliver initiatives and their experience and training for response to crisis and recovery efforts were invaluable.

Gathered outside on the back lawn that late afternoon, everyone was shocked yet already dealing with urgent priorities. As head of mission, I took the earliest possible opportunity to speak with everyone. We were still checking building safety and desperately locating and bringing home our family members, including children. There was anxiety in this suddenly new, unfolding situation, but I was peculiarly mentally ready, strengthened by recalling my young family's earthquake experience in Beijing in 1976.

Growing up as a rural Australian child introduced me to the anxieties of flood, bushfire, drought and even mice plagues, but not earthquakes. However, ironically, Tohoku 2011 in Japan was not the first catastrophic earthquake I had experienced in my lifetime. On 28 July 1976, at 3.42 am in China, the industrial city of Tangshan was flattened, killing 242,769 (according to Chinese official statistics). The nearby cities of Tianjin and Beijing were severely hit. With my young family, I had been posted to the Australian embassy in Beijing several years earlier. Tremors some months before had warned of possible major earthquakes. Important to understand in hindsight, this was not taken seriously, nor were contingency plans prepared. We believed that Beijing need not fear a major earthquake and were stupidly ignorant of what to do or how to act in the event, or even how to recognise an earthquake. At that time in a city like Beijing, earthquake provisions were not covered in building codes generally, nor earthquake preparedness drilled into us. That earthquake was 7.8 on the Richter scale, with early major shaking lasting for nearly two minutes in Beijing while major aftershocks followed.

While the Tangshan 1976 earthquake was of less magnitude than the Tohoku 2011 earthquake and there were no following tsunamis, it was hugely deadly and destructive, especially to old buildings and unreinforced structures in crowded cities unprepared for such a major event.

In the 1970s, the recently arrived foreign community in Beijing, like our family, lived in newly constructed apartment buildings. We scrambled from them in the dark as walls cracked and stairways became treacherous. Foreigners were evacuated after first camping outside, quite unprepared, in hot, humid conditions rife with mosquitoes and meningitis. Later, we returned to live in relative safety and comfort, compared to many in the local community who braved life on the streets for months in makeshift shacks facing great hardships into the coming winter as their lives were rebuilt. The humanitarian challenges faced by the government and people of China at that time could never be forgotten or underestimated.

That Tangshan 1976 earthquake experience, including the reality of the long-term recovery aftermath, deeply informed my awareness of earthquake treachery and of the need for preparedness to face danger and potential ensuing crisis, and for a ready responsiveness which could enable recovery and relief efforts. These memories set an invaluable personal benchmark for me in coping with the situation we now faced in Japan after the Tohoku 2011 earthquake. First, I was responsible, helped by others, for the wellbeing and safety of our embassy community. Then would come the task of guiding the broader consular and Australian humanitarian response to disaster recovery and relief, wherever possible.

In 2011 Japan, we had the confidence of our greater preparedness than in Beijing in 1976, but Tohoku's triple whammy of earthquake, tsunami and nuclear threat presented more of a challenge in recovery than anyone had anticipated. A decade later, we recognise the huge efforts that the survivors in Japan's devastated areas have made in rebuilding their lives and communities with great courage. On that first afternoon, which began Japan's long journey of recovery, with Blackberry phones not working and no immediate access to landlines, we relied on the few LES's personal mobile phones reconnecting to limited internet access more quickly. The reality of the multiple cascading tsunamis was only gradually comprehended in shock, while information about the 9.0 magnitude earthquake was hard to establish accurately.

A huge aftershock, 20 minutes after the earlier quake, triggered the worst escalation of the tsunamis. This shock heightened our vulnerable sense of critical danger and our awareness of looming emergency. We later learnt that Japanese news agencies had immediately taken helicopters to the scene of the developing tsunamis which had started to roll across the north-eastern coastline. International channels, less affected by communication difficulties than local channels, began reporting live to a global audience on the tsunamis as they rolled inland. Local channels were gradually restored but for the moment we had no reception.

Fortunately, there was no structural damage to embassy buildings as robust Japanese building codes had guided those who designed and constructed the embassy in the late 1980s. We returned to shelter indoors with caution, putting things in order, while still being hit by further, lesser aftershocks. More comprehensive communications were possible by then. By then we knew that a group of visiting Australian politicians was stranded on a stationary bullet train returning to Tokyo, while a senior business leaders' delegation, members of an Australia Japan Business Co-operation Committee group, were assisted in getting through gridlock to Narita airport departing late that night by air. Other visiting Australian senior officials in Tokyo were brought to the embassy for meals and rest, returning later to safe hotel accommodation. By late evening our staff finally met the politicians at Shinagawa station, accompanying them on the four-kilometre walk back to safe accommodation at the embassy.

Many of our local Japanese and locally engaged Australian staff who resided outside the embassy needed to return home urgently to check their families. Most public transport was halted for the next 48 hours, and some Japanese staff walked 30 kilometres or more to get to their families that evening. Others stayed to support the embassy staff, who began shifts to provide 24/7 consular service. Throughout the coming weeks, while facing their own local challenges, the embassy's Japanese staff contributed enormous capability and strong support to each undertaking, including logistics when our consular officials were in the field. Once systems were checked, our priorities were to monitor ongoing developments closely, and to maintain communications both within Japan and back to Australia. Emergency kits had been prepared and stocked, but there was an immediate need to procure further supplies, within thoughtful reason, particularly extra food for the many people now being fed and accommodated in-house at the embassy.

Australia in 2011 had the sad benefit of increased crisis response and recovery awareness and experience of such geophysical events in our region. Historic events such as the Indian Ocean Boxing Day 2004 tsunamis and the very recent Christchurch earthquake of February 2011 had deepened our understanding of how or where we might usefully assist. Knowledge of Japan's geography and history of earthquake and tsunami vulnerabilities prior to the events of March 2011 had guided our preparedness and plans for immediate action, but in this instance, not adequately.

Immediately on learning of the disasters, DFAT in Canberra and the embassy on the ground in Tokyo had swung into crisis response operation mode, particularly at a consular level. Concurrently, ideas were immediately considered as to how Australia could urgently deliver skilled search-and-rescue capabilities to Japan. By late Friday 11 March ADF colleagues in Tokyo and their Australian, Japanese and US counterparts were brainstorming possible plans for sending an experienced Australian search-and-rescue team into the tsunami-devastated region (referred to in some reports as urban search and rescue, or USAR). Responsible ministers and their various departments and agencies in Australia were coordinating and backing proposals for such a team's deployment in Japan. These ideas rapidly took shape and were confirmed.

From the outset, Prime Minister Gillard, who was about to return to Australia from New York, gave her full support and direction to all possible Australian crisis response efforts for Japan. An early decision promised a A$10 million donation to the Japan Red Cross. Further decisions then outlined the offer of a search-and-rescue team to be sent at once to the affected areas using a C-17 Royal Australian Air Force (RAAF) plane which, if needed, could remain in-country to work with US and Japanese counterparts transporting relief supplies around Japan. At a very early point, Australia informed the Japanese government that it was willing to do anything possible to help with the dire situation Japan faced. The RAAF, alongside the embassy and its Defence representatives, played a crucial role in delivering on that promise. The fact that Japan was a vital partner and friend to Australia meant that it was imperative we make major humanitarian efforts to provide support in its crisis recovery. We had well-structured relationships, shared experience and the necessary trust and goodwill to underpin those efforts and have our offers of help accepted.

On Saturday 12 March, as ambassador (head of mission) I was invited to join a meeting in Canberra, by videoconference link, of the National Security Committee of Cabinet. Australia's response plans were being fine-tuned and decisions made promptly at this most senior authoritative level. This was the first of several such Japan crisis-management cabinet meetings over the next few days, updating information and making necessary urgent decisions. Prime Minister Gillard, following her return from New York, and Ministers Rudd (foreign affairs) and Smith (defence), among others, participated. At one point in a video-linked meeting, I was forced to grab my safety hard hat with everything heavily shaking around me. Much to the bemusement of Prime Minister Gillard and others present I continued speaking to the meeting.

On 12 March, the Japanese government responded positively to accept the formal Australian offer of a search-and-rescue mission. Trilateral negotiations and arrangements between Australian, Japanese and US counterparts then settled the logistical details. Diplomatic clearances required for the RAAF C-17's landing in Japan were arranged. Since Japan's civilian airports were too stressed or unsuited to handle its arrival, identifying where the RAAF C-17 could land was a major planning dilemma. Helpfully, the Japanese government had provided a general conditional clearance for foreign aircraft to land at US bases in Japan. Painstaking negotiations undertaken by members of the ADF officers posted in Japan, coordinating closely with the embassy, achieved a trilateral agreement that the RAAF C-17 could touch down at the US Air Force Base at Yokota, west of Tokyo. This goodwill outcome was made possible through a complex matrix of the Australia–US and Japan–US alliances. The Yokota airbase provides facilities for the United Nations Command Rear (UNCR). At that time the UNCR Commander was a senior RAAF officer who played a key role as arrangements were coordinated among the embassy's defence adviser, the Japanese Ministry of Defence, the US Air Force and the embassy's senior diplomatic representations at the Japanese Ministry of Foreign Affairs (MOFA).

No matter how deep the formal structure and trust between two sovereign nations, any proposal involving non-routine deployment and entry across borders, even with great goodwill, must be correctly processed through the correct channels. Once accepted and agreed by senior levels of government, action may commence. With formal agreement in place, the plans for a search-and-rescue mission proceeded. Usually, Japan's MOFA is the formal frontline communication point or window in Japan for the Australian government's representations to the Japanese government, which by tradition are made by the ambassador or another diplomatic staff member. Senior officers from other agencies and each tasking or authorising hierarchy from non-DFAT agencies involved in Australia's crisis response and relief initiatives in Japan worked within the protocols of this framework. In turn, as ambassador, I left specialist technical matters to officers from those agencies appropriately skilled to deliver effective outcomes on the ground.

By 12 March, broad agreement between Australia and Japan on the search-and-rescue mission was in place. Coordinating closely with our ADF colleagues, including the RAAF, which would deliver the C-17 with the search-and-rescue team, the embassy began general oversight of the preparations for the operation, in-country, coordinated with senior command of NSW Fire and Rescue. So, as events unfolded during the weekend of 12–13 March, the very character and scope of the embassy's conventional role was changing. Overnight, diplomatic staff were meeting the challenge of major new demands, as the embassy became uncharacteristically a logistics hub for full-scale humanitarian response and recovery operations, at least for the immediate future.

Again, it is useful to put this in context. At the time of Tohoku 2011, as a major Australian post, the embassy in Tokyo and its regional consulates comprehensively supported business, trade and investment, security, multilateral commitments, and global and bilateral foreign policies. People-to-people strengths of goodwill, loyal friendships and mutual benefit were backed in countless ways. The embassy's consular services supported Australians who lived, worked, studied and travelled in Japan, while others in the embassy did a solid job of promoting and supporting diverse Australian interests in multiple fields of human endeavour, always with a positive attitude to negotiating constructive and mutually beneficial agreements with Japanese counterparts. We were good friends and strong strategic partners. The foundations of formal agreements and steady trust across multiple spheres of interest and long-shared experience underpinned the acceptance and the successful delivery of effective relief operations.

The embassy in Tokyo is Australia's official presence in Japan, headed by the ambassador, who is accredited to the Japanese government as the principal resident representative of the Australian government. The head of mission, assisted by DFAT diplomatic officers, leads an accredited senior advisory team of representatives of diverse government departments and agencies, including the ADF. Guided by the Australian prime minister's directive, it is the head of mission who carries ultimate responsibility for communications with the Japanese government, to uphold and represent Australian interests in Japan.

From the first earthquake on the afternoon of 11 March 2011, multiple aspects of the scope and scale of the embassy's daily work and its management realigned dramatically. Up to 120 Australian and Japanese staff, including some 40 DFAT officers with special skills from Canberra and other nearby posts, and over 20 staff from other agencies, were on the compound and in the Tohoku region each day working relentlessly over the intense weeks of this disaster. New undertakings like the search-and-rescue mission were planned in detail, and conventional consular work was radically adapted. Specialist staff were brought in, including Japanese linguists; experienced consular, passport and IT specialists; media liaisons; DFAT and Centrelink counsellors; and radiation health experts. As new systems were implemented and stretched to capacity to handle emergency demands, officers were tasked with unusual and challenging roles mastered on the run. Safety, health and wellbeing became critical factors for all.

Despite increasing tension and stress, everyone quickly adapted cooperatively and effectively to a schedule of round-the-clock shifts throughout the weeks of the crisis. As events unfolded, it was a priority to keep everyone fully updated on developments. Immediate personal needs were catered for as far as possible and reasonable, in crisis conditions. The embassy team's clear determination and sense of shared purpose to work flexibly, intent on finding workable solutions to problems, helped overcome the exhaustion and vulnerability which could have prevailed.

During the weekend of 12–13 March, what would become our greatest immediate concern emerged. Even before the largest explosion at the Fukushima Daiichi Nuclear Power Plant on 14 March, fears grew as we learnt more about the circumstances at Fukushima after the tsunamis, namely that unpredictable winds could carry developing clouds of radioactive fallout across Tokyo. A nuclear fallout shelter complex was quickly constructed in the sub-basement under the embassy as a contingency facility which in theory could shelter 200 people for two or three days. Canberra couriered stocks of potassium iodide to the embassy in case of a radiation emergency. Around Tokyo, and in the worst-affected areas, portable dosimeters were carried to detect radiation levels. Fortunately, there would be no total blowout of the Fukushima nuclear plant, nor the coincidence of winds potentially blowing fallout across Tokyo. However, the trepidation in anticipating and preparing for such prospects, when added to people's stress, became deeply worrying for the majority of Tokyo's community. Consideration of any possible potential radioactive fallout threat affected each of our crisis management and recovery response plans for many weeks. This silent, invisible threat was greatly feared. There was constant concern about contamination of the air, food chain and water supplies for everyone in the affected region.

As fears grew about the emerging crisis at the Fukushima, aided by a lack of accurate information, significant safety and welfare decisions had to be made on the run. Specialised briefings by the embassy for staff and the expatriate Australian community were regularly provided on nuclear fallout and health issues, assisted by medical experts and counsellors sent from Australia. On the ground we learnt quickly that in managing our response to such a crisis while assisting in complex relief initiatives, the need for immediate, practical action would increase. Newly arising problems, not dealt with adequately in our pre-planned manuals, demanded lateral thinking to deliver often ingenious, effective solutions quickly. Thoughtful concern for the welfare of all those impacted was essential. Issues in crisis risk management magnified, as fears about the possibility of nuclear explosions in the Fukushima region increased. Most difficult of all, tough decisions had to be made at times, based on limited or uncertain information about Fukushima.

Communications generally for those still in Japan presented huge difficulties. Along the north-east coastline many of the mobile towers were swept away by tsunamis. In 2011, DFAT had not yet implemented the use of social media such as Facebook and Twitter accounts. These were capabilities which some other embassies in Tokyo were able to use at the time of the quake. Our consular staff were limited to contacting all registered Australian citizens in Japan in person, by email or via telephones that were often not operating.

After the first quake, roads to Narita airport were clogged and others gridlocked with those seeking to leave Japan or the Tohoku region immediately. These included expatriate Australians many of them backed by their corporate employers. Extraordinary demand on our consular officers, to expedite paperwork and resolve identity issues for the growing number of Australian evacuees from Japan, necessitated expanded staffing levels in the embassy's consular office, and the stationing of consular officers at Narita airport.

As fears of nuclear fallout rose, discussions with Canberra led to an early decision, effected within days, that voluntary evacuation to Australia of any of our family members who wished to leave would be arranged and supported financially by the government. This offer was promptly taken up by the majority of families. The significant point was that return, again sponsored by the government, would only be enabled when the Australian government decided conditions were safe and manageable at the post in Tokyo.

For some families this became one of the delicate issues in personal life that such emergencies engender. It is extremely difficult to administer staffing policy decisions, which in an emergency are uniformly applicable to all concerned, without flexibility to accommodate individual requests. At the post in Tokyo, we had done our best to keep families fully informed and provided with relevant briefings or counselling when possible. At a distance in Australia not all home agencies kept up this level of support as rigorously as needed by anxious families, separated from their overworked spouses and partners. Sensationalist media did not always allay their concerns in Australia.

Multiple situation reports were prepared each day. The embassy maintained its 24/7 tempo, especially during the first two weeks after the 11 March quake, facilitating all forms of assistance which Australia was providing. Stress levels were high, and getting adequate sleep was a challenge. Increased tensions resulted from work pressures all hours of the day, exacerbated by relentless aftershocks and the increasing fears that the Fukushima disaster could worsen at any time. Some 400 shocks of 5.0 magnitude or greater were recorded over the first two months.

The time difference between Australia and Japan meant that each day's media reporting cycle from Japan started two hours earlier. There was intense pressure in reporting and responding to Australia's early morning news media enquiries following late nights of intense work. The extraordinary coverage of events by the Australian and international media raised awareness in communities Australia-wide and generated highly valued levels of support for our work and for the people of Japan. While the media's timely coverage was essential and appreciated, these constant media demands added a further burden to the relentless demands on our energies.

There was an overwhelming, spontaneous outpouring of sympathy and support from Australians, resident and offshore, including generous donations. Grassroots-inspired, and informed by the media, this response stemmed from decades of established friendship links between Japanese and Australian people and counterpart organisations. The Australian government could be confident that its proactive, generous and genuine support for the Japanese people at this time sat well with Australians. As soon as news of the disaster reached Australia, ministers, state premiers, business leaders, community groups with friendship arrangements with Japan sister cities, educational institutions and many others contacted the embassy to seek advice, to enquire about our wellbeing and to offer assistance in whatever way possible, to us and to the Japanese people.

Around us, meanwhile, Tokyo was maintaining a dignified and well-ordered response to the chaotic devastation. The resilience and community-minded strengths of local citizens was extraordinary as people remained calm and courteously patient in the face of increasing anxiety and adversity. While long queues formed to obtain basic provisions, which quickly ran out at supermarkets, there was no discernible state of disruptive panic. We knew that many, like ourselves, were anxious about the realities of Fukushima. Later, antinuclear street protests were held in upmarket shopping precincts of Tokyo.

The Japanese government and all senior business and industry leaders had long prepared crisis contingency management plans which supported the local community's response. As in our own case, the preparations were not fully adequate to the scale and enormity of the triple disasters which Tohoku 2011 brought. The combination of cascading disasters, starting with the earthquake followed by the catastrophic tsunamis and the damage and explosions at the Fukushima power plant, accentuated decision-making uncertainties in Tokyo. We knew that the government led by the Democratic Party of Japan, which was in government for the first time in decades and relatively inexperienced, did not enjoy the same strongly entrenched links with the industrial establishment which the Liberal Democratic Party always enjoyed when in office. Headed at the time by Prime Minister Kan, the government was greatly motivated to act effectively to address the crisis, but evidence soon emerged that the government was not being kept fully informed about the scale of the Fukushima disaster. The prime minister was frustrated by the lack of transparency from the Tokyo Electric Power Company (TEPCO). It became apparent that TEPCO was indeed withholding information and reportedly not briefing the government fully. This political situation trickled down to impact the information which the Japanese MOFA, as the key designated official contact point for the embassy, was able to provide at its regular briefings.

It became clear from various sources of information that after the tsunamis hit Fukushima initially, some smaller explosions resulting in fallout had occurred before the most significant blast of 14 March. These earliest clouds of radioactive fallout had blown out to sea. Prior to the worst fears of nuclear fallout increasing, the RAAF C-17, carrying the NSW Fire and Rescue task force, was in the air on Sunday 13 March with diplomatic clearance confirmed in consultation with the Japanese government for its arrival at Yokota US Air Base, west of Tokyo. The search-and-rescue team's ultimate destination would be Minamisanriku—one of the fishing villages of 20,000–30,000 people completely swept away, with huge loss of life and infrastructure, creating an eerily desolate, apocalyptic landscape.

The RAAF C-17 arrived safely at Yokota in the very early hours of 14 March, carrying a 76-strong task force from the NSW Fire and Rescue, together with two sniffer dogs from Queensland. That RAAF C-17 and its crew then opportunely remained in-country, working alongside the US Airforce and Japanese Self-Defense Force aircraft as personnel and tonnes of supplies were ferried relentlessly in repeat missions all over Japan, contributing massively to Australia's humanitarian assistance and disaster relief efforts in Japan and earning great appreciation.

As the fear of potential nuclear fallout deepened, the RAAF crews faced the same threats that the embassy dealt with on a daily basis—perhaps more so in flying. The critical ongoing unknown factor was potential wind direction at the time of any further explosion. Subsequent winds unfortunately did blow inland but towards the north-west, not north-east to the tsunami disaster zone.

On the ground, the embassy, with full responsibility, once the NSW Fire and Rescue team had arrived at Yokota, was preparing for the team's urgent deployment to Minamisanriku. Two groups, each comprising three fluent Japanese speakers from the embassy, were established to assist the specialist search-and-rescue team. A dedicated Japanese MOFA liaison officer joined the team travelling to the disaster zone, leaving in the very early hours of 15 March so that they would travel through the worst-affected zones further north during daylight. Since few normal supply chains in the community were fully functional and all necessities extremely scarce, food and medical provisions had been carried from Australia or sourced by the embassy. Negotiating special road permits, hiring buses and sourcing fuel presented constant challenges for the embassy. Our Japanese staff provided invaluable logistics support.

Before the search-and-rescue team could travel north in-country, numerous problems had to be resolved, including locating supplies of drinking water and fuel. Despite their own desperate circumstances, the Japanese provided fuel for the buses that took the search-and-rescue team up to Minamisanriku. The embassy's defence adviser purchased two tonnes of bottled drinking water from the US Commissary at Yokota airbase and Australian business assisted when Toll Holdings, whose logistic base was in Osaka, arranged to truck additional water supplies into Tokyo for the Australian team.

The embassy in Tokyo, working with the government in Australia, had become increasingly concerned about radiation levels in the disaster zone. In Australia, extensive consultations about radiation levels took place with the Australian Radiation Protection and Nuclear Safety Agency (ARPANSA), who were in close contact with their counterparts at the International Atomic Energy Agency and with US and Japanese agencies. ARPANSA helped coordinate the embassy's close monitoring of developments at Fukushima, and fully briefed the NSW search-and-rescue team prior to the team's agreeing to deploy in the affected regions. The embassy updated these briefings after the team's arrival in Japan.

Within days, the embassy had a special consular team actively locating Australians in the earthquake zone. This specialist team, augmented by officers from DFAT in Canberra and other regional posts, planned to set out on Sunday 13 March to travel north to Sendai. The team's objective was to locate people at home and, where necessary, to search evacuation centres, morgues and hospitals in the devastated areas.

At the embassy, in planning for the journeys of each team going north, we relied on the Bureau of Meteorology in Australia for its accurate forecasting of likely wind directions, in addition to ARPANSA's briefings. Main highways to the north were closed, with only limited access into the earthquake zone for emergency relief, including some diplomatic vehicles. Planning the routes to be taken north was complex for both the consular group and the search-and-rescue team, mindful that the earliest possible arrival time in the field was a critical factor for success of their missions.

Expert opinions varied as to what radius of safety exclusion zones around the Fukushima nuclear plant might be needed to avoid radioactive fallout exposure. Early assessments of 20–30 kilometres were quickly upgraded to 50 kilometres, then 80 kilometres, depending on the different criteria for gradations of safety levels from 'no go' evacuation to more moderate, or lesser exposure.

The consular team was ready to set out on the Sunday, aiming to travel along the main highway where possible, pausing occasionally for short periods through the perimeter of the 80-kilometre radius for radioactive fallout. During these incursions, additional precautionary measures to minimise any possible exposure were taken. The search-and-rescue team faced a similar dilemma, also taking appropriate precautions. A further challenge was the weather. March is officially the first month of spring but in northern Japan 2011 it was still late winter and icy cold.

There were many alliances that supported the embassy's work at this time. Close liaison had continued with those Australians remaining in Japan, including businesspeople. The head of Lend Lease Australia in Japan had called me, desperately seeking advice. His key regional office in Sendai was at the centre of the area most affected by tsunamis. He urgently needed to travel there, as Lend Lease was responsible for the reinstallation and restoration of mobile phone towers for one of Japan's major telephone operators. With the highway north closed except to emergency traffic, he was seeking advice as to how he might reach Sendai. Our special consular team's first destination to begin their search in the disaster areas was Sendai. Understanding the strategic importance of the Australian company's work in the affected region I offered him a seat in our bus but requested a critical reciprocal favour in return. Could our group set up a workstation in the Lend Lease office and camp overnight when scarce hotel accommodation was not available? This proved possible and provided an excellent example of the synergy during this crisis when business and government worked together effectively in ad hoc alliances. Flexibility was a key factor in finding effective solutions to new problems every day.

As planned, the consular team travelled far north visiting evacuation centres, morgues and hospitals in person, locating a few Australian citizens who had been injured. Fortunately, there were no recorded fatalities, and all known Australians were accounted for within two weeks. Meanwhile, it would be –5° C when the NSW search-and-rescue team arrived at the disaster area. Ironically, as they arrived at the staging point, Swiss and German teams who had arrived the previous day were departing, responding to reports of radioactive clouds from further Fukushima explosions blowing along the coast towards the disaster areas. The Australian team quickly took advice from Australia and, with their dosimeters showing only very low levels of radiation, continued conducting search and recovery operations over the next three days.

The role of the fluent Japanese speakers provided by the embassy to support the search-and-rescue team in the disaster zone was absolutely critical to its effective operation. Comprising fluent Japanese-speaking DFAT officers, the two teams faced extreme hardship and tragedy daily in bitter wintry conditions as they rotated to support the search effort, through that first week. While no further survivors were found, the search team, supported by the young linguists, sadly, but importantly and with care, was able to recover the remains of some who had died in the tsunami. Treasured family memorabilia and family photos were recovered where possible. These efforts earned tremendous goodwill. The team forged strong relationships with local survivors and authorities, including the town's mayor, Sato Jin. The work of the NSW Fire and Rescue task force, some of whom had only recently returned from the recovery efforts after the Christchurch, New Zealand, earthquake of February 2011, was exemplary. Their work, together with that of the young linguists, translated into lasting goodwill which underpinned the warmth of Prime Minister Gillard's visit to Minamisanriku six weeks later.

As the Fukushima crisis deepened in following days, Australia was able to play a further specific role in assisting the ongoing operation to cool the vulnerable reactors. Again, at every point, invaluable alliances, often ad hoc, between business, government, defence forces, people-to-people contacts and between embassies, proved critical in getting things done.

Regular meetings were held in Tokyo between the 'five eyes' embassies of the US, the UK, Canada, Australia and New Zealand. At one of those meetings the US ambassador approached me on behalf of Washington to ask if Australia might be able to transport by air from Western Australia extremely large, sophisticated fire-fighting water pump equipment operated by remote control. This pump, offered by its owner, the US multinational Bechtel, was stationed in Western Australia against the contingency of fire at a liquefied-natural-gas rig. It was hoped that this specialised equipment, the nearest situated to Japan of its type, could potentially help cool the Fukushima reactors by pumping and spraying huge volumes of water.

Immediate contact with Canberra led to a quick decision by relevant ministers and defence chiefs for Australia to air freight the equipment to Japan. Two further RAAF C-17 aircraft were available, into which the dismantled equipment could be loaded in a complex operation for shipment. After arrival, Japanese Self-Defense land forces transported it to Fukushima. At the time Australia had four RAAF C-17 aircraft, one already deployed to Japan and one out of commission. The Japanese appreciated as an extraordinary commitment of goodwill the fact that Australia provided its only two available C-17s for this purpose, with full RAAF technical skills and support.

After weeks of tension, marked by a deep sense of grief and massive upheavals, I was acutely aware of the need to move on with recovery, both in the wider community and in the embassy. Families were reunited, children back at school and staffing numbers at the embassy were realigned. Learning from our recent experience, we knew there were changes and upgrades to be implemented as soon as possible. My immediate challenge was to re-establish effective normality for the embassy in going forward.

Prime Minister Gillard's visit to Japan, 20–23 April 2011, marked a significant point of transition at the time. This visit had been tentatively planned prior to the earthquake crisis and the prime minister and others were highly sensitive to the importance of not hindering the Japanese government's recovery efforts by proceeding with the visit. After careful soundings with Japanese counterparts, I was delighted to report back that, very kindly, her visit would be welcome. The embassy and MOFA began the intensive work needed in preparation for the visit. Prime Minister Gillard handled the visit with dignity and an empathetic calm which was genuinely appreciated by her Japanese government hosts.

Figure 2.1: Australian prime minister Julia Gillard visits Minamisanriku, Miyagi Prefecture, north-east Japan, Saturday 23 April 2011.
Photographer: Toru Hanai.
Source: EPA/Toru Hanai/POOL.

This head of government visit, during which Prime Minister Gillard had an audience with Emperor Akihito and met Prime Minister Kan, was the first by any country's head of government after the Tohoku disasters. The embassy, with the Australian community in Tokyo, arranged a special earthquake relief dinner, at which the prime minister was the guest of honour, raising significant funds for the relief efforts. The central purpose of the event was the opportunity to bring together hundreds of Australian and Japanese friends in warmly shared appreciation of the enormous contribution to the relief efforts that everyone attending had given in the preceding critical weeks. For ourselves and our Japanese guests this was the first time we felt comfortable to relax and go out and meet friends over dinner. The extraordinary spirit of goodwill and shared endeavour felt at this function continued during the prime minister's visit to Sendai and Minamisanriku in the shocking face of such visible destruction. The prime minister established genuine rapport with the Japanese survivors she met during her visit to the disaster areas.

This visit required a great commitment on the part of the prime minister's Japanese hosts with whom we worked closely to ensure its success and safety for all. Major transport issues in Japan were further compounded by low cloud cover, which nearly prevented the prime minister's plane from landing at Sendai airport. A long bus drive to Minamisanriku followed. Here, Prime Minister Gillard gently embraced the town's mayor, Sato Jin, as they met in the devastated township. The photo of this sadly historic moment was carried front-page in Japanese, Australian and global media. Mayor Sato had established warm relations with the Australian search-and-rescue team during the time of their harrowing work in his community earlier and now expressed his deep heartfelt gratitude for the assistance his town had received from Australia. This visit truly captured the strong spirit of goodwill between Australia and Japan. Earlier, while in Tokyo, the prime minister planted a flowering crabapple tree in the beautiful traditional garden in the embassy compound, famous for its magnificent old cherry trees. This new tree was planted as a flowering symbol of the spirit of Australia–Japan relations during the crisis recovery period of 2011.

Figure 2.2: Julia Gillard with Sato Jin (left), the mayor of Minamisanriku.
Photographer: Takahiro Yamamoto.
Source: *Yomiuri Shimbun*; Associated Press.

Postscript for Times Recalled a Decade Later, 2021

This account must honour the lives that were swept away on that fateful day, 11 March 2011. They are never forgotten. It was a time of terrible grief. I have followed with deep respect the difficult journey which the survivors of devastated townships have taken to rebuild vibrant lives and communities with such courage and resilience. Recovery, and the return to a more normal life in the aftermath of crisis, is tough. It has been very important to me as chair (2012–20) of the Australia–Japan Foundation (AJF), that alongside many other business and community groups, AJF has played a central role on behalf of Australians through its grants program by supporting partnering projects assisting recovery of communities devastated by the triple disasters.

To serve as Australia's ambassador to Japan was a great responsibility and honour, always dependent on the skills, goodwill and loyalties of others, both Australian and Japanese. That would never have been truer than at the time of the Tohoku crisis. Those who shared that journey with purpose and determination know that the lessons learnt travel with us always, informing our work and enriching our lives. In this narrative it is impossible to recount all the daily events or to name the many individuals who played a crucial role in extending effective assistance to so many people, sharing a genuine regard for, and spirit of, humanity. Every word written brings back memories of faces and moments in time, with gratitude for shared endeavours well and meaningfully undertaken.

There were many ways that each of us, all quite ordinary, enlarged our courage by action. Some of the lessons we Australians learnt were essentially Japan context-specific, but many had universal impact and potential application. Looking to the future always, details of these past experiences, thoughtfully reviewed, can usefully inform us how to prepare for, or respond better to, the challenges that diverse crises will present in the future. State-of-the-art IT capabilities, for example, are vital in crisis response.

The critical role played by each Australian fluent in a language other than English, in this instance Japanese, and encompassing other culturally sensitive capabilities in their skill set, must be remembered as we educate tomorrow's Australians. Bilingual Japanese staff and counterparts working closely together with us in Australia-connected activities contributed invaluable strength to the embassy team's efforts and our shared wellbeing.

I have noted that at the time of the crisis the role of the Australian embassy, as it had evolved over the previous 60 years, took on new characteristics as it faced the complex challenges of a profoundly daunting period. We were backed from Australia by sound foreign policy and supportive government leadership. The solidarity of, and trust in, the Australia–Japan relationship with its diverse facets underpinned our cooperation at a crucial time and was strengthened on both sides. In particular, Australia's humanitarian response collaboration with Japan during the crisis recovery period led to broadening and deepening the substance of our joint security relationship.

I believe it is in the warmth of personal friendships shared across all of life's interests by so many Australian and Japanese people, long term, in boundless and curious ways, that the spirit of those Tohoku days shines.

The Embassy, Its People and Places

3

Ambassadors and Key Issues

David Lee and David Lowe

As Murray McLean recalls in relation to the Australian embassy's emergency response to the Tohoku earthquake and tsunami of 2011, relationships between Australia and Japan were notable for their breadth, depth and trust. The quality of these relationships, he argues, explains the readiness of Japanese authorities to accept Australian offers of help. In 2011, when the earthquake struck, the embassy was supporting 'trade and investment, security, multilateral commitments, and global and bilateral foreign policies' and enjoyed 'people-to-people strengths of goodwill'. The embassy was also a source of support for around 12,000 Australians resident in Japan. How did the Australia–Japan relationship recover from the depths of World War II enmity to blossom in such spectacular and multidimensional ways? This chapter investigates how we arrived at the situation that McLean recalls at the end of the first decade of the twenty-first century. It explores the main features of a changing Australia–Japan relationship, with special focus on the Australian ambassadors in Tokyo who navigated and helped facilitate these changes.

The challenges faced by Australia's ambassadors included not only establishing cordial relations after a bitter war with Japan but also, after 1952, encouraging Japan's active involvement in regional security matters and cultivating the trading relationship that saw Japan become Australia's most important economic relationship from the late 1960s to the 2000s. In the period from 1940 to the early 1970s, the Department of Commerce and Agriculture (and from 1956 the Department of Trade) vied with the Department of External Affairs to control the activities of the embassy in

Tokyo, which were dominated by matters of trade. This was despite the fact that heads of mission after Sir John Latham (August 1940–December 1941) were usually officers or former officers of either the Department of External Affairs or the Prime Minister's Department. Neil Currie (1982–86) was exceptional among former officials and was a former permanent secretary of the Department of Industry and Commerce. From the 1970s to the mid-1980s, the Department of Foreign Affairs won the contest with the Department of Trade. In 1987 the two departments were united in the Department of Foreign Affairs and Trade (DFAT), and thereafter the mission was staffed with diplomats, former politicians and former senior trade officials and controlled by a department with responsibility for both diplomacy and trade.

Unlike other high-ranking overseas posts such as London and Washington, the Australian embassy in Tokyo has been led predominately by career diplomats or senior civil servants, the two exceptions being Western Australian politicians Gordon Freeth (1970–73) and Richard Court (2017–20). Archival records occasionally reveal more of the diplomatic activities conducted below head-of-post level—at least up to around 2000, when records are publicly available for historians.

This chapter therefore covers a broad range of mutual interests and concerns for Australia and Japan. It includes the conclusion of the Peace Treaty with Japan in 1951 and the re-establishment of diplomatic relations. The Menzies government then needed to overcome popular hostility stemming from war-related memories in order to adopt a more liberal policy towards Japan from mid-1954. Prior to signing a significant trade agreement, the Commerce Agreement of 1957, it was not only those groups directly connected to the war, such as the Returned Servicemen's Leagues, that voiced displeasure; resistance from Treasury and Australian manufacturers also had to be overcome. David Walton's chapter, following this one, makes a compelling case for seeing this period from the early 1950s to the mid-1960s as special on account of the development of strategic and regional cooperation.

There developed a rough line of division within Australian government departments, with External Affairs, alongside Trade and Customs, on the one hand, pushing for more liberal treatment of Japan, including greater trade, and Treasury, on the other hand, opposing this. During the 1960s, the complementarity of Australia's and Japan's economies helped strengthen the relationship. Some of Australia's most important mining developments took place underpinned by Japanese contracts and new forms of state–federal cooperation. Western Australian iron ore mining was one celebrated example, but the minerals boom also saw new and highly profitable mining ventures in New South Wales and Queensland.

Japanese and Australian governments took different, but not opposing, approaches to the Vietnam War and related Cold War challenges in Southeast Asia, with Japan's economic engagement with the region roughly paralleling Australia's military involvement. By the mid-1970s, leaders of both countries welcomed the chance to articulate their desire for a broadening of the relationship based on shared principles, in the form of a Basic Treaty of Friendship and Cooperation—known as the NARA Treaty, from 'Nippon Australia Relations Agreement'—of 1976.

This chapter outlines how Australian ambassadors to Japan helped foster an increasing number of dialogues on ideas about regional cooperation from the mid-1970s. They also helped facilitate a huge expansion in the trade of Australian resources to Japan during the 1980s and 1990s, including new reserves of iron ore, coal and bauxite. In short, the embassy played a crucial role in the transition of the Australian–Japanese relationship from enmity to interdependence. At the core of this interdependent relationship was economic 'complementarity', but from this economic partnership developed a multifaceted relationship embracing regional and security cooperation and cultural and people-to-people linkages. Managing increasingly high expectations of the Australia–Japan relationship became a feature of work in the embassy by the 1990s; and economic shocks such as the downturn in the Japanese economy or imaginative misadventures such as the failed joint multifunction polis idea did not derail the continued growth and multidimensionality of the relationship.

By the turn of the century, the people-to-people dimension of Australia–Japan relations was striking. Movements between the two countries of students, teachers, working holiday visa holders, business leaders, tourists and a broader range of experts, especially economists and strategic analysts, demonstrated the expanded opportunities for regular exchange.

At the same time, the growth of China both challenged Australia–Japan relations—China overtaking Japan to become Australia's biggest trading partner in 2007—and strengthened an emerging cooperation between Australia and Japan in security policies. With China increasingly flexing its military muscles and with periodic North Korean expressions of belligerence as context, Australia has played a significant role in anchoring Japan's cautious re-emergence in security matters: regionally—especially as part of the Quad (Australia, India, Japan and the United States)—bilaterally and internationally, including in the context of United Nations actions.

The chapter concludes by noting how the Australia–Japan relationship has also been underpinned most recently by high levels of cooperation in responding to natural disasters. The Indian Ocean tsunami of 2004 set in train collaborative measures which, indirectly, led to the first version of the Quad. As we have seen in McLean's chapter, the disastrous Tohoku earthquake suffered by Japan seven years later, in March 2011, triggering a tsunami and meltdowns of the Fukushima Daiichi nuclear reactors, prompted a significant range of Australian actions to meet urgent needs. The Australian embassy was at the fore in how these various forms of assistance unfolded—just as the embassy has been central in much of the diverse and multifaceted forms of Australia–Japan connectedness since the 1940s.

Prelude

Australia's formal diplomatic relationship with Japan began as a result of the decision, taken by Prime Minister Joseph Lyons in 1939 and implemented by his successor, Robert Menzies, a year later, to establish direct diplomatic relations with foreign countries in Asia and the Pacific. Australia established legations in Washington and Tokyo that were headed by diplomats with the rank of minister. Menzies emphasised the status of the new diplomatic positions when in 1940 he appointed R.G. Casey, the minister for supply and development and a former federal treasurer, to Washington and Sir John Latham, the chief justice of the High Court of Australia, to Tokyo.

Latham was born on 26 August 1877 at Ascot Vale, Melbourne. He won a scholarship to the prestigious Scotch College, proceeded to the University of Melbourne and, after winning the Supreme Court Prize, was admitted to the Victorian Bar in 1904. During World War I, Latham was appointed head of naval intelligence with the rank of lieutenant-commander. Having come to the attention of the prime minister, W.M. Hughes, he was invited to join the Australian delegation to the Paris Peace Conference in 1919.

The delegation played a large part in gaining for Australia a League of Nations mandate over New Guinea but also in thwarting Japan's effort to enshrine racial non-discrimination in the League of Nations Covenant.[1] On his return to Australia, Latham championed the newly established League of Nations and entered parliament as an independent Liberal in 1922. He served as attorney-general and minister for external affairs in the Bruce–Page coalition government from 1925 to 1929 and led the Opposition to the Scullin Labor government from 1929 to 1931 before giving way to Joseph Lyons after the latter was appointed leader of the United Australia Party. At the end of 1931, having defeated James Scullin at the federal election, Lyons appointed Latham as attorney-general and, once again, minister for external affairs. In his external affairs capacity, Latham led a Goodwill Mission to Japan in 1934 before taking up an appointment as chief justice of the High Court of Australia in the following year.[2]

Because of Latham's longstanding interest in and understanding of Japan, his former political colleagues arranged for special legislation to be passed in 1940 to allow him to become Australia's first minister to Japan while remaining chief justice. Latham would not arrive in Tokyo, however, until December 1940, after Japan had reached a pact of mutual assistance with the Axis powers Italy and Germany. Latham was aware of criticism of Australia's policy towards Japan from influential voices in Australia. The young economist John Crawford argued that Australia should pursue 'economic appeasement' of Japan. Crawford's role in the changing Australia–Japan relationship was of such importance over the next three decades that he is the subject of Chapter 5 in this volume. In agreement was the Queensland historian A.C.V. Melbourne, who lobbied Lyons energetically to establish a separate Australian diplomatic mission in Tokyo in the late 1930s.[3] Both Crawford and Melbourne decried two Australian initiatives that had been taken without the benefit of an Australian diplomatic mission in Tokyo and had rankled Japan. The first was the diversion of trade away from

1   David Lee, 'Sir John Latham and the League of Nations', in *League of Nations: Histories, Legacy and Impact*, ed. Joy Damousi and Patricia O'Brien (Carlton: Melbourne University Publishing, 2018), 83–99; Naoko Shimazu, *Japan, Race and Equality: The Racial Equality Proposal of 1919* (London: Routledge, 2009).

2   Ruth Megaw, 'The Australian Goodwill Mission to the Far East in 1934: Its Significance in the Evolution of Australian Foreign Policy', *Journal of the Royal Australian Historical Society* 59, no. 4 (1973): 247–63.

3   James Cotton, *The Australian School of International Relations* (London: Palgrave Macmillan, 2013), 73–93; A.C.V. Melbourne, *Report on Australian Intercourse with Japan and China* (Brisbane: University of Queensland Press, 1932).

Japan towards Great Britain in the mid-1930s.[4] The second was the Lyons government's 1938 decision to stop the planned Japanese development of iron ore deposits at Yampi Sound, Western Australia, by prohibiting the export overseas of Australian iron ore.[5]

Latham shared their objective to conciliate Japan. He sought to help the Australian government to prevent war in the Pacific and discourage Japanese encroachment in Southeast Asia. He left Japan for consultations in Singapore in September 1941, but having fallen ill, returned to Melbourne before the outbreak of hostilities in the Pacific in December. The work of the newly created legation was suspended for the duration of the Pacific War and Latham's staff in Tokyo, including the diplomats Keith Officer and Patrick Shaw, were interned until an exchange could be arranged by the Allies with Japanese diplomats in August 1942.

The war in the Pacific was a profound break in these cautious first steps in official relations. As is now well known, the speed of Japan's success in capturing or controlling much of Southeast Asia from December 1941 through February 1942 shocked an Australian population beyond what they had thought possible, and the ease with which Japanese forces captured the British fortress island of Singapore was a huge blow to imperial pride and Australians' sense of security. Understandably, many Australians feared an attempted Japanese invasion of Australia was to follow. While Japanese high command had decided to isolate rather than invade Australia, this decision was not known in Australia, and aerial attacks on Darwin and midget submarine attacks in Sydney Harbour only fuelled Australians' worst fears. Through 1942 to the end of the war the ferocity of fighting in the Pacific and the brutal treatment of many Australian prisoners of war captured by Japanese, resulting in over 8,000 deaths in captivity, left a popular legacy of hatred and bitterness towards the Japanese.

There were hints, however, even in the approach to the Pacific War, of the possibility of a wholly different kind of relationship than that which developed during the Pacific War. This was presaged in the extraordinary personal relationship that developed between Tatsuo Kawai, Japan's minister to Australia, and John Curtin, leader of the Labor Opposition

---

4   D.C.S. Sissons, 'Manchester v. Japan: The Imperial Background of the Australia Trade Diversion Dispute with Japan, 1936', *Australian Outlook* 30, no. 3 (1972): 480–502, doi.org/10.1080/10357717608444583.
5   David Lee, 'Australia's Embargo of the Export of Iron Ore: A Reconsideration', *Journal of Australasian Mining History* 18, no. 1 (2020): 96–112.

3. AMBASSADORS AND KEY ISSUES

and then prime minister from 1941 to 1945. In the approach to war, Curtin sought to cultivate the personal relationship in the interests of preventing the outbreak of war in the Pacific. Curtin's idea was to reach an agreement whereby Australia boosted trade with Japan, including by allowing Japan access to Western Australia's iron ore resources, in exchange for Japan's guaranteeing Australia's safety. Curtin hosted Kawai as a guest of honour in Perth and at the Lodge in Canberra after he became prime minister. After the war, Kawai was ostracised in Japan and dismissed from the Foreign Office after calling on Japanese not to hate Australians. Towards the end of the war, he worked with future Japanese prime minister Yoshida Shigeru in the interests of peace and, after the war, became vice foreign minister under Yoshida.[6]

After the Japanese surrender in August 1945, the Australian government was determined to be fully engaged in the postwar occupation and planning for Japan. In 1946 Australian prime minister J.B. Chifley appointed the academic William Macmahon ('Mac') Ball as British Commonwealth member of the Allied Council for Japan and Australian minister to that country. The appointment of an Australian to the council was an acknowledgement of Australia's role in the Allied defeat of Japan and its leadership of the British Commonwealth Occupation Force (BCOF) in Japan from 1946 to 1952. At its peak, BCOF was about one-quarter the number of the US personnel in Japan and for most of the period of occupation Australians constituted most of BCOF's personnel.[7] Ball took up his position in Tokyo on 3 April 1946 but failed to make much headway in pushing Australian policy positions in the council.[8] US general Douglas MacArthur, the dictatorial supreme commander for the Allied powers, kept the most important policy decisions away from

6   See Bob Wurth, *Saving Australia: Curtin's Secret Peace with Japan* (South Melbourne: Lothian Books, 2006).

7   Peter Bates, *Japan and the British Occupation Force 1946–52* (London: Brassey's, 1993); George Davies, *The Occupation of Japan: The Rhetoric and Reality of Anglo-Australian Relations 1939–1952* (St Lucia: University of Queensland Press, 2001); James Wood, *The Forgotten Force* (Sydney: Allen & Unwin, 1998); Christine de Matos, *Encouraging Democracy in a Cold War Climate: The Dual-Platform Policy Approach of Evatt and Labor toward the Allied Occupation of Japan 1945–1949* (Sydney: Australia–Japan Research Centre, University of Western Sydney, 2001); Robin Gerster, *Travels in Atomic Sunshine: Australia and the Occupation of Japan* (Melbourne: Scribe, 2019); Julie Suares, *J.B. Chifley: An Ardent Internationalist* (Carlton: Melbourne University Publishing, 2019); and Jeffrey Grey, *Australian Brass: The Career of Lieutenant General Sir Horace Robertson* (Cambridge: Cambridge University Press, 1992).

8   Alan Rix, ed., *Intermittent Diplomat: The Japan and Batavia Diaries of W. Macmahon Ball* (Melbourne: Melbourne University Press, 1988); Ai Kobayashi, *W. Macmahon Ball: Politics and the People* (North Melbourne: Australian Scholarly Publishing, 2013).

the council's consideration while, at the same time, British diplomats were not averse to undermining Ball because of differences between British and Australian foreign policy towards Japan.[9] Ball resigned in August 1947 to be succeeded by Patrick Shaw, the diplomat who had first served in Tokyo under Latham. Shaw strove energetically, although unsuccessfully, to prevent MacArthur from marginalising Australian views on the reconstruction of Japan.[10]

In September 1949 Shaw was replaced by William Roy Hodgson, a former permanent secretary of the Department of External Affairs. Hodgson led Australia's mission in Tokyo during a period of dramatic change in East Asia. In October 1949 the People's Republic of China was established in mainland China after the Nationalists, under Chiang Kai-shek, had fled to the island of Formosa (Taiwan). In June 1950, when North Korea invaded South Korea, the United Nations Security Council authorised a group of countries, led by the United States and including Australia, to aid South Korea in resisting North Korean aggression.[11]

Developments in the Cold War in East Asia reinforced the reverse course to Japan taken by the United States in 1948 and 1949. This involved the progressive abandonment of the strict Allied policies followed between 1945 to 1947 to democratise and demilitarise Japan.[12] From 1948 onward the United States sought to build up Japan economically as an anti-communist bastion in the Cold War.[13] Australian governments, particularly the Chifley Labor government, had not been happy with aspects of the American reverse course on policy to Japan and wanted reassurances that there could be no revival of Japanese militarism.[14] Hodgson finished his term as minister to Japan in April 1952, just before two important developments. The first was ratification of the ANZUS

---

9   Christine de Matos, 'Diplomacy Interrupted? Macmahon Ball, Evatt and Labor's Policies in Occupied Japan', *Australian Journal of Politics and History* 52, no. 2 (2006): 188–201, doi.org/10.1111/j.1467-8497.2005.00414.x; Robert Harvey, *American Shogun* (London: John Murray, 2006); Michael Schaller, *Douglas MacArthur: The Far Eastern General* (New York: Oxford University Press, 1989); John Dower, *Embracing Defeat: Japan in the Aftermath of World War II* (Harmondsworth: Penguin, 2000).

10   David Lee, 'Shaw, Sir Patrick (1913–1975)' in *Australian Dictionary of Biography*, vol. 16, ed. John Ritchie and Diane Langmore (Carlton: Melbourne University Press, 2002), 220–21.

11   Robert O'Neill, *Australia in the Korean War 1950–1953* (Canberra: Australian War Memorial, 1981).

12   Walter LaFeber, *The Clash: U.S. Japanese Relations Throughout History* (New York: W.W. Norton & Company, 1997), 262–70.

13   Ibid., 270–83.

14   David McLean, 'ANZUS Origins: A Reassessment', *Australian Historical Studies* 24, no. 94 (1990): 64–82, doi.org/10.1080/10314619008595832.

Treaty between Australia, New Zealand and the United States, which was seen partly in terms of Cold War alliance, defending against the threat of communism in Asia, and partly as addressing Australian fears of a remilitarised Japan. The second and related development was the signing of the Japanese Peace Treaty, which ended the Allied occupation and enabled the restoration of Japan's full sovereignty.

Restoration and Trade

Hodgson was succeeded in Japan by E. Ronald Walker, who was Australia's first head of mission of ambassador status. Walker was an eminent economist and head of the National Security Resources Board, which advised the Menzies government on the balance between civilian and military spending during the Korean War.[15] His term in Tokyo ran from 1952 to 1955, a period coinciding with Japan's resumption of its prewar place as a significant trading partner with Australia. In 1948 Japan's industrial production was no more than two-fifths of its 1937 level and export trade was minimal. It was thus fortunate for Japan that US spending in Japan during the Korean War provided a boost to its economy.[16] As Japan's economy steadily recovered, it emerged once again as a substantial international purchaser of Australian raw wool, wheat and barley. The balance of trade ran heavily in Australia's favour. In 1952/53 Japan's purchases from Australia were valued at A£83,958,000, while Australian imports from Japan were limited to a mere A£4,692,000.[17] Already, less than a decade after the end of the Pacific War, were signs of the development of an important economic and trading relationship between two erstwhile enemies.

Despite the boost that the Korean War boom had given Japan, many diplomatic observers considered the country unstable, and that a leftist takeover was a possibility. Between 1952 and 1959 the left-wing Social Democratic Party increased its representation in the Diet and led agitation against both the terms of the Japanese Peace Treaty and a Security Treaty

---

15 David Lee, 'The National Security Planning and Defence Preparations of the Menzies Government, 1950–1953', *War & Society* 10, no. 2 (1992): 119–38, doi.org/10.1179/072924792791198913. Walker was the author of several books on economics and economic history, including *The Australian Economy in War and Reconstruction* (New York: Oxford University Press, 1947).

16 LaFeber, *The Clash*, 283–95.

17 Sandra Tweedie, *Trading Partners: Australia & Asia 1790–1993* (Sydney: University of New South Wales Press, 1994), 155.

made between Japan and the United States in 1954.[18] Moreover, some Japanese businessmen and politicians, including Yoshida Shigeru, prime minister of Japan from 1948 to 1954, agreed with elements of the left in calling for a revival of trade with mainland China in defiance of the wishes of the United States.[19] In 1953, Walker warned the Department of External Affairs of the American view that Japan urgently needed to wean itself off American aid and find trading partners other than the People's Republic of China.[20] The minister for external affairs, R.G. Casey, accepted the advice and told cabinet in July 1954 that Australia should work actively to make sure that Japan retained a democratic government. Australia's restrictions on Japanese trade, through tariff, import licensing and sterling-area payments, worked against such efforts. As a consequence, in 1953 and 1954 the Japanese sought to have trade talks with Australia. Although Japan made no headway in trade discussions in those years, it was successful in negotiating an agreement with Australia about resuming pearl shell fishing off the north coast of Australia.[21]

By the end of 1954, New Zealand and Canada had made trade agreements with Japan while the United States had reached with Japan the much stronger treaty of friendship, commerce and navigation (FCN). Australia, by contrast, had not reached any such agreement, and there were several obstacles in the way. A decade after the end of the Pacific War there was considerable resistance in Australia from manufacturing interests, protectionist-minded public servants and the Returned Services League to a national trade agreement with its former enemy. Many Australian manufacturers were averse to the prospect of more Japanese imports coming into Australia, and within the federal bureaucracy the Treasury and the Department of Trade and Customs worked to oppose a trade agreement with Japan. The Treasury feared that imports from Japan would exacerbate Australia's balance of payments problem and Trade and Customs sought to safeguard Australia's manufacturing and the trading relationship with Britain.[22]

---

18   LaFeber, *The Clash*, 296–324.

19   Extract from submission to cabinet by R.G. Casey, 21 September 1951, Department of Foreign Affairs and Trade (DFAT), *Documents on Australian Foreign Policy: The Australia–Japan Agreement on Commerce* (Canberra: Australian Government Publishing Service, 1997), 11–12.

20   Ibid., cablegram from Walker to Department of External Affairs, 30 January 1953, 33.

21   Alan Rix, *The Australia–Japan Political Alignment: 1952 to the Present* (London: Routledge, 1999), 43–70.

22   Alan Rix, *Coming to Terms: The Politics of Australia's Trade with Japan 1945–1957* (Sydney: Allen & Unwin, 1986).

Taking an opposing view was the Department of Commerce and Agriculture, now led by John Crawford, and the Department of External Affairs. The Department of Commerce and Agriculture was particularly worried about possible Japanese retaliation against wool exports. The Department of External Affairs, advised by Walker and his colleagues in Tokyo, wished to prevent Japan from aligning with Communist China and to keep it within the Western bloc. In the second half of 1955 Australian and Japanese officials began informal trade discussions, and bureaucratic opposition to a trade agreement diminished when, at the beginning of 1956, the Department of Commerce and Agriculture and the Department of Trade and Customs merged to form a unified Department of Trade headed by Crawford and under the former minister for commerce and agriculture, John McEwen. The new Department of Trade commenced its work at the same time as a new Australian ambassador, Alan Watt, arrived in Tokyo.

Watt was a highly experienced diplomat and a former permanent secretary of the Department of External Affairs.[23] As Watt took up his position in Tokyo, a small team was set up in Australia to negotiate with Japanese officials. It was headed by the deputy secretary of the Department of Trade, Alan Westerman, under the direction of Crawford and McEwen. Australian negotiators had three main objectives: to bind duty-free entry into Japan of raw wool; to persuade Japan to protect Australia from foreigners dumping their exports in the Japanese market; and to ask that Japan accord Australia most-favoured-nation status, or at least minimum quotas for wheat, barley and sugar.[24] In return, Japan sought from Australia most-favoured-nation status and non-discriminatory access to Japanese imports.

Early in 1957 several developments contributed to the conclusion of an agreement. One was a decision of the Japanese cabinet in January to reject surplus US farm imports, thus clearing the way for Japan to be able to accept the necessary quantity of Australian wheat imports.[25] Second was the dispatch of a Japanese goodwill mission to Australia in February. Third was a visit to Japan by the Australian prime minister, Robert Menzies—including a meeting between Menzies and the Japanese

23 See Sir Alan Watt, *Australian Diplomat: Memoirs of Sir Alan Watt* (Sydney: Angus and Robertson in association with the Australian Institute of International Affairs, 1972).
24 Tweedie, *Trading Partners*, 165.
25 Ibid., 166.

prime minister, Kishi Nobusuke, that helped smooth the path to final agreement.[26] Despite his success in organising Menzies's visit, Watt had cause to complain that he had had no role in negotiating the Commerce Agreement until the document had been completed. McEwen treated the trade agreement as exclusively the preserve of the Department of Trade.

In the wake of the Commerce Agreement, Japanese trade missions started purchasing quantities of hard coking coal from the south coast of New South Wales. At the same time, in the process of the annual review of the Commerce Agreement, the Japanese pioneered the development of long-term contracts for their importation of Australia coal and this mechanism was later replicated for other minerals such as iron ore and bauxite.[27] Matters of trade and defence were prominent issues for Australia's embassy in Tokyo in the late 1950s.[28] Watt was keen, however, for Australia to broaden the relationship and develop positive plans to help shape postwar Japan. He believed Australia should work harder to convince Japan that Australia was geographically part of Asia and not merely a European outpost.[29] As David Walton outlines further below, Watt's style and experience assisted in his building of good relationships in Tokyo.

The Minerals Boom and Regional Security

Between 1960 and 1965, a period coinciding with the tenure of Laurence McIntyre as ambassador to Japan, a minerals boom began in Australia that was spurred by a resource-poor and rapidly developing Japan's thirst for Australia's natural resources. McIntyre was a career diplomat born in Hobart in 1912 and educated at the University of Tasmania. He joined the Department of External Affairs in 1940 and was Australia's ambassador to Indonesia from 1957 to 1960, immediately before his posting in Tokyo. As ambassador in Tokyo much of McIntyre's time was devoted to managing various aspects of Australia's mining boom.

---

26 Record of conversation between Kishi and Menzies, 12 April 1957, National Archives of Australia (NAA): A1838, 3103/10/11/1/1 PART 2. See also A.W. Martin, *Robert Menzies: A Life, Volume 2 1944–1978* (Carlton: Melbourne University Press, 1999), 35–45.
27 Don Fitch, 'Review of Japanese Trade Agreement—Coal', NAA: A1313, 1959/2017 PART 1.
28 Memorandum from Watt to Arthur Tange, 27 September 1956, DFAT, *The Australia–Japan Agreement on Commerce*, 260.
29 Ibid., 260–1.

The 1960s was a decade of mineral discovery and development that helped Japan displace the United Kingdom as Australia's largest trading partner in the early 1970s, a position it would retain for the next quarter of a century. In the year that McIntyre took up his position, Japan welcomed the decision of the Menzies government to relax the iron ore embargo, implemented by Lyons in 1938.[30] Following this decision, the Japanese steel industry signed long-term contracts that enabled mining companies in Australia to borrow the capital needed to finance building railways, mines and ports in Western Australia's Pilbara region. Cooperation between the Japanese steel industry, mining companies and the Western Australian government saw the establishment of a major new export industry geared to supply the Japanese steel industry. A Japanese steel mission to Australia in 1960 also spurred federal–state cooperation to revamp the New South Wales coal ports of Port Kembla, Balmain and Newcastle. McIntyre hosted visits by the federal minister for national development, William Spooner, and the New South Wales minister for mines, James Simpson, to foster the bulk export of Australian black coal to Japan. In Queensland, Japan's Mitsui combined with US company Peabody and Australia's Thiess brothers to develop the pioneer coking coal export industry in the Bowen Basin, Thiess Peabody Mitsui.[31] Not long afterwards, Mitsubishi collaborated with a US company, Utah, to form Central Queensland Coal Associates and develop even larger and more lucrative mines in the Bowen Basin coal province.[32] Japan also became a substantial importer of bauxite developed for export in North Queensland and Western Australia.[33]

Although much of the business of Australia's embassy under McIntyre was concerned with trade and economic matters, regional disputes, including Indonesia's struggle to incorporate West New Guinea and its confrontation of the Malaysian Federation between 1963 and 1966, loomed large on the foreign policy agenda of both Australia and Japan. Important for the embassy too was Japan's successful hosting of the Olympic Games in October 1964. This first Olympics ever held in Asia showcased Japan's phenomenal technological development through the

---

30 David Lee, 'Reluctant Relaxation: The End of the Iron Ore Export Embargo and the Origins of Australia's Mining Boom, 1960–1966', *History Australia* 10, no. 3 (2013): 149–70, doi.org/10.1080/14490854.2013.11668485.

31 See David Lee, *The Second Rush: Mining and the Transformation of Australia* (Redland Bay: Connor Court, 2016), Chapter 1.

32 Brian Galligan, *Utah and Queensland Coal: A Study in the Micro-Political Economy of Modern Capitalism and the State* (Brisbane: University of Queensland Press, 1989).

33 Lee, *The Second Rush*, Chapter 4.

years of the 'Japanese Economic Miracle', symbolised in the construction of its high-speed train network, the *Shinkansen*.[34] The embassy was also engaged with the question of who should occupy the China seat in the United Nations Security Council. Three ambassadors to Japan wrestled with the China question: McIntyre (1960–65), Sir Allen Brown (1965–70) and Gordon Freeth (1970–73).[35] After 1961, Japan, which had been the occupying power in Taiwan up to World War II, agreed with Australia and the United States on a procedure in the General Assembly of the United Nations that made it necessary for two-thirds of the General Assembly to vote to unseat the Nationalist Chinese government in China in the United Nations. This mechanism would keep Nationalist China in the United Nations China seat until 1971.

Allen Brown succeeded McIntyre as ambassador to Japan in 1965. Born in Melbourne in 1911, Brown was educated at Caulfield Grammar and the University of Melbourne and was director-general of the Department of Post-War Reconstruction from 1948 to 1949 before taking up the position of permanent secretary of the Prime Minister's Department from 1949 to 1959.[36] He then served as deputy high commissioner in London, before succeeding McIntyre in Tokyo in 1965. During Brown's term as ambassador, Australia and Japan both joined a new regional organisation: the Asian and Pacific Council (ASPAC), a group of nine anti-communist nations in the Asia-Pacific region that first met in Seoul in June 1966.

During this period Japan was stepping up its engagement with the countries of Southeast Asia. This was expressed through economic means, while Australia's engagement with these nations was substantially military. Japan's pacifist postwar Constitution meant that it eschewed military involvement in its region. This meant that Japan was even chary of using its navy's vessels to evacuate its nationals from Hong Kong in 1967 during China's Cultural Revolution.[37] The Australian and Japanese

---

34 Alexander Martin, 'The 1964 Tokyo Olympics: A Turning Point for Japan', *Wall Street Journal*, 5 September 2013; Christopher P. Hood, *Shinkansen—From Bullet Train to Symbol of Modern Japan* (London: Routledge, 2007), doi.org/10.4324/9780203180389.

35 See Stuart Doran and David Lee, eds, *Documents on Australian Foreign Policy: Australia and Recognition of the People's Republic of China 1949–1972* (Canberra: Department of Foreign Affairs and Trade, 2002).

36 Sir Peter Lawler, 'Sir Allen Brown: An Exemplary Public Servant', in *The Seven Dwarfs and the Age of the Mandarins: Australian Government Administration in the Post-War Era*, ed. Samuel Furphy (Canberra: ANU Press, 2015), 183–89, doi.org/10.22459/SDAM.07.2015.09.

37 Cablegram from Brown to Department of External Affairs, 18 September 1968, NAA: A1209, 1964/6661.

governments diverged over the American-led intervention in Vietnam. While the Japanese government appreciated the overwhelming military superiority of the United States in South Vietnam, it always doubted that the Americans would be able to defeat the insurgency there. Brown, while conveying to the *Gaimusho* (Japan's Ministry of Foreign Affairs) Australia's firm support for the US (and Australian) defence of the Republic of Vietnam, also observed elections in South Vietnam in 1967. In the late 1960s Australia shared with Japan an ambivalence about whether to ratify the Nuclear Non-Proliferation Treaty, with Australia wanting to retain the option to develop a nuclear deterrent and Japan mindful of its civilian atomic program.[38] Japan would not ratify the treaty until 1976, three years after Australia did so.[39]

In 1970 Gordon Freeth, the Western Australian Liberal politician and a former minister for external affairs, succeeded Brown as head of mission in Tokyo. Freeth headed the embassy in very turbulent times for both Japan and Australia, providing added incentive for the two governments to institute better ways of consulting with each other. In 1971 the president of the United States, Richard Nixon, broke the connection of the dollar with gold and left the dollar to float, a process aimed at raising the value of the yen. He combined this with a 10 per cent surcharge on imports.[40] The effect was to make Japanese exports less competitive than they had been in the 1950s and 1960s. This first 'Nixon shock' was quickly followed by a second and even greater one. In July 1971 Nixon's national security adviser, Henry Kissinger, announced that Nixon would visit Beijing in 1972 to bring about a rapprochement with the People's Republic of China. The announcement caught both Japan and Australia off guard. Both governments were, at US request, supporting Taiwan's position in the United Nations without any forewarning of Nixon's intention to allow China to take its place among the Great Powers on the Security Council. In October 1971 the General Assembly finally voted to put the People's Republic of China in the UN seat. In 1972, a year in which the increasing volume of diplomatic exchange between the two countries was remarked on in an Australian Senate Committee, the two governments established

38 Ibid.
39 Wayne Reynolds, 'Australia's Quest to Enrich Uranium and the Whitlam Government's Loans Affair', *Australian Journal of Politics and History* 54, no. 4 (2008): 562–78, doi.org/10.1111/j.1467-8497.2008.00516.x.
40 LaFeber, *The Clash*, 352–53.

an annual meeting of ministers from both countries.[41] In the nearly three decades from 1945 to 1972, the relationship had metamorphosed from wartime hostility into a vital economic partnership that was strengthened by shared political and regional interests.

From NARA Treaty to Regional Planning

At the end of 1972 the Gough Whitlam Labor government was elected to office. In the following year the seasoned diplomat K.C.O. 'Mick' Shann succeeded Freeth as ambassador in Tokyo, a position that he held until 1976. Shann helped Whitlam to implement his wish, imposed on an unwilling bureaucracy on John Crawford's advice, to negotiate with Japan a Basic Treaty of Friendship and Cooperation (also known as the NARA Treaty).[42] The treaty, which was eventually signed by Whitlam's successor Malcolm Fraser, established a broad framework of principles to guide and strengthen future bilateral relations with Japan.[43] One area of the bilateral relationship that had become more complicated since 1972 was 'resources diplomacy'. In an effort to maximise the value of the resources exported to Japan, Whitlam had instituted export controls on all minerals exported from Australia as a lever to bargain for higher resource prices and had imposed restrictions on the level of foreign ownership of Australian mineral resources.[44] Although these policies were deeply concerning to Japanese companies, particularly the steel industry, Australia's mineral exports to Japan increased in the 1970s as black coal emerged as Australia's most valuable traded commodity in the 1980s. It was the delayed effect of the rise in the price of petroleum in the early 1970s that prompted Japan to search for oil substitutes such as thermal coal.[45]

Prior to his posting to Tokyo, Shann had, as deputy secretary of External Affairs (Foreign Affairs from 1973), promoted measures designed to improve dialogues on these and other developments in the

41 See Shann's comments to the Senate Standing Committee of Foreign Affairs and Defence, in Rix, *The Australia–Japan Political Alignment*, 72–73; 'Japan and Australia', *Canberra Times*, 12 October 1972.
42 Moreen Dee, *Friendship and Co-operation: The 1976 Basic Treaty between Australia and Japan*, Australia in the World: The Foreign Affairs and Trade files no. 3 (Canberra: Department of Foreign Affairs and Trade, 2006).
43 Peter Drysdale, 'Did the NARA Treaty Make a Difference?' *Australian Journal of International Affairs* 60, no. 4 (2006): 490–505, doi.org/10.1080/10357710601006994.
44 Lee, *The Second Rush*, Chapter 6.
45 Ibid, Chapter 7.

relationship. An Australia–Japan Ministerial Committee and a Standing Interdepartmental Committee on Japan were the result. Neither proved long-lasting but foreshadowed later efforts to establish more regular and internally coordinated forms of dialogue.

One of the most active senior bureaucrats in Australian public life, John Menadue succeeded Shann and served as ambassador from 1977 to 1980.[46] Of all the public servant appointees to Tokyo, Menadue was the least in the mould of a diplomat or trade expert. He was born in South Australia in 1935 and graduated from the University of Adelaide in 1956 with a bachelor of economics. His path to Tokyo was foreshadowed in two ways. His first sortie was while working for press owner Rupert Murdoch managing the *Australian* newspaper in the late 1960s. In recognition of Japan's growing importance to Australia, Menadue established a new bureau for the newspaper in Tokyo in 1969.[47]

The second lure of Tokyo came while Menadue was secretary of Prime Minister and Cabinet, both before and after the Whitlam government's dismissal. In 1974–75 Menadue threw his support behind Ambassador Shann's proposal for what became the Basic Treaty of Friendship and Cooperation. The passage of the bill to establish the treaty was suspended by the dramatic dismissal of Whitlam in November 1975. There was a risk of it languishing, but Menadue and others ensured that it secured passage in 1976; they then supported, under Prime Minister Malcolm Fraser's government, the work and recommendations of another committee, led by retail businessman Kenneth Baillieu Myer, for a separate Standing Committee on Japan comprising permanent heads of departments, and a Consultative Committee on Relations with Japan, supported by a permanent secretariat.[48]

---

46   Oral history transcript, Menadue interviewed by Ray Aitchison 19 February 1985, National Library of Australia (NLA): ORAL TRC 2158/1, Bib ID 1658940; Oral history transcript, Menadue interviewed by Daniel Connell, 7 August 1995, NLA: ORAL TRC 3307, Bib ID 2207502; John Menadue, *Things You Learn along the Way* (Melbourne: David Lovell Publishing, 1999); see also *Pearls and Irritations* (blog): johnmenadue.com/about-pearls-irritations/. John Menadue's wife, Cynthia, also wrote an account of their time in Japan, *Shadows on the Shoji: A Personal View of Japan* (Sydney: John Ferguson, 1985) (published in Japan as *Ambassador's Wife*). Menadue returned to senior positions, including secretary of the Department of Trade in 1983, and during the 1990s served as head of major companies Qantas and Telstra.
47   Menadue interviewed by Daniel Connell, TRC 3307, p. 262. He appointed as the bureau's first chief Greg Clarke, former diplomat and outspoken critic of Menzies-era governments' tendencies to view Asia primarily through a Cold War lens.
48   Ibid., 262–65; and Menadue, *Things You Learn along the Way*, 183–84; Rix, *The Australia–Japan Political Alignment*, 78–80.

When Fraser suggested in October 1976 that Menadue succeed Shann as ambassador in Tokyo he relished the chance to move on. Although he recalled getting little in the way of strategic direction from Foreign Affairs and other departments in Canberra by way of preparation, this was not unwelcome. Menadue enjoyed the sense of license that came with his being neither a professional diplomat nor politician. Being 'not particularly attracted to the dreary round of diplomatic dinners and parties which are so much the life of bored diplomats', he balanced procedural necessity with his inclination to do things his way.[49]

Menadue was in Tokyo during a time of increased international admiration for Japan's economic growth, high exchange rates, increased Japanese investment in Australian ventures, and a two-to-one trade surplus ratio. His tenure was especially marked by the new resources diplomacy, including greater activity by Western Australian and Queensland governments trying to shape the conditions of trade deals with Japan. In the late 1970s Australia provided around 80 per cent of Japan's wool, 50 per cent of its iron ore and 40 per cent of its coking coal, and more than 50 per cent of its bauxite. As Menadue recalled: 'Embassy staff used to lay bets that I couldn't make a speech about Australia–Japan relations or answer questions without mentioning dollars or tonnes. I always lost.'[50]

Within the strong flow of trade, contractual sticking points relating to Japan's importing of sugar and beef demanded attention, and the Department of Trade was continuously engaged. Trade minister Doug Anthony and secretaries Doug McKay and Jim Scully stood out as the top Australians most sensitive to negotiations with Japan.[51] In 1978 the Japanese steel mills managed to divide the three main Australian iron ore companies in reaching lower-than-expected prices for ore contracts. This led to something of a showdown between Canberra and the Western Australian government of Charles Court, which was anxious to proceed as it also needed Japanese investment for further development of the Pilbara mine region. Doug Anthony was furious that the usual practice of federal government endorsement of broad parameters governing such export contracts had been circumvented, but, in recognition of the Japanese bargaining position, was forced to concede.[52]

---

49   Menadue, *Things You Learn along the Way*, 193; Menadue interviewed by Daniel Connell, TRC 3307, pp. 265–67.
50   Lee, *The Second Rush*, 255; Menadue, *Things You Learn along the Way*, 196.
51   Menadue interviewed by Daniel Connell, TRC 3307, pp. 266, 272–73, 288–89.
52   Lee, *The Second Rush*, 287–89.

Menadue kept pressing for greater breadth in the Australia–Japan relationship, involving more, and especially younger, Australians. He supported the new Australia–Japan Foundation (with the help of Neil Currie, who succeeded him in Tokyo) to develop education kits about Australia for Japanese teachers. In part, the education kits were a response to one of the least satisfactory experiences Menadue had in Japan—the recurrence of what he called 'the ghost of "White Australia"'. So often, after giving one of his many public talks, he said, and especially after a drink or two, he would be questioned about the White Australia policy. The production of education kits would go some way to relaying a broader Australian history. He also worked with his counterpart in Canberra, Japan's ambassador Yoshio Okawara, to conclude a working holiday 12-month visa scheme between the two countries for those up to the age of 25, along the lines of similar schemes operating between Australian and European countries. The Australia–Japan working holiday scheme was announced during the visit to Australia by Japanese prime minister Masayoshi Ōhira in 1980.[53]

By this time, the Australia–Japan relationship benefited from more high-level meetings, a broader group of political and economic policy thinkers joining some of these, and a joint focus on conceptual thinking about the Asia-Pacific region. Outcomes included a major report recommending more interchanges on policy to both Australian and Japanese governments by Sir John Crawford and Dr Saburō Ōkita, *Australia, Japan and Western Pacific Economic Relations*[54] in 1976; Whitlam's speech, 'Australia and Japan and their Region', delivered at the 7th Australia–Japan Relations Symposium, at The Australian National University (ANU), 29 March 1979; the Pacific Basin Cooperation Concept, an agreement made between Prime Ministers Malcolm Fraser and Masayoshi Ōhira in Canberra, in January 1980; and the Pacific Community Seminar at ANU in Canberra in September 1980, which is regarded as the first meeting of the Pacific Economic Cooperation Council (PECC). In Tokyo, Menadue hosted quarterly breakfasts with Japanese politicians, including with the secretary-general and others from the ruling Liberal Democratic Party.

---

53 Menadue interviewed by Daniel Connell, TRC 3307, pp. 281–82, 290–91; Menadue, *Things You Learn along the Way*, 204.
54 Sir John Grenfell Crawford and Saburō Ōkita, *Australia, Japan and Western Pacific Economic Relations: A Report to the Governments of Australia and Japan* (Canberra: Australian Government Publishing Service, 1976).

The secretary-general, Masayoshi Ōhira, became prime minister in 1978, and another who occasionally attended, Yasuhiro Nakasone, rose to this position in 1982.

Menadue concluded his term in Tokyo in 1980, returning to Australia to become secretary of the Department of Immigration. His continuing seniority in Canberra therefore enhanced the standing of the embassy in Tokyo. James Plimsoll's appointment to Tokyo in 1981 confirmed this high standing as he was one of Australia's most senior public servants and diplomats. Born in Sydney in 1917, he graduated from the University of Sydney in 1941 with bachelors of economics and arts. A captain in the Citizen Military Forces, during World War II he worked in the Directorate of Research and Civil Affairs and at the end of the war was posted to the Australian Military Mission in Washington, DC. For a little over a year, he was the Australian representative on the Far Eastern Commission there, working on Allied policy towards occupied Japan, before returning to Australia at the end of 1947 and soon afterwards joining the Department of External Affairs. His talents as a diplomat emerged quickly, first accompanying the minister, Dr H. V. Evatt, to UN meetings in New York, then as Australia's representative in Korea on the UN commission for unification and rehabilitation, and as permanent representative to the UN in New York, 1959–63. Plimsoll served as high commissioner to India, 1963–65; secretary of External Affairs, 1965–70; ambassador in Washington, 1970–74, Moscow, 1974–77, and Brussels, 1977–80; and high commissioner in London, 1980–81.[55]

Indeed, 'Jim Plim' was the consummate diplomat and brought to the post the highest standards in his profession.[56] The circumstances of his arrival were less than ideal—having been appointed the first career high commissioner in London he was forced to leave London early as Prime Minister Fraser needed to move a controversial minister, Victor Garland, out of the way and the solution was to send him to London. Plimsoll's stay in Tokyo, seen widely as a compensatory measure, was also brief as he then accepted an offer to become governor of Tasmania. By mutual

---

55   Jeremy Hearder, 'Sir James Plimsoll (1917–1987)', in *Australian Dictionary of Biography*, vol. 18, 2012, adb.anu.edu.au/biography/plimsoll-sir-james-15471, accessed 8 July 2020.
56   See, generally, Jeremy Hearder, *Jim Plim: Ambassador Extraordinary: A Biography of Sir James Plimsoll* (Ballarat: Connor Court Publishing, 2015).

agreement, and with a view to the importance of the Australia–Japan relationship, Plimsoll served in Tokyo for 18 months before taking up his new post in Tasmania.[57]

This was time enough for Plimsoll to send back to Canberra two long reports on a delicate aspect of Japan's potential role in regional security: the future of Article 9 of the Japanese Constitution, renouncing war and prohibiting Japan from having the potential to prosecute war. Plimsoll arrived in Japan after some constitutional challenges to the existence of Japan's Self-Defense Force had failed, and amid recurring discussion of Japan's obligations as an ally of the United States. It was, argued Plimsoll, reasonable to suggest that Japan should be capable of defending its home islands, and that the United States should not have to bear the burden of this. What was less desirable was an increase in Japanese production of military equipment beyond this measure, and the sending of Japanese forces beyond the home islands. The Japanese he asked assured him that memories of the military regime were still strong, and there was no likelihood of a military group in Japan re-emerging to wield political influence again. Plimsoll later recalled that his reports along these lines were well received in Canberra.[58]

His successor, Neil Currie, was the first ambassador to arrive with some proficiency in Japanese language. Being appointed ambassador to Japan in 1982 was, for Currie, like a wheel turning full circle. He was born in Mackay, Queensland, in 1926, and moved in his childhood with his family to Perth. He joined the small Department of External Affairs in 1948, and his first overseas posting was to Tokyo, as third secretary, in 1950. Even before then he had developed a strong attraction to Japan, having enjoyed studying Asian history under the inspirational John Legge at the University of Western Australia, and then taking a language course in Japanese prior to joining External Affairs. During that initial posting, 1950–53, his interest was further stimulated by firsthand observation

---

57   Oral history transcript, James Plimsoll interviewed by Clyde Cameron, 26 March 1984, NLA: ORAL TRC 1967, nla.gov.au/nla.obj-215722006/listen/38-2539. In fact, Plimsoll received the offer just three months after this arrival in what was to be his final overseas posting of three years in Tokyo. Scrupulous as ever, Plimsoll sought advice from departmental secretary Peter Henderson, who in turn consulted the foreign affairs minister, Tony Street. Relayed back to Plimsoll, Street's advice was candid: if Fraser had upended him once to solve a political headache, there was no guarantee it would not happen again.
58   Ibid., nla.gov.au/nla.obj-215722006/listen/38-1371.

of the gargantuan task of postwar reconstruction. Currie married his wife Geraldine while in Tokyo and three of their four children were born during this time there.

After Tokyo, Currie joined the Department of Trade, working under the strong leadership of Sir John Crawford, and then Sir Alan Westerman. This saw him engaged on the implications of Britain's application to join the Common Market, the Kennedy Round of the General Agreement on Tariffs and Trade (1964–67) and annual reviews of the trade agreement with Japan. Within Trade, he became deputy secretary of the Department of Secondary Industry in 1968, and then secretary, successively, of the Departments of Supply (1971), Manufacturing Industry (1974), and Industry and Commerce (1975). He headed the new Department of Industry and Commerce until his appointment as ambassador to Japan in 1982.

Currie was thus well placed to help foster the Australia–Japan trading relationship and it continued to grow during his term, being valued at the seventh largest in the world.[59] Much of the expansion in Western Australia's iron ore mining was linked to Japan's needs. The 1980s also saw a broadening of the base in the relationship, as Whitlam and others had hoped. One focal point was ANU, where Sir John Crawford and Peter Drysdale initiated a series of conferences on Pacific cooperation. The idea flowed from the visit to Australia by Japanese prime minister Masayoshi Ōhira in January 1980, taking into account Ōhira's enthusiasm for an 'open' form of regionalism in the Pacific. It evolved into a series of PECC conferences during the 1980s, building towards Australian prime minister Bob Hawke's suggestion in 1989 of a more formal, ministerial body: Asia-Pacific Economic Cooperation (APEC). The conferences leading up to this point, and thereafter, enabled influential bureaucrats, business leaders and academics to exchange policy ideas more readily between Australia and Japan. They complemented the work of an Australia–Japan Ministerial Committee established in 1972.[60]

After Currie left Tokyo in 1986, Japan remained a constant in his life. In retirement he chaired the Australia–Japan Foundation, 1989–93, and was an executive member of the Australia–Japan Business Co-operation Committee, 1993–97. He was working on a novel set in postwar Japan when he died in July 1999. The Australia–Japan Foundation established

---

59 Lee, *The Second Rush*, 255.
60 Rix, *The Australia–Japan Political Alignment*, 135–36.

the Sir Neil Currie Australian Studies Award Program in 2000 to commemorate Currie's life and to promote academic exchanges and research and teaching about Australia at tertiary institutions in Japan.

Managing High Expectations, Bilateral and Regional

Succeeding Currie, Geoff Miller, born in 1934, was educated at the University of Tasmania, where another inspiring history lecturer, George Wilson, helped spark an interest in Asia. In December 1956 he joined a pioneering tour of Southeast Asia with the National Union of Australian University Students that furthered this interest; and a long conversation with a fellow Tasmanian, journalist Dennis Warner, led him to connect his regional fascination to a possible career in External Affairs. Before joining the department, he took up the offer of a Rhodes Scholarship to Oxford (making him the first of three successive Rhodes scholars as ambassadors to Japan between 1986 and 1998).[61] After a short posting to Kuala Lumpur, Miller was then sent to Jakarta. His time there coincided with the so-called attempted coup of 30 September 1965, leading to Suharto's rise to power, at the expense of Sukarno, and the murder of upwards of 500,000 Communist Party of Indonesia members, supporters and others. In the chaotic aftermath he and other members of the Australian embassy drew on information gathered by their counterparts in the Japanese embassy who they held in high regard. After further postings to the United Nations in New York and New Delhi, Miller served as ambassador to the Republic of Korea, 1978–80. Indeed, all of his overseas postings excepting New York were to Asia.

Recent progress towards regional cooperation, expanded trade for Australian resources and the thickening of Australia–Japan cultural ties continued but were also buffeted somewhat by sharp economic shocks during Miller's term as ambassador, 1986–89. Foremost were the consequences of the sudden appreciation of the Japanese yen. Longstanding Japanese importers of Australian coal and iron ore were desperate to bring prices of these down. At the same time, the recession in Australia led the Hawke government to inflate its expectations of

---

61 Oral history transcript, Geoff Miller interviewed by David Lowe, 28 August 2017, NLA: ORAL TRC 6870/5, Bib ID 7464418.

Japan, both as buyer of commodities and as a model of high technology manufacturing that Australia might emulate. Japan took more than one-quarter of Australia's exports in the late 1980s. The collective cartel buying by Japanese importers made for tough, even 'quite edgy' negotiations on prices, and this absorbed a good deal of Miller's time. He recalled efforts in joining US pressure for Japan to open up to foreign imported beef, at the same time as he argued that opening up was not to be confined to US exporters.[62] It ended satisfactorily for Australians, and trade relations settled reasonably well after the alarms about the higher yen, but the negotiations were testing, especially on agricultural products. When Prime Minister Bob Hawke visited in December 1987, he was even more strident in his insistence that Australia not suffer from Japan's need to respond to US pressures about their imbalanced trade with Japan.[63] Future ambassador in Tokyo Peter Grey was deeply involved, as he was then agricultural attaché in the embassy.[64]

Japan's influence in the Pacific grew during this period, especially through increased levels of Japanese aid for the South Pacific, a region of immediate strategic concern to Australia. This was accompanied by mostly fruitful Australia–Japan consultation and information-sharing, even if both governments were clear that their respective aid programs were in no way coordinated.[65]

Two further issues were the sale of a portion of the embassy grounds (as discussed in Chapters 6 and 7) and the rising levels of Japanese investment in Australia, including the ill-fated Australia–Japan proposal to build what was called a multifunction polis (MFP) in South Australia. On the issue of demolishing the old mansion building serving as the chancery, Miller acknowledged that it had become too small. But he was opposed to the sale of a great slice of the property, no matter that land prices had skyrocketed and the sale was seen as addressing Australia's national debt. He registered his opposition to the sale of part of the property but it did not change Canberra's determination to sell.[66]

---

62   The Americans reached agreement in 1985 to supply Japan with one million tonnes of steaming coal at prices higher than current market prices. The Australian government understandably saw this as a threat. See Lee, *The Second Rush*, 301–03.

63   Rix, *The Australia–Japan Political Alignment*, 35–37.

64   Miller interviewed by David Lowe, TRC 6870/5.

65   Rix, *The Australia–Japan Political Alignment*, 140–42.

66   Geoff Miller, 'Diplomatic Reflections: An Australian View from Tokyo', *Japanese Studies* 24, no. 2 (2004): 169–75, doi.org/10.1080/1037139042000302474; Miller interviewed by David Lowe, TRC 6870/5.

The rising Japanese investment in Australia was a welcome development, but also posed questions for Australia–Japan relations more generally. Japan's share of total investment in Australia rose from 8.7 per cent in 1981 to 17.9 per cent 10 years later.[67] Japanese tourist visits to Australia rose spectacularly at the same time. The MFP was an innovative and big idea, envisaging a new community in Australia, built jointly by Australian and Japanese firms, combining high tech industry, education, research and lifestyle. On the one hand, it was a measure of the success in the annual Australia–Japan Ministerial Committee meetings that such an ambitious project was raised—at the ninth such meeting in January 1987. But it also brought to a head a growing backlash in Australia against rising levels of conspicuous Japanese real estate investment, especially on the Gold Coast. During his visit to Australia in 1988, Prime Minister Noboru Takeshita witnessed anti-investment rallies.[68] Another site near Adelaide was selected for the MFP, but the proposal rapidly fell apart in the early 1990s as the bursting Japanese economic bubble took its toll on investors; and popular opposition in Australia and then withdrawn government funding combined to deliver fatal blows. Instead of constituting a new height in Australia–Japan multilayered cooperation, the MFP became an embarrassment to both governments.[69]

In 1989, Miller was succeeded in Tokyo by Rawdon Dalrymple. A Rhodes scholar from New South Wales who joined the Department of External Affairs in 1957, Dalrymple first visited Japan in late 1965. He was in charge of the Economic Policy Unit, and he made two trips, travelling with Treasury officials, first Colin Konran and then Harold Heinrich, to discuss the Japan-led proposal for what became the Asian Development Bank, launched in December 1966, and to consider the economic implications of the deteriorating situation in Indonesia. There, the worsening economic outlook and failure to repay loans coincided with volatile politics. This was in the wake of the events of 30 September 1965

---

67 Rix, *The Australia–Japan Political Alignment*, 107.
68 Ibid., 37.
69 On the MFP, see Ian Inkster, *The Clever City: Japan, Australia and the Multifunction Polis* (Sydney: Sydney University Press, 1991); Walter Hamilton, *Serendipity City: Australia, Japan and the Multifunction Polis* (Sydney: ABC Books, 1991); and Gavan McCormack, ed., *Bonsai Australia Banzai: Multifunction Polis and the Making of a Special Relationship with Japan* (Sydney: Pluto Press, 1991).

and subsequent turmoil. On the second of these two visits to Japan, he stopped in Jakarta on his return journey and saw firsthand the last days of Sukarno's tenure.[70]

From the mid-1960s Dalrymple was engaged more than others in the Department of External Affairs in development economics, and this led to his being appointed alternate director for Australia on the Asian Development Bank in Manila in 1967, before he was posted to Jakarta as minister, 1969–72. He therefore developed a keen awareness of the nexus between Japan's regional engagement, US policy towards Asia, and international economic development thinking and policy.[71] He subsequently served as ambassador to Israel, then to Indonesia, and then the United States, prior to his term as ambassador to Japan, 1989–93. Upon arrival in Tokyo he had to spend considerable time making adjustments to the new chancery and residence, and fielding complaints from staff unhappy at some of the apartments they had to occupy, and which did not always compare well with their previous accommodation in Tokyo suburban houses. The senior trade commissioner was perhaps the most affected, having previously been living and working very separately from the old embassy, and with a sense of license to work independently.[72] The new buildings meant that the Tokyo embassy was quite literally shadowing the merging of the Departments of Trade and Foreign Affairs in Canberra in 1987.

Managing one of the biggest of Australia's embassies that suddenly required all staff to be housed in its new residential block on the embassy grounds soaked up a considerable portion of Dalrymple's time. Nor did he recall it as a time of breakthroughs in trade on some of the commodities Canberra was eager to see Japan import. Dalrymple recognised early on that asking the Japanese to purchase Australian rice was an uphill task, and not one that saw rewards in his time.

Nevertheless, his term was notable for the growing sense of Australia–Japan partnership in ways that reached beyond trade and investment. An example of this was Australian support for Japan's provision of peacekeeping forces in the Gulf War, a move approved after difficult debate in the Diet in 1992. In the same year, Australia's defence minister

---

70 Oral history transcript, Rawdon Dalrymple interviewed by David Lowe, 23 May 2017, NLA: ORAL TRC 6870, Bib ID 7385848.
71 Ibid.
72 Ibid.

Robert Ray visited Tokyo and flagged Australia's readiness to increase defence contacts on a number of levels, an important step towards gradually broadened defence cooperation that would continue to unfold thereafter. It was also a partnership informing the two governments' approaches to regional cooperation, particularly in the new APEC. Japan's strong support for APEC ensured that this body would take precedence over any involvement in the Malaysian-sponsored alternative, the East Asian Economic Caucus. The focus on APEC also saw agreement on trade liberalisation as an essential component of regional cooperation.[73]

The growing people-to-people and cultural connections between Australia and Japan, including sister cities and school exchange programs was another feature of the early 1990s, as is discussed in Chapter 9. Charismatic figures stood out in the cultivation of people-to-people connections. Dalrymple recalled the outstanding efforts of Australian Catholic priest Father Tony Glynn, who had been based in Nara since 1953, and whose work in reconciliation, interfaith cooperation and fund-raising attracted widespread admiration. John Menadue also recalled Father Glynn's work as a highlight in Australia–Japan relations.[74]

In October 1993 Ashton Calvert was appointed to succeed Dalrymple. Miller, Dalrymple and Calvert all shared an appreciation of an Australia–Japan relationship that went far beyond economic and strategic factors. In this sense, they expanded on the approach of earlier diplomat-ambassadors, perhaps with the exception of Alan Watt, who had urged the importance of cultural ties in the 1950s. Of all Australia's ambassadors to this date, Calvert was the most Japan-oriented. As a Rhodes scholar, he gained a doctorate in mathematics at Oxford. He joined External Affairs in 1970, was selected to learn Japanese, and was very quickly posted to Japan, for four years, 1971–75. During this first posting he played a crucial role in negotiating sticking points needing to be addressed before the Basic Treaty could be agreed.[75] He spent 14 of the next 37 years in Japan, serving next time as counsellor for labour relations, 1984–85. His wife, Mikie, was Japanese-born. He became fluent in Japanese, a talent that

---

73 Alan Rix, 'Australia and Japan', in *Seeking Asian Engagement: Australia in World Affairs, 1991–95*, ed. James Cotton and John Ravenhill (Melbourne: Oxford University Press in conjunction with the Australian Institute of International Affairs, 1997), 134–48.
74 Sydney *Sunday Telegraph*, 11 December 1994. Glynn died in Nara in 1994, having been made an honorary citizen of Nara.
75 The full story is told in Moreen Dee, *Friendship and Co-operation: The 1976 Basic Treaty between Australia and Japan,* Australia in the World: The Foreign Affairs and Trade files no. 3 (Canberra: Department of Foreign Affairs and Trade, 2006).

proved invaluable for his four postings to Tokyo, the last as ambassador. He is fondly remembered there on account of his linguistic fluency and astute reading of Japanese politics and society, and his constant attention to Australia–Japan relations, including during his seven years as secretary of Foreign Affairs and Trade beginning in 1998. It was perhaps fitting that a very public declaration of the importance of the Australia–Japan relationship emerged during his time in Tokyo. In May 1995, at the time of Prime Minister Paul Keating's visit to Tokyo, the two governments issued a 'Joint Declaration on the Australia–Japan Partnership'. They described the relationship as one of 'unprecedented quality' and pledged to build on the foundation they had built, including with others in the region. The Japanese government added that Australia was 'an indispensable partner in regional affairs'.[76]

Building on earlier foundations continued, but within constraints. Calvert was in Tokyo as Japan experienced economic reversal and the collapse of real estate prices in a period of deflation. This would have consequences for Australia's resource exports but the percentage share for Japan slowed from a high point—of 25 per cent in 1980 to 20 per cent in 1997.[77] The security dialogue between the two governments also grew during his term. Having passed the hitherto strict barrier of 1 per cent GNP spending on self-defence in 1987, Japanese governments continued their cautious but steady moves towards greater involvement in international (primarily UN peacekeeping) and bilateral and regional security measures. Following the Ray visit and developments in 1992, in February 1996 Tokyo hosted the first annual official talks on politico-military matters, following Australian prompting. Thereafter, Prime Minister Howard and official defence statements stressed the logic of both Japan's increased involvement in regional security, and the defence relationship becoming a stronger part of Australia–Japan relations.[78]

Calvert left Tokyo to become secretary of DFAT from April 1998 to January 2005. He died in November 2007 from an aggressive form of cancer. In paying tribute to his life and work, Australian foreign minister Alexander Downer described his contribution to Australia–Japan relations as 'immeasurable'.[79]

---

76 Quoted in Rix, 'Australia and Japan', 138–39.
77 Lee, *The Second Rush*, 307.
78 Rix, *The Australia–Japan Political Alignment*, 169–70.
79 Alexander Downer, DFAT, Media release, FA 142, 16 November 2007.

Calvert was followed in Tokyo by Peter Grey,[80] from 1998 to 2001. A University of Sydney graduate (bachelor of economics, with honours), Grey also completed a master of business administration at Stanford before joining the Department of Trade. In the wake of the merger of the Department of Trade with Foreign Affairs in 1987 he emerged as one of Australia's most senior trade negotiators. In addition to being departmental deputy secretary in the mid-1990s, he was Australia's first ambassador for APEC and led negotiations on World Trade Organization matters. Grey's time in Tokyo coincided with the aftermath of the 1997 Asian financial crisis, compounding the economic downtown in Japan. It was harder to maintain the recent energy behind regional cooperation in these circumstances, and harder also with less enthusiasm for regional/multilateral diplomacy by the Howard government.

In Grey's area of special expertise, trade, the turn of the century saw slight declines in overall Australian market share, but familiar exports of wheat, coal, iron ore and now also liquefied natural gas held their places in Japan. While the Australia Trade Commission (Austrade) tried to sound upbeat about the prospects of diversifying the range of exports to Japan to include foods, manufactures and other goods, there was little actual progress in this direction.

Among the most significant developments of this period was the continued strengthening of defence ties. In brief, it was a case of the tentative talks and regularised meetings becoming even more substantive and envisaging higher levels of politico-military coordination in response to regional security issues. The very visible growth of China's military capability and North Korea's testing of sophisticated missiles over Japan in 1998 provided important context.

At the same time, the two governments initially responded very differently to the emerging crisis in East Timor. Australian support for East Timor's self-determination and lead role in securing a UN-backed military intervention was very different from Japan's more hands-off approach. Taken together with an apparent Australian readiness to intervene in the name of regional security in conjunction with the United States

---

80   Peter Grey and his successor, John McCarthy, benefited from Tokyo's inclusion in a group of posts that were deemed by DFAT secretary Ashton Calvert to be of special standing, warranting a higher remuneration for the head of post. The initial five were Beijing, Tokyo, Washington, Jakarta and London, and New Delhi was added later. This special listing operated from 1997–98 to 2004–5, when it ceased for budget reasons: Oral history transcript, John McCarthy interviewed by David Lowe, 8 May 2017, NLA: ORAL TRC 6870/1, Bib ID 7384295.

(Prime Minister Howard did not reject the title of sheriff given to him in a media report in 1999, and this became 'deputy sheriff' in Indonesian commentary in 2002), it seemed that Australia was less concerned to act in concert with regional allies. In practice, however, Japan soon cooperated, in the form of financial aid, with both the Australian-led International Force East Timor (INTERFET) operation in East Timor and the UN Transitional Administration in East Timor (UNTAET).[81]

Partnership Expansion

Grey returned to Canberra in 2001 to senior trade roles and then as chief executive officer of Austrade. He was succeeded by John McCarthy, one of the department's most senior diplomats. McCarthy grew up in England, graduating from Cambridge with a master of arts and bachelor of laws. He worked briefly as a lawyer in New York before joining External Affairs in 1968. Prior to his arrival in Tokyo, McCarthy had served as Australia's ambassador five times, to Vietnam, Mexico, Thailand, the United States and, prior to Japan, Indonesia. After Jakarta, McCarthy found Tokyo very quiet. He recalled it as busy but in a predictable way, rather than frenetic, and without the need for frequent briefings for the local and Australian media that had punctuated his life in Jakarta. It took him some months to adjust. Secretary Ashton Calvert instructed that he wanted more political content to inform the relationship, but trade was the foundation for much of the embassy's work.

Just prior to McCarthy's departure from Australia in 2001 there was a conference organised in Sydney to promote broader, two-way dialogue between the two countries. What became the first of eight such Australia–Japan conferences was initiated by Prime Ministers Howard and Koizumi and brought together members of the two governments with participants from business, media, academia and elsewhere, to exchange ideas. The initial conference held at the end of April 2001 was subtitled, 'Australia–Japan creative partnership'. It ranged broadly from strategic and trade and economic relations to cultural, social, science and technological relations.[82]

81   Rikki Kersten, 'Australia and Japan', in *The National Interest in the Global Era: Australia in World Affairs, 1996–2000,* ed. James Cotton and John Ravenhill (Melbourne: Oxford University Press in association with the Australian Institute of International Affairs, 2001), 72–90.
82   Summaries of the eight meetings are provided on the DFAT website: www.dfat.gov.au/geo/japan/Pages/australia-japan-conference, accessed 2 September 2020.

McCarthy recalled that it involved Australian business leaders, including Hugh Morgan, and Japanese representatives from major companies such as Tokyo Electric, Kobe Steel and Nippon Steel. Morgan was especially bullish about the prospects of a free trade agreement (FTA) and the need to aim for this rather than something less.[83]

In the early 2000s, the sense of trade complementarity between the two countries was slipping, as Japan looked to restructure its economy and Australia focused on an FTA with the United States (achieved in 2004). During his term, McCarthy's team made steady progress towards the more modest, but important, Comprehensive Economic Partnership. Prime Minister Howard acted against McCarthy's advice in pressing for an FTA during the visit by Japanese prime minister Koizumi in 2002. Howard's insistence resulted in awkwardness and back-pedalling rather than forcing the pace. But the Koizumi visit was notable for his envisaging and supporting a strong role for Australia in annual meetings of what he had earlier called an East Asian Community—what became the East Asia Summit, the first of which was held in Kuala Lumpur in December 2005. Japanese support for Australian membership of the East Asia Community, at its foundation, was gratefully received. Australian support for Japan's bid for a permanent seat on the UN Security Council, while not resulting in success, was equally appreciated in Tokyo.

The attacks on the United States of 9/11 in 2001 might have added to the US orientation of Australian policymakers, but they also assisted in the building of defence ties between Australia and Japan during this period. The dialogues were primarily at ministerial level, but they paved the way for stronger measures, such as when Australia provided security for the Japanese Self-Defense Forces deployed to Iraq in 2005, and a broad-ranging Joint Declaration on Security signed in 2007. Before then, the two governments took part in exchanges on combatting terrorism, sharing intelligence and strengthening ties between military colleges. In addition to academic events, and with the encouragement of the US government, Japanese military officers joined with Australia and other nations in naval exercises in the Coral Sea in 2003. In the wake of the 9/11 events and the Bali bombings of 2002, both Australian and Japanese governments were acutely aware of the importance of their respective security alliances with the United States but were also keen to develop a trilateralism unhindered

---

83   McCarthy interviewed by David Lowe, TRC 6870/1.

by these longstanding agreements, and to foster regional security. During McCarthy's term, both the cautious and limited enhancements in security cooperation and the prospects of what might lie ahead were front of mind in Australia–Japan relations.[84]

The two ambassadors succeeding McCarthy, Murray McLean (2004–11) and Bruce Miller (2011–17), both provide accounts of their respective terms elsewhere in this volume—contributions that are especially welcome given the longer terms that both served. The major developments in Australia–Japan relations during their terms, and during the term of the recently returned ambassador Richard Court (2017–20), are outlined very briefly here.

During the last 15 years Australia's trading relationship with Japan has continued to be the subject of much diplomatic activity. A major milestone, building on steady and patient work, was the Japan–Australia Economic Partnership Agreement (JAEPA) that entered into force in January 2015. JAEPA resulted in some immediate tariff reductions and removals and anticipated more in the following years. From the Australian perspective, exports such as wine, milk protein, select horticultural goods and seafood enter Japan with reduced or no tariffs; certain energy-related and manufactured products enjoy tariff reductions or eliminations; and a range of services, including education, finance and legal, enjoy greater access to Japanese markets. From the Japanese perspective, Australia allows a broader range of automotive and other manufactured products to be imported with removed or phased out tariffs.[85]

For both countries, but for Japan in particular, the continued rise of China and the Chinese readiness to flex their military muscle in the region was a crucial factor in Australia–Japan relations. China also overtook Japan to become Australia's biggest trading partner in 2007, a milestone that perhaps fed into thinking already underway in Tokyo about different forms of partnership that might unfold in the relationship with Australia. One outcome was the Australia–Japan Joint Declaration on Security Cooperation (JDSC) signed in March 2007. This declaration trod a careful path between not diverging from crucial alliances with the United States and asserting that Australia–Japan security and defence cooperation

---

84   David Walton, 'Australia and Japan', in *Trading on Alliance Security: Australia in World Affairs, 2002–2005*, ed. James Cotton and John Ravenhill (Melbourne: Oxford University Press, 2007) 72–88.
85   DFAT, 'JAEPA Outcomes at a Glance', October 2018, www.dfat.gov.au/trade/agreements/in-force/jaepa/fact-sheets/Pages/jaepa-fact-sheet-outcomes-at-a-glance, accessed 20 June 2020.

needed to become more multidimensional and more connected to security for the Asia-Pacific region. While the JDSC attracted Beijing's criticism, the new means of dialogue it fostered, an annual '2+2' dialogue of foreign and defence ministers, was quickly valued by both Japanese and Australian governments. The JDSC opened the door further to levels of security coordination such as increased interoperability between defence forces. Beyond the JDSC, at a broader level of thinking, it also made very good sense from Tokyo's point of view to broaden security thinking to include food and energy security, the latter being a longstanding strength in the Australia–Japan relationship.[86]

It proved harder for Australian and Japanese governments to agree on ideas about regionalism during the first decade of the new century. In June 2008 Australian prime minister Kevin Rudd set out his vision of an Asia-Pacific Community, but in doing so, took his Japanese counterparts (and others) by surprise. Rudd's ideas were soon overtaken in the following year by Japanese prime minister Yukio Hatoyama's vision of an East Asian Community—a concept doubly troubling to Canberra, as it did not include the United States and might have also excluded Australia. In the event, neither version of regionalism gained broader support and from 2005, both Australia and Japan joined in the annual meetings of the East Asia Summit, held in conjunction with annual ASEAN (Association of Southeast Asian Nations) leaders' meetings.[87]

Although it has taken two attempts, what is known as the 'Quad', the Quadrilateral Security Dialogue between Australia, Japan, India and the United States, is the strongest expression of shared thinking about regional security. The first iteration of the Quad took shape in the aftermath of emergency responses to the 2004 Indian Ocean tsunami, the coordination of the four governments in this emergency suggesting what might be possible in more structured manner. Prime Minister Shinzō Abe first proposed the Quad in the middle of 2006, and it took shape through a joint naval exercise the following year. What exactly it

86 Rikki Kersten, 'Australia and Japan: Mobilising the Bilateral Relationship', in *Middle Power Dreaming: Australia in World Affairs, 2006–2010*, ed. James Cotton and John Ravenhill (South Melbourne: Oxford University Press, in association with the Australian Institute of International Affairs, 2011), 93–100.

87 Baogang He, 'Australian Ideas of Regionalism', in *Navigating the New International Disorder: Australia in World Affairs, 2011–2015*, ed. Mark Beeson and Shahar Hamieri (South Melbourne: Oxford University Press, in association with the Australian Institute of International Affairs, 2016), 105–23.

was meant to entail was vague beyond envisaging diplomatic and security (naval) cooperative elements. It did not take the Americans long to cool on the idea; and then the new Rudd government confirmed in 2008 that it was not pursuing the Quad, something Rudd's political opponents seized on as constituting a snub to Tokyo and New Delhi.[88] The revival of the Quad in 2020, or what is sometimes called Quad 2.0, is an important new feature of Australia–Japan relations, even as it attracts predictable hostility from China.

A Reciprocal Access Agreement, flagged in June 2020 and signed at the beginning of 2022, has been central to the most recent measures on security cooperation. The agreement provides for greater interoperability of Australian and Japanese forces, and faster deployments for training and in response to disasters. Japanese disappointment at not securing a huge contract to help build Australia's next generation of submarines was a bump in this road to closer security coordination, but what is more remarkable is how quickly the two governments have continued to strengthen their security ties and present a united view on key issues since April 2016, when news of the submarine contract not going to Tokyo was announced. On matters such as the curtailing of freedoms in Hong Kong, maintaining peaceful relations across the Taiwan Strait and condemning North Korean ballistic missile testing, Japanese and Australian governments, often coordinated with the US government, have issued joint statements or used common language to express their concerns for regional security. At the end of 2021 Japan was Australia's only 'special strategic partner' in Asia; and from Tokyo's perspective, Australia was the only other security partner, besides the United States, with which such comprehensive levels of cooperation had been established.

One persisting issue of contention between Australian and Japanese governments, Japan's commercial whaling, has proved challenging at times, but not to the extent of derailing the above-mentioned progress on trade, security and multilateral regional cooperation. Having led the establishment of a whale sanctuary in the Southern Ocean in 1994, Australian governments have tried to invoke this sanctuary, as well as the Whaling Convention and the Convention on International Trade in Endangered Species (CITES), to halt Japanese whaling in this area. After Australian-initiated legal proceedings in 2010, the International Court

88   Daniel Flitton, 'Who Really Killed the Quad 1.0?', *Lowy Interpreter*, 2 June 2020, www.lowy institute.org/the-interpreter/who-really-killed-quad-10, accessed 2 November 2020.

of Justice (ICJ) ruled in 2014 that Japan must cease its whaling in the Southern Ocean, in accordance with the moratorium on commercial whaling. A year later, however, Japan resumed whaling, claiming to be meeting conditions set by the ICJ. At the end of 2018, Japan withdrew from both the International Whaling Commission and CITES but resumed whaling in northern Pacific waters rather than the Southern Ocean. Australian opposition to any form of commercial whaling has meant that the issue remains a point of contention. But the lack of Japanese vessels in the Southern Ocean, so often captured dramatically by Greenpeace and media groups in a manner that roused public feeling and prompted stronger language by Australian leaders, has helped in the management of tensions.

Finally, Australia–Japan cooperative assistance in the face of natural disasters, already evident in the wake of the 2004 Indian Ocean tsunami, has been a most prominent feature of the relationship since the earthquake and tsunami, and subsequent nuclear reactor meltdowns, in Tohoku, north-east Japan, in March 2011. As Murray McLean has recalled in vivid detail, the scale of the disaster—nearly 20,000 people killed, more than 2,500 missing and large areas left uninhabitable for some years—prompted both immediate and ongoing forms of support from Australia. The Australian government donated A$10 million to a Red Cross appeal; a search-and-rescue team, supported by the Australian embassy, helped search for survivors; and the Royal Australian Air Force was quickly deployed to provide food, water and other supplies to the worst-affected Miyagi Prefecture. Notably, Australian prime minister Julia Gillard was the first foreign head of government to visit Tohoku, in April 2011. In the wake of these measures, many Australian schools, businesses and organisations, especially those that had been enriched by increasing people-to-people connections with Japan, also helped with donations of funds, services and time. The Australia–Japan Foundation funded a series of relief, reconstruction, research and community building initiatives in the following years.[89]

---

89   This summary is drawn from the AJF–DFAT report, *The Reconstruction Initiative: Australia–Japan Foundation's Response to the 2011 Japan Earthquake and Tsunami* (Canberra: Australian Government and AJF, 2015), www.dfat.gov.au/sites/default/files/the-reconstruction-initiative.pdf, accessed 15 August 2020.

The chapters that follow flesh out in greater detail the lineaments of Australia–Japan relations as core business of the embassy that made such a fulsome response to the earthquake disaster possible. They also demonstrate how the themes of mutual assistance, security, economic cooperation and regional thinking have been increasingly underpinned by a rich array of people-to-people connections between Australia and Japan. The work of the embassy in facilitating this broader sphere of connections beyond officialdom, as well as government-to-government relations, is arguably one of the most prominent features of its 60-year history.

4

Early Australia–Japan Postwar Relations: The Role of the Australian Embassy in Tokyo, 1952–65

David Walton

The Australian embassy in Tokyo has been one the of most important postings for Australian diplomats in the postwar era. Yet surprisingly little is known of the private thoughts of key Australian diplomats, including Ambassadors E. Ronald Walker, Alan Watt and Laurence McIntyre. Using embassy dispatches, cables, memoirs and interviews, this chapter attempts to capture the 'mood' in Tokyo during the period 1952–65 to give a fuller picture of these important early ambassadors. Primary sources provide valuable and unique insight into how Australian diplomats coped in what was a hardship posting, their personal views on Japan and the Japanese people they had direct contact with, and how their views of Japan developed over time. As might be expected, strong biases are evident in early dispatches and cables as Australian views were seen through the prism of the Pacific War and subsequent Allied victory and occupation of Japan.

By the early 1960s, however, a more nuanced understanding of Japan and Japanese foreign policy was becoming evident in diplomatic reports. The change in tone on Japan in diplomatic dispatches was indicative of the beginnings of a transformative moment that laid the foundations for future milestones in the bilateral relationship such as the Nippon Australia

Relations Agreement (NARA) Treaty signed in 1976.[1] The Tokyo embassy posting, accordingly, moved from a hardship post to a prized post by the mid-1960s. A key factor in the changing tone and style of reporting was the growing awareness among embassy staff of Japan's emergence as a significant economic power and a potentially important strategic partner in the Asia-Pacific region.

Departmental Rivalry in Canberra: Setting the Scene

The Department of External Affairs was, during the 1950s, small, made up of talented people dealing with 'big' foreign policy issues. An important dimension to the study of Australian diplomacy and Australia–Japan relations during this period was interdepartmental rivalry between Trade and External Affairs. Clearly this was a highly controversial and problematic affair. External Affairs during this period was not particularly powerful within the bureaucratic structure. The policies of trade pursued by the Department of Trade and Industry, by contrast, were deemed to be central to Australia's national interests. Moreover, the department was led by John McEwen (leader of the Country Party and deputy prime minister) and, consequently, was very powerful and influential within Canberra circles. As such, an analysis of the role of key individuals in the embassy in Tokyo offered in this chapter provides insight into policy development and efforts by the department to remain relevant.

Within External Affairs, Arthur Tange (later Sir) played a key role. As secretary (or head of department) from January 1954 to April 1965 he oversaw major developments in foreign policy matters during this period. Tange met with successive Japanese ambassadors Nishi, Suzuki and Ohta in regular ad hoc meetings. He was involved in the profound changes in Australian views towards Japan and in the bilateral relationship. Notably Tange sent two of the most experienced and senior officials at

---

1   For a comprehensive overview of the NARA Treaty see Moreen Dee, *Friendship and Cooperation: The 1976 Basic Treaty between Australia and Japan,* Australia in the World: The Foreign Affairs and Trade files no. 3 (Canberra: Department of Foreign Affairs and Trade, 2006); and David Walton (special editor) 'The NARA Treaty: 30 Years On', special issue, *The Australian Journal of International Affairs* 60, no. 4 (December 2006).

his disposal (Watt and McIntyre) to represent Australia in Japan. Tange saw Japan as a great power and played a more active role than has been assumed in improving overall bilateral relations.[2]

Until 1963, Tange monitored bilateral relations and noted the shifts and tended to support the proposals put forward by senior staff. According to Tange, during his period as secretary the bulk of the discussions between Australian and Japanese officials in Canberra were carried out at the division-head level.[3] However, from August 1963, in the aftermath of the amendment to the trade agreement, the secretary took a more active role in relations with Japan. The trade amendment was the last major impediment in overall bilateral relations and Tange was keen to look for new means to further broaden relations and engage Japan on regional matters.[4] In particular, Tange was interested in finding new opportunities and forums for direct discussion with Japanese counterparts on regional developments. It is from this period that there was a significant expansion in political dialogue.

Among senior diplomats, there were several that had extensive experience in the Asian region who were able to offer External Affairs expert comment and policy direction at a critical juncture in Australian postwar history with Japan and the region. Given the small size of the department, these leading senior officials were actively involved in policy discussions in Canberra or from their post. Thomas Critchley (Kuala Lumpur, 1955–65, London and later Bangkok and Jakarta), James Plimsoll (UN, India and later Tokyo) and Keith Shann (Philippines, Jakarta and later Tokyo), for example, had served in several critical posts. Each officer had years of in-country experience and had developed a wealth of personal contacts. Their background knowledge and capacity for constructive analysis were immensely useful. Accordingly, these outstanding officers were capable of dealing with emerging regional 'crises' such the West New Guinea dispute, *Konfrontasi* and of course the subsequent conflicts in Indochina, with a sound knowledge of regional issues and of the respective leaders involved.

Efforts by officials in External Affairs to engage in policies concerning Japan sparked an intense bureaucratic rivalry with their counterparts in Trade and Industry. From an External Affairs perspective, there was open

---

2   Sir Arthur Tange, correspondence with author, 30 November 1999.
3   Ibid.
4   Tange to McIntyre, 4 June 1964, National Archives of Australia (NAA): file no 3103/10/6 pt. 2, CRS A1838/280.

and frank acknowledgement that trade was the most important aspect of the relationship with Japan. Indeed, External Affairs officials were often sidelined and viewed as 'irrelevant' by officials in Trade and Industry who viewed commercial issues as the focus of bilateral relations.

Nonetheless, Cold War developments in the Asia-Pacific and the actions of Indonesia in West New Guinea were a source of discussion and mutual interest between Canberra and Tokyo.[5] By 1959 there was agreement on a regular exchange of information on a wide range of topics. The agreement to broaden consultation reflected the importance of the trade relationship and an acknowledgement in Canberra that Japan had something to offer in terms of political information, and demonstrated that both governments could work together effectively at the official and political level. By 1962, there was broad agreement within the Department of External Affairs that the political dimension of the relationship was important and worth cultivating as part of the overall bilateral relationship. This, of course, meant that External Affairs was becoming more relevant and in direct competition with the policies pursued by McEwen and his secretary, John Crawford (and later Alan Westerman), who saw the relationship with Japan primarily as their domain.[6]

Early Views: Dr E. Ronald Walker, 1952–56

[It is] difficult to make an objective assessment of Japan due to the long tradition in Australia of distrust and aversion towards Japan.[7]

This comment by Walker on his posting to Tokyo is revealing and worthy of reflection. In the early 1950s, wartime memories in Australia were still relatively fresh. Fear and residual anger towards Japan and the treatment of Australian prisoners of war were a lingering source of tension. During this period, moreover, Tokyo was a hardship post for Australian diplomats. The city was still undergoing a massive rebuilding phase after destructive wartime bombing campaigns and subsequent fires that destroyed much of

---

5   For a detailed coverage of the West New Guinea dispute see W. Henderson, *West New Guinea: The Dispute and Its Settlement* (South Orange, NJ: Seton Hall University Press, 1973).

6   For insightful accounts of the bureaucratic politics of the time see Peter Golding, *Blackjack McEwen: Political Gladiator* (Carlton: Melbourne University Press, 1996); Alan Rix, *Coming to Terms: The Politics of Australia's Trade with Japan, 1945–1957* (Sydney: Allen and Unwin, 1986).

7   Walker to R.G. Casey, 'Reflections on Three and a Half Years in Japan', 31 January 1956, NAA: A 4231 Tokyo 1956 Despatch No JI /56.

greater Tokyo. No doubt the city felt like a very large construction zone—noisy, bustling and dirty. The houses were mainly made of wood and were flimsy in appearance. Roads were full of potholes and dangerous to drive on. Electricity was erratic outside Tokyo. In the mid-1950s, televisions were a luxury item, with one diplomat noting that a village he frequented just outside Tokyo had its only television set mounted on a pole in an open square for all to share.[8] Luxuries from home and foreign foodstuffs more generally were available but could become scarce, and public transportation was slow, tedious and overcrowded. The summer months, with their high temperatures and oppressive humidity, would have made daily life extremely difficult. A clearly agitated Watt noted that in his first summer in Tokyo, he was not allowed to turn on air conditioning at the Australian embassy in August until the Australian mission in Washington did so.[9]

This is not to say that life was always difficult for diplomats. The embassy was a grand European-style house located in the Mita district of central Tokyo. As described in Chapter 1, the embassy had an extensive and beautiful garden, including a tennis court. Life in central Tokyo meant proximity to numerous restaurants, bars and clubs, and diplomats had the advantage of a highly favourable exchange rate that allowed them access to upmarket weekend and holiday accommodation in lovely locations such as Karuizawa (a resort town in Nagano) to escape the summer heat.

Initially the numbers at the embassy were small, consisting of the ambassador, head of chancery, a second secretary, two third secretaries, a consular attaché, an administrative officer and a cypher clerk. According to Richard Austin, who had a posting in Tokyo in 1955:

> The Ambassador worked from his study in the house and the rest of us from small rooms in an annex behind, which had been added later. On Monday mornings we joined the Ambassador to discuss the events of the previous week and to prognosticate about those of the coming one.[10]

---

8   Hugh Dunn, *The Shaping of a Sinologue of Sorts,* Australians in Asia Series No. 1 (Nathan: Centre for the Study of Australia-Asia Relations, 1988), 34.

9   Oral history transcript, Alan Watt interviewed by Bruce Miller, 11 December 1974, National Library of Australia (NLA): ORAL TRC 306, Bib ID 788329.

10   R.W.L. Austin, *The Narrow Road to a Far Country: Intimations of Things Japanese,* Australians in Asia Series No. 7 (Nathan: Centre for the Study of Australia-Asia Relations, 1991), 34.

Key issues in the first few years after normalisation of relations in 1952 included dealing with war criminals, pearling, compensation for former Australian prisoners of war, discussions on Japanese war dead in Australian territorial waters, concern about Japan as a potential military threat, and the possibility of Japan turning 'Communist'.[11] The most sensitive issue, however, was over pearl fishing, which highlighted the ongoing distrust between the two nations. The dispute was essentially over the exploitation of pearl shell resources off the coast of northern Australia and Australian fears of Japanese intentions as Japanese boats were only 160 kilometres north of Darwin. Although the issue became a protracted legal dispute, it nonetheless lost its intensity by 1957 as the demand for pearls dropped and in December that year, Prime Minister Kishi accepted the territorial limits set by Australia.[12]

For External Affairs officials in Tokyo, there was a great deal of uncertainty and suspicion about Japan, but also awareness of Japan as a rising power. Walker, as part of his reflections on his period in Tokyo, commented that it was: 'Most desirable that we get to know the Japanese intimately for they are going to play a leading role in the political and industrial development of Asia.'[13]

There was also a strong sense of frustration that Australia was not able to exercise much influence over Japan's future developments and that Australian views were not carrying any weight in Washington. The number one fear in Canberra was that Japan would rearm and pose a future security threat. Walker, reporting on this sensitive topic, noted that despite understanding Australian concerns, United States officials had no fear of Japan as a possible menace. In fact, he reported that pressure on Japan to rearm was coming from Washington and was met with resistance in Japan.[14] Accordingly, there was considerable pressure on Australia to alter its position towards Japan. In Washington there was concern that Japan may turn communist through an alliance with China. Both the British and Australian embassies expressed early concerns about this potential development and that Australia may be isolated if there was persistence with opposition to Japan in Canberra.[15] Walker raised

---

11 External Affairs internal report: *Australia–Japan Relations—A Balance Sheet*, 27 September 1957, NAA: A1838/280, 3101/10/11/2 Pt.1.
12 For more detail see Rix, *Coming to Terms*, 45–52.
13 Walker to Tange, 21 August 1953, ANZUS Papers, NAA: A9564, 221/4/2 Pt 2.
14 Ibid.
15 Casey to Tange, 28 July 1954, NAA: A4940/1, 1009.

this issue and reported on the view of the Italian ambassador to Japan, who argued that Australia should make a volte-face and create a new relationship with Japan.[16]

By the mid-1950s the rebuilding and the redevelopment phase across Japan was clearly making substantial progress. Ambassador Walker noted in his review of his three and half years in Japan that:

> Japanese people are now sensing that they are making solid progress after the surrender. Cities have been rebuilt and the average Japanese person is better fed and clothed than ever before. General level of health has improved. Trade has improved and the political situation steadied by the merger of conservative and socialist parties.[17]

Japan's postwar reconstruction and alignment with the United States led to a change of view and the support for closer ties with Japan in Canberra. These decisions were made for pragmatic reasons, based on new Cold War security concerns, including the emergence of Communist China, the Korean War and endorsement of the American-led policy that Japan would play a critical role in the postwar stability in the Asia-Pacific. According to Thomas Critchley:

> [the ill feeling towards Japanese officials in Canberra] evaporated when I returned from Korea in 1954 and amended the view on Japan. It was not just based on trade as I said, I think the people who have represented Australia in Japan really enjoyed being there; the job, the relationship and attached great emphasis to Japan. I always thought Japan would be of critical importance.[18]

In line with this sentiment, External Affairs Minister Richard Casey advocated that Australian policy should:

> pay special attention to prevent a close alliance between Japan and China, support Japan to have reasonable facilities for own defence (in cooperation with non-communist countries) and expanding export trade.[19]

---

16   Walker to Tange, 11 September 1952, NAA: A9564/2, 221/4/2 Pt 4.
17   Walker to R.G. Casey, 'Reflections on Three and Half Years in Japan', 31 January 1956, NAA: A 4231 Tokyo 1956 Despatch No JI /56.
18   Thomas Critchley, interview with author, 16 June 1998.
19   Casey to cabinet, 'Australian Policy Towards Japan', 28 July 1954, NAA: A4940/1, 1009.

Australian prime minister Robert Menzies's 'Man to Man' radio address on Japan in March 1954 symbolised the new postwar arrangements, calling for a new relationship with Japan free of wartime enmities. The subsequent commerce treaty (1957) and reciprocal visits by Menzies and Kishi, in 1957, moreover, were watershed moments.

Adjustment to a New Relationship: Alan Watt, 1956–59

> The International position of both Japan and Australia is qualified by their dependence on the United States for security. Japan's strategic position, the size of her population and her industrial power have resulted in more direct interest being shown in her than Australia. East Asia is a more critical area for the United States than Southeast Asia.[20]

The nature of Australia's bilateral relationship with Japan was rapidly changing after 1957, as demonstrated in the above cabinet report by External Affairs Minister Casey in July 1954. The reset in bilateral relations and full-scale trade agreement gave impetus for a broadening of bilateral ties. Australian public commentary on Japan was less vocal and Australia's position had changed from that of a member of a victorious coalition overseeing the occupation of Japan to one of a small to middle power with a mission in Tokyo. These developments, and the perception in External Affairs that Japan would become increasingly central to Washington's planning in East Asia, appeared to have irritated Watt. A common theme in the bulk of his reports to Canberra was annoyance at what he saw as Japanese lack of appreciation of Australian support. As a former secretary of the department, his views also reflected his frustration at having limited power to influence the relationship with Japan given the emphasis on trade. Watt lamented that he had no role in the Commerce Agreement until the document had been completed. The problem, as Watt saw it, was that McEwen was not only powerful, but also handled the trade treaty extremely well.[21]

20 External Affairs internal report: *Australia–Japan Relations–A Balance Sheet*, 27 September 1957, NAA: A1838/280, 3101/10/11/2 Pt.1.
21 Watt interviewed by Bruce Miller, TRC 306.

Watt's frustrations that Australia was losing influence in Japan were evident in his reporting. For example, annoyed that Japan chose Iran and Peru over Australia to sponsor its application for UN membership, Watt wrote in his dispatch to External Affairs:

> If those who control policy in Japan believe that we can be fobbed off with polite words they will continue to do this in the future when it suits them. If they learn in some polite but firm way that their words are not deceiving us, it will help them to understand that international friendship depends on acts rather than words.[22]

Clearly, there were a wide range of competing interests in the Japanese Ministry of Foreign Affairs and Japanese policymaking communities more generally. Rapid economic development, domestic political realignments with the merger of parties on the left and right of the political spectrum, focus on postwar rehabilitation and acceptance into the international community would have been compelling factors. Nonetheless, Watt wanted to ensure that Australia was noticed and appeared perplexed when this was not the case. In preparation for Prime Minister Menzies's visit to Japan in March 1957, Watt commented in his report that the newly appointed Japanese prime minister, Nobusuke Kishi, had not seemed conscious of Australia while serving as foreign minister. Watt's recommendation was that:

> A valuable consequence of the PM visit to Japan could be a realisation by Kishi personally that Australia exists, that our friendship is worth having and that our reactions and interests could have some consequence for Japan.[23]

In the following year, Watt reported that the Japanese economy was still wobbly and that the Japanese government remained susceptible to 'play' with communist countries offering tempting trade deals. Even more concerning, from his perspective, was Japan's drift as an 'Asian Nation'. Although couched in rather vague language, Watt appeared to be worried about Japan's identity and how it promoted its interests in political forums. He noted that:

22 Watt to Tange, 'Japanese Membership of United Nations', 12 December 1956, NAA: A5105/3, 223/1 Pt 2.
23 Department of External Affairs, 'Prime Minister's Brief–Japan', March 1957, NAA: A1838/278, 3103/10/11/2/1 Pt 1.

[the] need to press the US at the next ANZUS meeting for comments on recent Japanese policy and diplomatic assistance. Since the last election Japan has stressed her position as an 'Asian Nation' disproportionately to her association with Free world countries and even her support for the United Nations.[24]

Staff at the Tokyo embassy were given the task of enhancing Australia's understanding of Japan. At this time Japanese culture was considered alien. Indeed, knowledge of Japan in Australia was, in most cases, based on ignorance, wartime enmities and propaganda. Reports to Canberra, accordingly, provided useful information, adding insight into Japanese thinking and Japan's future policy orientation.

By his own account, Watt was reluctant to take the head of mission role in Tokyo as he found Japanese people difficult to understand. Nonetheless, he made the effort, including reading about Japanese history and culture, and becoming president of the Tokyo Lawn Tennis Club as a means of socialising with Japanese elites.[25] According to Austin, a second secretary at the embassy, 'Walker asked for reports on things that mattered. Watt [by contrast] was a worrier who demanded reports on everything, no matter how trivial'.[26]

In this respect, Watt's reporting to Canberra on a wide range of issues offered useful insight into life in Tokyo and of a foreign diplomat's perception of Japan. For example, within three weeks of his arrival in Tokyo to commence his posting, Watt gave his impressions on meeting the Japanese Imperial Family and on social protocol at the palace. His report included a discussion on lack of a dress code for women (who could wear both long dresses and dresses with shorter sleeves), the failure of clear rules when presenting the Letter of Credence, and uncertainty as to whether one should curtsy in front of the other members of the Japanese Imperial Family. Watt sensed that Japanese restraint on imposing clear guidelines was based in part on a fear that foreigners might regard them as 'undemocratic'. He noted:

---

24 Watt to Tange, 'ANZUS Meeting—Japanese Problems', 31 July 1958, NAA: A9564/2, 221/4/2 Part 4.

25 Watt interviewed by Bruce Miller, TRC 306.

26 Austin, *The Narrow Road to a Far Country*, 34. In terms of temperament, Austin compares Walker to a basset hound and Watt to a terrier. These views were corroborated by Hugh Dunn, a third secretary at the Tokyo embassy, 1954–58, in his oral history interview. Oral history transcript, Hugh Dunn interviewed by Michael Wilson, 27 August 1993, NLA: ORAL TRC 2981/1, Bib ID 396635.

There is, I feel, a certain lack of confidence in Japan following upon its first military defeat in history. I shall have occasion on other despatches to refer to this 'lack of confidence' of the Japanese in dealing with matter of greater importance than Palace protocol, namely the handling from day to day of significant international problems.[27]

It was fortuitous for Watt that circumstances aligned that allowed him to meet the emperor and the Japanese Imperial Family three times not long after his arrival. Emperor Hirohito was described as a shy and retiring person and his son, then Crown Prince Akihito, as an easygoing and more composed person than his father. Much to Watt's delight, Prince Akihito was a keen tennis fan and Watt noted that his membership of the Tokyo Lawn Tennis Club was a useful way to maintain contact.[28] On his second meeting at the emperor's birthday reception, Watt was given the opportunity for a direct conversation with the emperor in a small group. To Watt's surprise, the emperor engaged in a political conversation on the Malay Emergency and the communist threat:

I remain surprised that he not only asked questions but clearly had a political view. This view could, I think, safely be described as uneasiness regarding the expansion of Communist Chinese influence. I should add that the conversation took place in the presence of the Chief of protocol, so that presumably, its substance will be known to the Foreign Minister.[29]

Watt was, in many respects, an excellent choice as ambassador to Japan during this period. He had seniority within Canberra circles, which was important as the relationship was about to take off with the Australia–Japan Agreement on Commerce. Watt was also 'old fashioned' in many respects and his anti-communist stance and elite attitudes would have also been appreciated among conservative Japanese elites who shared similar values.

---

27 Watt to Casey, 3 May 1956, NAA: A4231, Tokyo 1956.
28 Ibid. Watt was a quarter finalist at Wimbledon in 1923.
29 Ibid.

Japan as a Regional Partner in the Making: Laurence McIntyre, 1960–65

> Five years in Japan was satisfying professionally and agreeable in social and human terms. I found myself liking Japanese people which I had not expected to.[30]

McIntyre's arrival in Tokyo in 1960 was well timed. His previous posting was to Jakarta and Indonesian policy under President Sukarno was the pressing issue of the day. By the early 1960s the trade relationship between Australia and Japan was becoming lucrative and a sense of change in bilateral relations was palpable. The Japanese economy was growing, and Japanese people were becoming more prosperous every year. Moreover, trade with Australia was flourishing. By 1962, much of the attention in dispatches from Tokyo centred on Japanese domestic developments and its regional diplomacy. External Affairs Minister Casey's visit to Tokyo in March 1959 was a turning point in developing the political relationship. Casey and his Japanese counterpart had agreed to exchange political information on regional developments at a broader level, which included Indonesia and mainland China.[31] Casey's visit sparked an increase in political consultation between Australian and Japanese officials. Between 1959 and 1962 there was considerable debate about the security of information discussed and the process involved in setting up a reciprocal arrangement for the exchange of information. By February 1962, there was broad agreement for regular exchange of information among relevant section heads.

The view within External Affairs was that Japan, in overall terms, supported the Western position. A ministerial brief in March 1959 noted that Japan took an anti-Soviet line and offered a moderating role within the Afro-Asian group. Moreover, it was noted that Japan supported the Western position on pressing issues such as Chinese representation at the United Nations.[32] As consultation became more regular, the UN was seen as an important vehicle for discussing, and, where possible, coordinating

---

30 Laurence McIntyre interviewed by Mel Pratt, 9 September–27 November 1975, NLA: ORAL TRC 121/67, Bib ID 727969.

31 Record of conversation between Casey and Foreign Minister Fujiyama at the Gaimusho, Tokyo, 25 March 1959, NAA: 3103/10/1 pt. 7, CRS 1838/283.

32 Japan was also sympathetic towards the United Kingdom on the Cyprus question at the United Nations. See Ministerial brief, 25 March 1959, NAA: A1838, 3103/10/1 Pt 7.

policies on issues of mutual interest. The regular exchange of views at this forum was, in this respect, a logical extension of the commitment by Australian officials to expand relations with Japan. Furthermore, the sharing of information had practical benefits as the Japanese delegations were renowned for their ability to gather information. Alf Parsons, who had a posting to the UN from 1962 to 1964, commented that the Japanese delegates were the people to go to if you were unsure of technical issues or the substance of issues. They were well informed and masters of publishing documents and reading the entire range of materials.[33]

In the 1962–63 Japan Post Review, McIntyre reflected on this trend and referred to the decision in 1960 and 1961 to supply the Japanese Ministry of Foreign Affairs (MOFA) with advanced notes on Australian agenda items for UN General Assembly meetings. The Australian ambassador noted how the exercise assisted in opening discussions with the Japanese Foreign Ministry on a wide range of issues and generally added to the climate of cooperation in bilateral relations. Indeed, McIntyre stated that the MOFA was clearly expecting (and hoping) that the advanced notes would become a regular part of two-way exchanges.[34] One area for further development suggested by McIntyre was discussion of matters arising from the Economic Commission for Asia and the Far East. In 1962, Australia was reclassified as a member of the Asian and Far Eastern region and the Australian ambassador reported that Japanese officials had expressed interest in a preliminary exchange of opinion before the completion of national briefs.[35] From an Australian perspective, such collaboration offered insight into Japanese thinking on regional issues and the opportunity for Australians to influence the Japanese position.

The process towards closer cooperation on UN matters continued to develop. In the 1964 Japan Post Review, McIntyre commented that Japan's views on how the various agenda items should be handled were in most cases quite close to those of Australia. Moreover, McIntyre emphasised in his report that there had been frequent and close collaboration on a range of issues at the UN. Notably, this included the controversial question of the occupancy of the China seat.[36] These developments were in line with planning within External Affairs. In 1963, an internal report argued that

---

33 Alf Parsons, interview with author, 12 May 2000.
34 Shaw to Tange, 'Japan: Post Review 1962–63', 4 June 1964, NAA: A1838, 3103/10/21 Pt1.
35 Ibid.
36 Ibid.

the removal of final trade barriers in July that year was a watershed moment in the bilateral relationship. The report stressed how Japan was of national importance to Australia's future security and economic wellbeing:

> Japan will increasingly occupy a position of influence and power in the Pacific and Asian areas because her economic strength and ability and drive of her people. Her continuing friendship with the West is a matter of vital importance to Australia. What happens to Japan may determine Australian physical and economic security. Every effort is essential to influence the present and potential leaders of Japan on lines favourable to Australia and to secure close political and economic collaboration.[37]

The Australian view of changes in Japanese policy was, by late 1964, taking shape. According to Richard Broinowski, who was a third secretary in Tokyo in 1965, McIntyre was well connected in the ministries and Diet and throughout the Japanese community.[38] In particular, his personal friendship with Takio Oda (vice minister of the Japanese Ministry of Foreign Affairs, 1964–65) was a major asset. McIntyre and Oda had developed their friendship while on postings to London and Jakarta. As a result, McIntyre was able to directly contact Oda and key MOFA officials quickly and without making formal appointments at a time where there where more than 60 foreign missions in Tokyo. McIntyre commented:

> I could pick up a telephone and get straight through to Oda and he would usually say well come over and see me in ten minutes time. It was a very good working relationship.[39]

The networking carried out by McIntyre was viewed in External Affairs as a crucial step in closer political relations. Tange noted in a report on Australia–Japan relations in 1964 that the McIntyre–Oda relationship was the only close contact on the political side.[40] As a result, Australians were starting to gain a clearer sense of MOFA policy and access to their thinking, which laid the foundations for regular institutionalised bilateral political consultation.[41]

---

37 External Affairs talking points for call by Ambassador Ohta, 6 August 1963, NAA: A1838, 3103/10/1/ pt. 9.
38 Richard Broinowski, former DFAT official, interview with author, 12 May 2000, Canberra.
39 McIntyre interviewed by Mel Pratt, TRC 121/67.
40 Tange to McIntyre, 4 June 1964, NAA: file no. 3103/10/6 pt2, CRS A1838/280.
41 McIntyre's networking role continued during his next posting to the United Nations in 1970s. According to former Japanese diplomat Shizuo Saito, the two worked closely at coordinating Australian and Japanese policy while in New York. Former diplomat Shizuo Saito, interview with author, Tokyo, 24 April 1998.

Indeed, Australian policy was affected by the broadening of the bilateral relationship with Japan and the prevailing view within External Affairs was that closer alignment would make it easier to coordinate policies. Throughout 1964, officers were examining ways to develop such closer political relations to ensure that Japanese policymakers took more account of Australian points of view. The perceived need to engage in more consultative arrangement with Japan amounted to an admission by External Affairs that Australians had minimal influence on Japanese policymakers. Suggested strategies within the department included increasing the number of ad hoc meetings, enhancing the exchange of confidential political information, and advanced consultation with the Japanese on UN matters. In addition, the possibility of regular ministerial meetings was seriously considered.[42]

The United States also endorsed the push for a more consultative arrangement with Japan. A prevailing view in the American State Department was that the Japanese had decided that they were not strong enough to follow a foreign policy that might involve them in criticism and controversy. Thus, the Japanese were seemingly unlikely to take a firm position over Malaysia as it would endanger their good relations with Indonesia. The influential American ambassador to Japan, Edwin O. Reischauer (1964–67), supported this view. He argued that Japan still required a feeling of confidence and reassurance, and this would occur through further bilateral and multilateral dialogue on a wide range of fields.[43] The US view was also made clear to Australian officials during the July 1964 ANZUS meeting, held in Washington. US secretary of state Dean Rusk commented that he would like to see Japan increase its foreign aid commitment and play a more active political role in Asia.[44] In any event, this process was already well advanced in Australian thinking. Such plans had been discussed at the departmental level in preparation for the 1963 Ikeda visit. Moreover, in December 1964, discussions on an annual

---

42   Tange to McIntyre, 4 June 1964, NAA: A1838, 3103/10/6 Pt 2.
43   A.J. Melhuish to Department of External Affairs, 22 September 1964, NAA: A1838, 250/10/4/4 Pt 5.
44   Rusk, in an apparent disregard for Japanese constitutional limitations, commented at the 1964 ANZUS meeting that he would like to earmark a Japanese battalion or two for United Nations service. Department of External Affairs file note: ANZUS meeting 17–18 July 1964, 25 January 1965, NAA: A1838, 3103/11/2 Pt 1.

ministerial meeting were held between the newly appointed Australian minister for external affairs, Paul Hasluck, and his Japanese counterpart, Etsusaburo Shiina.[45]

By late 1964, the Australian position on exchanging information with Japanese officials on regional developments was under review. Regional issues where Japanese information was of particular interest included the Indonesian embrace of China by late 1964, and the withdrawal of Indonesia from the UN in January 1965. The geopolitical importance of a stable Indonesia and the possible expansion of communist influence in the region would have been a source of concern in Canberra. Australian reports now indicated a renewed appreciation of Japan's information and role as a potential moderating influence on President Sukarno. From an Australian perspective, the appointment of Shizuo Saito as ambassador to Indonesia was a positive development. He was viewed by the pro-Western faction within the MOFA as a more moderate and sensible diplomat, likely to put relations with Indonesia on a new footing.[46] In any event, Saito was the consummate diplomat who managed to balance relationships during a difficult period in Indonesian history. He maintained a personal friendship with President Sukarno, developed during the Japanese occupation period, and built on ties cultivated by his predecessors, including with Dewi, one of Sukarno's polygamous wives, who was Japanese. As well, by early 1965, as events in Jakarta became more complex, Saito ensured that information was being passed on to American and Australian officials. During this period, the Japanese ambassador had developed a good working relationship with Shann. According to Saito, the two had 'frank and direct consultations and exchange of views on a regular basis and at any time'.[47] This proved to be an invaluable source of information as the tumultuous events unfolded in Jakarta later in the year.

Accordingly, the Australians were more relaxed than they had been in the past about Japanese motives and policy and were more focused on working with Japanese officials. The shift in the Australian view represented a new approach which was more accepting of Japanese foreign policy objectives as they became more aligned to Australian policies. This also reflected the Japanese relationship with the United States. Prime Minister Sato's

---

45 Hasluck suggested that such meetings cover issues of mutual interest to both countries and the situation in Asia. Record of discussion between Hasluck and Japanese foreign minister Shiina at the United Nations, 4 December 1964, NAA: A3092, 221/12/5/5/1.

46 McIntyre to Department of External Affairs, 4 September 1964, NAA: A1838, 3103/11/108 Pt 1.

47 Shizuo Saito, interview with author, Tokyo, 24 April 1998.

visit to Washington in January 1965 was seen as indicating a new ease in relations. According to American observations of the meeting, both sides treated each other as equals. The United States did not lecture or hector the Japanese and the Japanese did not show any signs of timidity or humility. Indeed, most of the meeting was reportedly taken up with international issues, unlike previous meeting devoted to bilateral matters.[48] McIntyre was nonetheless dubious about a rapid transformation of Japanese policy. He was positive, however, about the long-term implications. He wrote:

> They [the Japanese] have not yet reached the point of abandoning the caution, amounting at times to timidity, that had characterised their posture in past years. When they do, they may well pose problems for us as well as for the United States but this is no reason to consider the prospect unwelcome. Provided relationships with Japan continue to develop on their present sound and amicable basis, the advantages of having a more incisive Japanese voice should surely outweigh the disadvantages.[49]

Impact of the Embassy on Bilateral Relations

Several factors are evident in an assessment of the Australian embassy in Tokyo between 1952 and 1965. First, key policymakers in External Affairs demonstrated foresight, strength of character and creativity. This attitude was important in the success and staffing of the embassy. The decision within External Affairs to enhance relations with Japan, given the lingering postwar animosity towards Japan within the general community, would have been a difficult decision.[50] However, the fact that a majority of the key policymakers were supportive of developing closer ties made the process less arduous to implement. Moreover, the overall positive attitude towards Japan in Canberra, which was based on trade, led to a rapid improvement in the quality and quantity of bilateral dialogue. In this context, the embassy was a vital link in enhancing understanding

---

48 'Australian Embassy: Washington to External Affairs: Report on Prime Minister Sato's visit to Washington', 15 January 1965, NAA: A1838, 250/10/4/4 Pt 5.
49 McIntyre to Department of External Affairs, 25 January 1965, NAA: A1838, 3103/11/161 Pt 15.
50 Alf Parsons commented that in the early postwar period he knew of several senior public servants who would turn their back on Japanese officials at international conferences. Alf Parsons, interview with author, 12 May 2000.

of Japan and Japanese culture. The insights of embassy staff became more nuanced over this first decade. Successive ambassadors Walker, Watt and McIntyre were instrumental in this process.

Second, and interrelated, key individuals assisted in institutionalising bureaucratic links between Tokyo and Canberra. Indeed, key senior officials largely drove these policies. For example, Tange and Shaw in Canberra were receptive to the arguments to further develop the political as well as economic links with Japan and were looking for new initiatives. In Tokyo, Watt and, in particular, McIntyre were committed to developing personal ties with a wide range of key Japanese elites and officials in the MOFA. The regular exchange of political and security information after 1962 represented a gradual maturation in postwar relations.[51]

Third, the emerging policy networks, although not properly developed during this period, were to become an important feature in bilateral relations. Individuals in Canberra and Tokyo fostered these connections for reasons of mutual self-interest and shared values. The embryonic policy networks that emerged provided a framework for the further expansion of consultation within the bilateral relationship. The high calibre of Australian diplomats in Tokyo and their exceptional performance was critical in this development, which has had profound implications for postwar bilateral relations.

Finally, the Australian embassy in Tokyo was an influential source of information on Japan. Embassy dispatches were providing the basis for policy developments. As diplomats became more proficient in understanding Japanese culture and layered meanings, the reporting became more nuanced. Staff were clearly enjoying their experience in Japan and the post became highly prized. Staff were committed to developing these ties as Japan was an emerging power and an important country for Australian regional diplomacy and long-term national interests.

In this context, the embassy played a vital role in normalising bilateral relations and offering valuable in-country experience for both highly experienced and up and coming junior diplomats. The experiences and impressions presented in this chapter showcase the range of information gathered and its significance for an Australia still coming to terms with

---

51 For a detailed analysis of the Australia–Japan postwar relationship, see Alan Rix, *The Australia–Japan Political Alignment: 1952 to the Present* (London: Routledge, 1999).

the growing importance of Japan as a 'rock solid' US ally and an emerging economic power. The efforts by External Affairs officers to make the department relevant, moreover, were clearly successful. By the early 1970s the burgeoning trade relationship and shared political values received broad recognition in Australian policymaking circles. Accordingly, a new bureaucratic framework was implemented designed to capitalise on these developments. The new structure also attempted to deal with the long-term rivalry between the Departments of Trade and Foreign Affairs. In 1971, the Department of Foreign Affairs (as it was renamed in 1970) was given the role of chairing an interdepartmental committee on policy towards Japan. The committee also included Prime Minister and Cabinet, Treasury, and Trade and Industry and effectively gave Foreign Affairs the role of coordinating policy.[52]

---

52 Lingering hostility between the two departments remained, however. In many respects, the problem of departmental rivalry was not resolved until the forced merger between the two departments for practical reasons in 1987.

5

Sir John Crawford and Japan, 1953–77

David Lee

As a senior Australian public servant in the 1950s and then as leader of The Australian National University (ANU) in the 1960s and 1970s, Sir John Crawford played a crucial role in helping Australian governments to build the architecture of the post–World War II Australia–Japan relationship. Crawford had been engaged in thinking about Australia's long-term relationship with Japan even before the Pacific War from 1941 to 1945. As a young academic, he presented a paper to the Australian Institute of Political Science in 1938, when Japan was at war with China, calling for what he called 'economic appeasement' of Japan. By this he meant that the Western nations, including Australia, should seek to satisfy Japan's legitimate demand for industrialisation in return for political agreements to limit its aggressiveness.[1] Economic appeasement was an idea before its time. Japan's interests increasingly diverged from the Western powers leading to the Pacific War from 1941 to 1945. By the end of the Pacific War, Crawford had joined the Australian Public Service and would ascend to the position of permanent secretary of the Department of Commerce and Agriculture (1950–56) and then of Trade (1956–60). In this position he carried a substantial responsibility for Australia's mission in Tokyo and played an important role in making

---

1   See Peter Drysdale, 'The Relationship with Japan: Despite the Vicissitudes', in *Policy and Practice: Essays in Honour of Sir John Crawford*, ed. L.T. Evans and J.D.B. Miller (Canberra: Australian National University Press, 1987), 66–71.

policy relating to Japan during that time, most notably in successfully arguing for a trade agreement. In 1960 he joined ANU and became its vice-chancellor from 1968 to 1973 and chancellor from 1976 to 1984. As an academic leader he was also an adviser to Australian governments. This chapter examines Crawford's key role in the making of the Australia–Japan Agreement on Commerce of 1957, the NARA (the Nippon Australia Relations Agreement) Treaty of 1976 and the formation of the Australia–Japan Foundation, also established in 1976. Because of his key role in the two treaties and the foundation, Crawford must be regarded as the key architect of one of Australia's most successful postwar bilateral relationships, Australia's relationship with Japan. This chapter draws out the difference made by one man, Sir John Crawford, to the making of the Australian–Japanese relationship.

The Problem of Australian Trade with Japan

Crawford's consciousness of the need for action on the trading relationship with Japan, after the disasters of trade diversion in the 1930s and the Pacific War, started early in the 1950s. In 1953, Japan was already Australia's second-best customer after Britain, largely because of its healthy postwar purchases of Australian wool.[2] Despite this, the trading relationship was heavily weighted in Australia's favour, with Australia sending several times in value to Japan what it imported from it. In this respect, the Australia–Japan trading relationship was the reverse of the Anglo-Australian relationship, where British imports into Australia considerably outweighed Australian exports to Britain. Less than a decade after the end of the Pacific War, there was lingering resentment towards Japan and concern that liberalised trade might damage Australian industries. From 1953 onward, against these headwinds, Crawford set about reforming Australia's fragile relationship with Japan. In doing so, he was helped by his connections with Australia's heads of mission in Tokyo. By 1953 Crawford was not only one of Australia's leading agricultural economists but also a member of the coterie of powerful

---

2   Unsigned notes by the Department of Commerce and Agriculture, 4 August 1953, Papers of Sir John Crawford, National Library of Australia (NLA): MS 4514/6/18.

heads of department who were dubbed the 'seven dwarfs'.[3] E.R. Walker, ambassador to Japan from 1952 to 1955, was a fellow economist and executive member of the National Security Resources Board that advised the Menzies government on balancing the civilian and military sectors during the Korean War; Allen Brown, ambassador from 1965 to 1970, was a former head of the Prime Minister's Department and another of the 'seven dwarfs'; and Alan Watt, ambassador from 1956 to 1959, had been secretary of the Department of External Affairs and a peer when Crawford started as secretary of the Department of Commerce and Agriculture in 1950. The embassy in Tokyo, moreover, was largely staffed by officers of the Department of External Affairs and the Department of Commerce and Agriculture (Trade from 1956) and both these departments were in accord about the need for development of a more positive relationship with Japan.

Though Australia had supported Japan's admission to the UN and the Colombo Plan in the 1950s, the question of Japanese accession to the General Agreement on Tariffs and Trade (GATT) was much more difficult. Once Japan became a member of GATT, the Australian government would have to give it the same treatment as other foreign countries through the intermediate tariff. The Department of Trade and Customs and manufacturing interests in Australia feared that opening the floodgates to Japanese imports could damage not only Australian industry but also the exports of Australia's major trading partner, the United Kingdom. On the other hand, the view of Crawford's Department of Commerce and Agriculture was that:

> exclusion of Japan from GATT settles no problems, but the application of GATT as between Australia and Japan may offer possibilities of controlling to some extent Japan's general export and import policies. Any retaliatory measures by Japan against any move by Australia to restrict Japan's exports to Australia, provided these are based on reasonable grounds, should also be subject to more control than if GATT did not apply.[4]

3   See Samuel Furphy, ed., *The Seven Dwarfs and the Age of the Mandarins: Australian Government Administration in the Post-war Reconstruction Era* (Canberra: ANU Press, 2015), doi.org/10.22459/SDAM.07.2015.
4   Ibid.

In the end, the Australian government hedged its bets by supporting Japan's accession to the GATT in 1955 but invoking its Section XXXV, which meant that it could avoid according Japan most-favoured-nation treatment. Essentially, this meant that Australia had elected that the principles of the GATT would not apply between Australia and Japan.[5]

By 1953, the Japanese had become concerned about Australia's discrimination in its trade relations with Japan. This discrimination had two key aspects. First, there were few countries trading with Australia that did not enjoy the benefit of either the British preferential tariff or the most-favoured-nation rates. Japan was the only major trading country to which the highest general tariff applied. Secondly, the import licensing system accorded Japan less advantageous treatment than to other non-dollar countries.[6] In 1953, the Japanese government asked the Australian government for trade talks to bring an end to the discriminatory treatment against Japan in import licensing and the tariff.

After this request was made, Harry Menzies warned Crawford that Japan, which was one of the principal textile countries in the world, had the capacity to experiment with substitute fibres other than wool or to source its wool from competitors such as Argentina.[7] Harry Menzies, a trade commissioner in Crawford's department, urged a sympathetic response to Japan's complaints about Australia's import licensing on the ground that 'we can do a great deal to safeguard our position in the immensely important market for Australian wool'.[8] Crawford agreed. Though the Department of Commerce and Agriculture was not responsible for import licensing, he persuaded his minister, John McEwen, to write to Senator George McLeay, acting minister for trade and customs, warning that:

> it may be helpful if I set down my view that a study of Japan's import trade in wool makes me believe that Japan could take reprisals against Australian trade. Moreover, if action is once taken to restrict imports from Australia, I would fear that our trade might receive some permanent injury. I therefore wish to stress that we

5   Minute from Crawford to McEwen, 5 February 1953, Papers of Sir John Crawford, NLA: MS 4514/9/33.
6   Letter from Tange to Watt, 10 April 1956, National Archives of Australia (NAA): A1838, 3103/10/1 PART 4.
7   Minute from H.C. Menzies to Crawford, 28 May 1953, NAA: A609, 317/20/7.
8   Ibid.

should examine the possibility of offering some concessions to the Japanese with a view to forestalling any Japanese action to reduce imports from Australia.[9]

In November 1954, in large part because of Crawford's urging, Prime Minister Robert Menzies's cabinet agreed to informal trade talks with the Japanese. The commencement of the talks, however, was delayed by continuing differences between the Australian trade departments and the preoccupation of both the Australian and Japanese governments with Japan's accession to the GATT. This would not take place until September 1955.

In September 1955, despite Japan's prospective admission to GATT, fundamental differences between the Department of Commerce and Agriculture and the Department of Trade and Customs were still holding up the government conveying a response to the Japanese on the start of informal trade talks. The Department of External Affairs by this time was fretting about the future of Australia's relations with Japan and sought to arrange interdepartmental discussions to take place as soon as possible to prepare for the talks. External Affairs complained that these discussions had been postponed essentially because Crawford had been unable reach agreement with his counterpart, Frank Meere, the secretary of the Department of Trade and Customs.[10] On 5 September 1955, Crawford wrote to Meere, expressing his concern that time was 'slipping away' and that, when Japan acceded to the GATT, the Japanese government would come under pressure at home to discriminate against countries continuing discrimination against it.[11]

On 29 September 1955 Crawford was finally able to meet with Meere. At this meeting he pressed his views that purely informal trade talks should begin between Australia and Japan. The Australian government, he thought, should be represented only by officers of the Department of Trade and Customs and the Department of Commerce and Agriculture. Crawford indicated that because the Australian government had already taken the decision that GATT would not apply between Australia and

9   Letter from McEwen to McLeay, 6 June 1953, NAA: CP553/1, BUNDLE 21/194/B/10/35; Minute from Crawford to McEwen, 1 June 1953, NAA: A609, 555/120/4 PART 1.
10   Minute from Shaw to Tange, 'Informal Trade Talks with Japan', 30 August 1955, NAA: A1838, 759/1/7 PART 2.
11   Department of Foreign Affairs and Trade, *Documents on Australian Foreign Policy: The Australia–Japan Agreement on Commerce 1957* (Canberra: Australian Government Publishing Service, 1997), 189.

Japan, it could scarcely ask Japan for a guarantee of non-discriminatory treatment. Rather, Crawford considered that Australia's representatives should deal with export commodities one-by-one, indicating the kind of treatment Australia sought from the Japanese. The Japanese would then be invited to outline the problems they faced in the Australian market and table their requests.[12]

Accompanied by Arthur Tange, the permanent secretary of the Department of External Affairs, and Meere, Crawford met the Japanese ambassador to Australia, Tadakatsu Suzuki, in October 1955. The three permanent secretaries agreed with Suzuki that informal trade talks should commence with officials from the Japanese embassy in Canberra. They also agreed among themselves that Alan Westerman of the Department of Commerce and Agriculture and Hudson Heyes, first assistant secretary in the Department of Trade and Customs, should be the Australian government's senior representatives in the informal talks.[13] Crawford had achieved a breakthrough of immense importance to the future of Australian trade policy and Australian engagement with Asia.[14]

The Australia–Japan Commerce Agreement

From August to October 1956, Crawford's Department of Trade (a new department created in January 1956 by merging the Department of Commerce and Agriculture and the Department of Trade and Customs) led an Australian delegation of officials in negotiations with officials from the Japanese embassy in Canberra. Crawford had conceived the idea of a unified Department of Trade, and Menzies had carried it out largely because of his unhappiness with the way that the Department of Trade and Customs was administering Australia's system of import licences.[15] The creation of this new Department of Trade was an indispensable prerequisite for the negotiation of a trade agreement with Japan, because

---

12   Minutes of meeting at Department of Trade and Customs, 29 September 1955, NAA: A1310, 810/1/39.

13   Minute from Crawford to Westerman, 21 October 1955, Papers of Sir John Crawford, NLA: MS 4514/9/33.

14   J.G. Crawford, 'Matters for Writing and or Annotation of Files', 14 June 1983, Papers of Sir John Crawford NLA: MS 4514, Box 193.

15   Note by Crawford for McEwen, 'Departmental Changes in the Commonwealth Service', 17 May 1955, NAA: A463, 1957/2193 Part 1.

it removed the bureaucratic impediment of two trade departments arguing different and sometimes contradictory positions in respect of Japan. The unification of the Department of Trade was important, too, because Menzies needed to be persuaded that a trade agreement with Japan was not an unacceptable political risk for him. Menzies, in addition to having concerns about Australian public opinion, was more willing than McEwen to listen to British arguments about protecting their own trade with Australia against Japanese incursions. After 1956 McEwen, speaking in cabinet on behalf of a unified trade bureaucracy and backed by the Department of External Affairs, was better able to respond to the political concerns of Menzies and other ministers about a modified trade relationship with Japan.

After the informal talks between officers of the Department of Trade and its counterparts finished, Japan sent out its formal delegation. It was chaired by Nobuhiko Oshiba from the Japanese Foreign Office and included representatives from the Japanese Customs, Finance and Trade and Industry ministries. On 1 November 1956 a counterpart Australian delegation, chaired by Crawford's deputy secretary Alan Westerman, started negotiations with the Japanese. The Japanese were particularly appreciative of Crawford's nomination of Westerman, the second most senior official in the Department of Trade, to lead for Australia as showing the importance that the Australian government was attaching to the negotiations.[16]

The Japanese asked Australia for most-favoured-nation tariff and licensing treatment and Australia reciprocated. However, because of state trading activities in Japan and Japan's reception of surplus American agricultural products under US president Dwight D. Eisenhower's 1954 'Food for Peace' legislation, the Australian delegation considered that the goal of most-favoured-nation tariff and licensing treatment would not be sufficient. Consequently, it aimed at Japan's accepting targets on individual commodities—23 million bushels of wheat, 350,000 tons of barley, 900,000 bales of wool and a quota of 100,000 tons of sugar. The Australian delegation also revealed that the Australian government was negotiating lower preferences on British imports into Australia, which would enable Australia to increase benefits to countries like Japan.[17]

---

16 Cablegram from Stuart to the Department of Trade, 5 November 1956, NAA: A1209, 57/5473.
17 Minute from Jones to Durie, 'Japanese Trade Negotiations', 2 November 1956, NAA: A1209, 57/5473.

By 14 June 1957, negotiations were substantially concluded. The Commerce Agreement, eventually signed by McEwen on 6 July 1957, comprised seven articles. Under the first four, each government undertook to extend most-favoured-nation treatment in tariff and import licensing to the other, but in Australia the tariff preferences for British imports were retained. Both parties, moreover, undertook to conduct state trading on non-discriminatory and commercial principles and to base their commercial relations as far as possible on GATT principles, while preserving the right of each to invoke Article XXXV. Articles VI and VII of the Commerce Agreement provided for regular consultations and for a term of at least three years for the agreement. The most contentious provision was Article V. It provided safeguards in the case of serious injury caused by the exports of either to the industries of the other, first by consultation and then by an attempt to renegotiate the agreement. In 1986 Alan Rix provided a comprehensive account of the negotiation of the trade agreement with Japan.[18] This chapter focuses on the role of Crawford in Australia's 'coming to terms' with Japan in the 1950s. His major accomplishments were first to argue the case for a more liberal trading relationship with Japan against bureaucratic and political opposition between 1953 and 1955 and then to convince Menzies and McEwen to create a new Department of Trade that would negotiate it. Crawford left the actual negotiations to his deputy, Westerman, but he worked successfully with McEwen in Canberra to shepherd the agreement through cabinet. In doing so, he used his contacts in the embassy in Tokyo to full effect.

In 1962, when looking back at the negotiation of the agreement with Japan, Crawford recalled the apprehensions felt in 1956 and 1957, mainly by manufacturers and by consumers, who feared an inrush of cheap, low-quality Japanese imports. This fear had not been realised. Australia had gained a stronger market for wool, foodstuffs and, increasingly, minerals, and Japan had obtained the end of discrimination in tariffs and import licensing.[19] In the years from 1957 to 1962 Japan and Australia both made rapid progress under the treaty, Japan proportionately more than Australia and Australia more in absolute terms. Declared Crawford:

---

18 See, generally, Alan Rix, *Coming to Terms: The Politics of Australia's Trade with Japan 1945–1957* (Sydney: Allen & Unwin, 1986).

19 See, generally, David Lee, *The Second Rush: Mining and the Transformation of Australia* (Redland Bay: Connor Court, 2016).

> Neither side expects nor can expect a neat balance for the very reasons that make us 'natural' trading partners. Japan needs industrial raw materials and foodstuffs which we can supply in good quality and competitively. It can fairly be said that our wool and industrial minerals, our scrap and, indeed, our raw sugar, are exports vital to the employment of Japanese people. We export employment to Japan's growing population.[20]

Crawford was here giving expression to what was described as economic 'complementarity'. Another Crawford protégé, Ross Garnaut, would make use of the term and the concept in describing the nature of Australia's relationship with the countries of Northeast Asia in the 1980s.[21] Crawford also thought in 1962 that Australia's continued invocation of Article XXXV was invidious and called for its removal, a decision which the Menzies government would take in 1963.[22] In a newspaper article that year, Crawford noted that Japan was taking 17.5 per cent of Australian exports and that it would 'almost certainly' replace Britain as the leading market for Australian exports.[23] It took only four more years for Crawford's prediction to be realised. By that time Crawford had made the transition from the Australian Public Service to ANU.

Beyond the Commerce Agreement: Australia and Japan, 1968–76

As director of the Research School of Pacific Studies and later vice-chancellor of ANU, Crawford strongly encouraged the academic study of Australian–Japanese relations, setting up a new school of economists at the ANU in the field of international economic studies at the centre of which would be one of his protégés, Peter Drysdale. Drysdale would work closely under Crawford on a project announced by the Liberal minister for foreign affairs Nigel Bowen in 1972—the Australia, Japan and Western Pacific Economic Relations Research Project. The project,

---

20 J.G. Crawford, 'Speech to Welcome Japanese Sugar Mission: CSR Dinner', 8 August 1962, NAA: M58, 402.
21 See, for example, Ross Garnaut, *Australia and the Northeast Asian Ascendancy: Report to the Prime Minister and Minister for Foreign Affairs and Trade* (Canberra: Australian Government Publishing Service, 1989).
22 'Amendment to Agreement on Commerce Between Australia and Japan, Joint Communiqué on Protocol, Signed 5 August 1963', in *Australian Trade Policy 1942–1966*, ed. J.G. Crawford (Canberra: Australian National University Press, 1968), 383.
23 J.G. Crawford, 'The Jolt of the Common Market', *Sunday Review*, 2 January 1963.

running for an initial three years from 1973 to 1976, was conceived by Crawford and Saburō Ōkita, president of the Japan Economic Research Centre, in Japan. Ōkita was born in Dalian, Kwantung Leased Territory, on 3 November 1914. Before World War II, he worked as an engineer with the Ministry of Posts and after the war he held government research positions that were similar to the ones held by Crawford in Australia in the 1940s. Ōkita was chief of research for the Economic Stabilization Board in 1947, head of the economic cooperation unit for the economic planning agency in 1953, director-general of the planning bureau in 1957 and, in 1963, director-general of the development bureau. In these roles Ōkita played an important part in implementing the economic plans of Japanese prime minister Hayato Ikeda (minister for international trade and industry from 1952 to 1956 and from 1959 to 1960, and prime minister from 1960 to 1964), in reforming the Japanese economy and creating what had become known as the Japanese 'economic miracle'.

Ōkita would go on to become Japan's minister for foreign affairs from 1979 to 1980 and continued after that to be one of Japan's foremost economic spokesmen. Ōkita and Crawford first met in 1967, when Ōkita attended a conference sponsored by ANU on Australia's relations with India. Several months afterwards, in January 1968, Crawford met up with Ōkita in Tokyo when he attended the first meeting of the Pacific Trade and Development (PAFTAD) Conference at the Japan Economic Research Centre in Tokyo.

Crawford and Ōkita initiated the Western Pacific Economic Relations Research Project to bring together studies by Australian and Japanese economists on the policy issues of importance in Australia–Japan and regional relationships. In the initial three-year project running from 1973 to 1976, an Australian group of researchers based in Canberra and a counterpart group in Japan examined the general nature of the Australia–Japan relationship and undertook specific studies. These studies were in areas such as the approach of Australia and Japan to world trade and adjustment policies and trade; investment, monetary and foreign exchange policies; foreign aid and technology transfer; resource goods trade and the role of long-term contracting; problems of structural adjustment in the agricultural and manufacturing sectors of both economies; and more detailed industry studies.[24] The program of research

---

24 'The Australia–Japan Research Centre', *Australian Foreign Affairs Record* 52 (December 1980): 595.

established by Crawford and Ōkita was completed jointly by Australian and Japanese economists. Drysdale and Professor Kiyoshi Kojima of Hitotsubashi University, Tokyo, undertook most of the drafting and they were joined by J.W. Neville, H.W. Arndt, E.S. Crawcour, Stuart Harris, Hisao Kanamori, Kenzo Hemmi, Chikashi Moriguchi, Makoto Ikema and Koichi Hamada.[25]

The outcome of the 'Crawford–Ōkita' report was formally entitled 'Australia, Japan and the Western Pacific Economic Relations'. It contained a detailed analysis followed by conclusions and recommendations on Australia–Japan economic relations in a long-term framework, on means of providing resource and food security for Japanese consumers and market assurances for Australian producers, and on proposals for closer economic cooperation with countries in the Western Pacific region. Crawford and Ōkita would subsequently publish the report commercially as *Raw Materials and Pacific Integration*.[26] Arising from his thinking about Japan and the Australia–Japan research project, Crawford came to the view that a new treaty with Japan was desirable. Such a treaty was being pressed insistently by Japan but was being adamantly resisted by the Australian government and particularly by the Department of Foreign Affairs. During 1973 to 1977, the senior diplomat K.C.O. 'Mick' Shann was ambassador to Japan. Shann fully shared the Foreign Affairs scepticism about a treaty with Japan. Crawford's relationship with Shann and other senior officers of the Department of Foreign Affairs, such as Keith Waller and Alan Renouf, was less close, in part because Crawford differed emphatically with them on the need for a treaty with Japan that went beyond the Commerce Agreement.

In the years after the conclusion of the 1957 Commerce Agreement the question of a 'treaty of friendship, commerce and navigation' (FCN) had arisen from time to time. The FCN had developed in the nineteenth century as a type of treaty that safeguarded the persons and activities of merchants and traders and generally covered matters such as immigration and residence, protection of property, taxation, exchange control, customs duties and import quotas, restrictive trade practices, shipping, civil liberties and the judicial process. Countries that negotiated FCNs

---

25   J.G. Crawford and Saburō Ōkita, *Australia, Japan and Western Pacific Economic Relations: A Report to the Governments of Australia and Japan presented by Sir John Crawford and Dr Saburo Okita* (Canberra: Australian Government Publishing Service, 1976), vii.

26   J.G. Crawford and Saburō Ōkita, *Raw Materials and Pacific Economic Integration* (Canberra: Australian National University Press, 1978).

achieved equality of treatment between nationals of the beneficiary state and nationals of any third state. Australian governments, however, were not in favour of FCNs because of the extreme difficulty of gaining agreement among Commonwealth departments and the various states.

By 1970, nevertheless, Japan had concluded FCNs or similar treaties with 26 countries, eight of them after the end of World War II. The economic relationship with Japan had broadened from agriculture to mineral commodities such as black coal, iron ore, bauxite, nickel and alumina. In 1962–63, a few years after Crawford's retirement from the Department of Trade, Australian exports to Japan were A$346 million, or 16 per cent of the total. Ten years later, in 1972, they were nearly A$2 billion, almost one-third of total exports.[27] Japan had by that stage taken over the position which Britain had hitherto had with Australia.

In May 1970, at the eighth meeting of the Australia Japan Business Co-operation Committee in Kyoto, the Japanese again requested that Australia and Japan examine the idea of an FCN. The matter was raised formally at official talks in Tokyo on 29 and 30 October when a senior Japanese official of the Foreign Office argued for the need to go beyond the 1957 Commerce Agreement, believing it 'highly desirable to go further to create an environment conducive to the stable development of a close and friendly economic relationship' and that an FCN would 'complete the chain of friendly agreements' already concluded between Australia and Japan. Australian government departments were suspicious. The Standing Inter-Departmental Committee on Japan was worried in March 1972 that an FCN would touch on questions such as immigration, investment policy, shipping and state interests such as property and resource development.

Crawford did not agree with prevailing orthodoxy and spoke out strongly against the consensus among federal departments. Crawford's essential views about Australia and Japan had at its core the arguments he had expressed about Japan as a young man in the 1930s when he urged a policy of 'economic appeasement'. Crawford would confide to Gough Whitlam in 1974 that:

---

27 Letter from Cairns to Whitlam, 1 October 1973, NAA: A1209, 1973/6986.

I regard Japan as one of the most vulnerable advanced powers in the world and a failure to indicate a positive willingness to help her by way of assurances could endanger what I believe to be a needed political relationship. A negative course on our part might contribute to driving Japan into other political relationships inimical to our long-term interests. At the worst Japanese could be made to feel that the pre-war policy of Lebensraum had some justification after all.[28]

Two years before writing that letter, as a witness in 1972 before the Senate Standing Committee on Foreign Affairs and Defence, Crawford was alone in urging that Australia needed a 'framework of principles' on which to base negotiation of specific agreements with Japan.[29] Crawford was scathing about the negative attitude of departments to a new treaty typified by the refrain—there was nothing in it for Australia. He told the Senate:

it is a fairly typical comment: 'There is nothing in it for us.' Now I have never heard such nonsense in my life as to say that there is nothing in a negotiation over a general treaty with Japan … I doubt if even the trade expansion that we want and an understanding on investment policy can be adequately achieved on an ad hoc basis. I do believe we do need some framework of principles against which to negotiate … This adhocery is quite dangerous if a very powerful trading partner is left to believe that we do not much care what happens.[30]

For Crawford a framework treaty with Japan was necessary and should combine a 'general understanding about [the] relationship with a recognition that in fact we are going to negotiate over a number of very specific things'.[31] An ad hoc approach was no basis either for the orderly and stable development of Australian industries or of a major trading partnership. Instead, Crawford urged that Australia needed to foster and maintain long-term interests with Japan through consultative machinery enabling the discussion of matters of mutual interest affecting bilateral relations as well as with third parties.

---

28 Letter from Crawford to Whitlam, 11 October 1974, NAA: A1209, 1974/6573.
29 Senate Standing Committee on Foreign Affairs and Defence, Japan, 26 July 1972, NAA: A1838, 759/1/9 PART 6, pp. 990–93.
30 Quoted in D.C.S. Sissons, 'Japan', in *Australia in World Affairs 1971–1975*, ed. W.J. Hudson (Sydney: George Allen & Unwin, 1980), 256.
31 Ibid.

Without such a treaty, Crawford thought that Australia would not have the means to press for bilateral discussions whenever Australia considered that its interests were involved. In the absence of such a treaty, he feared that Japan would have the latitude to negotiate deals with third parties to Australia's detriment. He cited the example of Japan, in the absence of a framework treaty with Australia, possibly making an agreement with the European Economic Community to take its surplus agricultural produce at dumped prices. Crawford continued:

> I think we have to remember that Japan is still feeling its way somewhat into a policy which suits it admirably but which is the complete antithesis of pre-war where it felt the only way it could be sure of adequate supplies of raw materials and goods was through a policy of imposing its will. Now it is finding it possible to trade in the world and succeed. But every now and then the Japanese are perplexed, non-plussed by an inability to understand the attitude of foreign governments on matters affecting trade relations. I think a large element in the Japanese anxiety, perhaps, is the very same as my anxiety—to have a framework within which it is known that things can be rationally discussed ...[32]

Crawford's approach to managing Australia's relations with Japan on an orderly basis and over the long term paralleled his approach to long-term economic planning in the Vernon Committee of Enquiry and his approach to government assistance to industry. While Crawford's views were resisted in the Commonwealth public service, elements of Australian business were becoming more receptive to accommodating the Japanese pressure for an FCN. In 1972, Sir James Vernon, chairman of the Colonial Sugar Refining Company and Mount Newman Mining and Crawford's former colleague on the Committee of Economic Enquiry, became chairman of the Australia Japan Business Co-operation Committee. In discussions with the Inter-Departmental Committee on Japan on 24 October 1972, Vernon argued that it was important that the Japanese request for an FCN not be dealt with in 'such a way that the Japanese lost face'. Vernon wondered whether contentious issues in an FCN could be put to one side and then to 'see whether there was anything left that might be included in a harmless FCN treaty'.[33] The Senate committee was also persuaded

32 Ibid.
33 Summary Record of a Meeting between Representatives of the Australia Japan Business Co-operation Committee (AJBCC) and the Inter-Departmental Committee on Japan (IDCJ) held in the Department of Foreign Affairs, Canberra, 24 October 1972, NAA: A1838, 759/1/9 PART 6.

by Crawford's arguments. One of its recommendations in January 1973 was 'that a treaty could be devised which would confer equal and mutual benefits to both parties'.[34]

Crawford and Whitlam: Towards the Treaty of NARA

Crawford's arguments in favour of a new treaty fell on even more receptive ears when the Whitlam Labor government was elected in December 1972, the first federal Labor government elected since the defeat of the Chifley government in 1949. Whitlam—in an initial duumvirate in which he and Deputy Prime Minister Lance Barnard shared all ministerial portfolios—moved quickly to recognise and establish diplomatic relations with the People's Republic of China. On 6 December 1972, Whitlam also asked the Department of Foreign Affairs, of which he was the minister in 1972 and 1973, for a paper on an FCN with Japan. He asked for the paper to be presented not to the duumvirate with Barnard but to the full Labor cabinet when it was appointed. Whitlam indicated that he had 'no personal inhibitions' about such a treaty but called for a paper setting out the pros and cons.[35]

The secretary of the Department of Foreign Affairs, Keith Waller, was sceptical that such a treaty would ever see the light of day. He noted:

> The real problem is political will. If the PM wants an FCN, then we can give him one. If he lets the matter be sorted out on basis of balance of advantage as seen by Depts (& other Ministers) on details, then we will not have one.[36]

But some other voices were now becoming more optimistic about the practicability of negotiating a new treaty. One of them was Jim Cairns, the presumptive minister for overseas trade, who declared in Tokyo on 12 December 1972 that he was in favour of a broader treaty with Japan.[37] Despite such calls for a new treaty, the bureaucracy in Canberra remained

---

34 Quoted in Sissons, 'Japan', 256.
35 Minute from R.S. Laurie to Waller, 7 December 1972, NAA: A1838, 759/1/9 PART 6.
36 Ibid.
37 *Sydney Morning Herald*, 13 December 1972; Cablegram from Australian embassy in Tokyo to Department of Foreign Affairs, NAA: A1838, 759/1/9 PART 6.

adamantly opposed to an FCN with Japan. J.W.C. Cumes, first assistant secretary of the International Organisations Division of the Department of Foreign Affairs, summed up the case against an FCN:

> The basic argument against our accepting a Treaty is that the Japanese see a Treaty as improving their position in Australia (otherwise why would they bother to seek a Treaty), either by having concessions—especially in the immigration and financial field—written into the Treaty itself or by building on the general wording and spirit of the Treaty to seek concessions later.[38]

For Cumes the issue which confronted Australia was whether to formalise an arrangement with Japan that would be taken, domestically or internationally, to constitute a 'special relationship' ahead of other significant relationships such as Australia's relationship with Indonesia.[39] Reviews prepared by the interdepartmental committee in May 1973 showed no change in the position of departments on an FCN with Japan.

Whitlam was not happy with the interdepartmental committee's advice, which he later described to Indian prime minister Indira Gandhi as 'appalling'. Whitlam passed the interdepartmental committee's advice on to Crawford, whom he knew from his remarks in the Senate to be a supporter of a new treaty with Japan, and invited his comments.[40] Crawford agreed with Whitlam's assessment, noting that Commonwealth departments had identified 'problems and difficulties but [were] far from being conclusive about the policy to be followed—whether in general political terms or in economic terms'.[41] Crawford recommended to Whitlam that, before the government could examine the feasibility of a treaty, the interdepartmental committee should 'examine more deeply a treaty designed to meet our interests and then to explore what sort of price we might have to pay in terms of Japan's interests'.[42] Crawford thought that the examination should include three parts: what Japan has sought; what the pros and cons would be of meeting the Japanese wishes in the terms so far suggested by them; and then what sort of treaty would serve Australian interests and what price might be sought for one.[43]

---

38 Minute from J.C.W. Cumes to Whitlam, 19 December 1972, NAA: A1838, 759/1/9 PART 6.
39 Ibid.
40 Minute from R.S. Merrilees to Feakes, 19 June 1973, NAA: A1838, 759/1/9 PART 8.
41 Letter from Crawford to Whitlam, 17 June 1973, NAA: A1838, 759/1/9 PART 8.
42 Ibid.
43 Ibid.

Whitlam accepted all of Crawford's advice. He instructed the Department of Foreign Affairs to compile a report on the lines that Crawford had recommended—one that did not negotiate compromises and that would be placed in the hands of one man who would seek advice from inside and outside the public service.[44] Whitlam's decision to seek advice from outside the public service was an explicit acceptance of another suggestion of Crawford's. This had been devised to overcome departmental constraints on individual public service members of interdepartmental committees 'to prepare reports in which the debate [was] pursued to a clear conclusion'.[45] Whitlam and Crawford were crucial in overcoming bureaucratic opposition to a new treaty with Japan, a treaty eventually signed by Whitlam's successor, Malcolm Fraser, in 1976. Just as Crawford and McEwen were the fathers of the 1957 Agreement on Commerce, so Crawford and Whitlam may be regarded as the fathers of the 1976 NARA Treaty.

The new report that was commissioned by Whitlam on Crawford's advice paved the way for the NARA Treaty. It was prepared not by an interdepartmental committee and nor by one man but rather by the Economic Policy Branch of the Department of Foreign Affairs, which consulted several people outside the public service on the terms of the draft treaty. The Economic Policy Branch was particularly anxious to consult Crawford, its head, Philip Flood, noting:

> Unless you think otherwise, I propose to send a copy of the F&C report to Crawford. I think we should make an effort to outline our thinking to him, rather than have him head off on his own comments to the PM.[46]

Crawford happened to be overseas at the time that the new report was being prepared.[47] Although Crawford did not see the Economic Policy Branch's report, he was consulted while abroad on its broad shape and on the terms of the economic component.[48] Also consulted was Peter Drysdale, along with Peter Robinson, editor of the *Australian Financial*

---

44   Memorandum from Whitlam to Waller, 20 June 1973, NAA: A1838, 759/1/9 PART 8.
45   Letter from Crawford to Whitlam, 17 June 1973 NAA: A1838, 759/1/9 PART 8; Briefing Note for Deputy Secretary A, n.d. 1973, NAA: A1838, 759/1/9 PART 8. Whitlam asked for a report seeking advice inside and outside the Public Service on (a) what has Japan asked for? (b) what are the pros and cons of meeting their wishes in the terms so far suggested by them? (c) what sort of treaty would serve our interests and what sort of price might be sought for this?
46   Handwritten minute from Flood to Acting Deputy Secretary, Department of Foreign Affairs, n.d. 1973, NAA: A1838, 759/1/9 PART 9.
47   Minute from A.D. Brown to Philip Flood, 28 June 1973, NAA: A1838, 759/1/9 PART 9.
48   Cablegram from Crawford (Rome) to K.C.O. Shann, July 1973, NAA: A1838, 759/1/9 PART 9.

Review, and Max Suich, editor of the *National Times*. The Economic Policy Branch, in addition to its report, prepared a preliminary draft of the treaty on 16 July 1973.[49] Copies were then circulated to Sir James Vernon and to Bob Hawke and Harold Souter, respectively president and secretary of the Australian Council of Trade Unions (ACTU). K.C.O. Shann, deputy secretary of the Department of Foreign Affairs, cabled the text of the draft treaty to Crawford in Rome.[50] Drysdale, when consulted in Canberra, held the same opinions as Crawford of the need for

> an umbrella Treaty which encompasses the operation of established specific agreements and, at the same time, envisages, under that umbrella, the negotiation of new specific agreements or the re-negotiation of established agreements as required.[51]

Hawke, though he was a great admirer of Crawford, saw little that would be worthwhile in such a broad-ranging treaty with Japan, fearing the competition of Japanese with Australian workers.[52]

After Crawford's return to Australia, Flood sent Crawford a full copy of the report that accompanied the draft treaty.[53] Crawford found it a 'far more satisfactory approach than was evident in earlier documents' and thought that that draft was an 'excellent basis for opening talks about a Treaty with the Japanese Government if this proves to be the decision of the Government'.[54] He recommended listing all treaties already negotiated in an annex and added:

> I would also like to see … a clause which requires each country to consult with the other before imposing new quantitative restrictions or embargos likely to impair the interest of the one or the other. I do this especially because of the fright Japan got when the U.S.A. arbitrarily stopped the export of soy-beans.[55]

---

49   'Future Development of Australia's Relations with Japan', 16 July 1973, NAA: A1838, 759/1/9 PART 8.
50   Cablegram from Shann to Crawford, 19 July 1973, NAA: A1838, 759/1/9 PART 8.
51   Memorandum from Drysdale to the Secretary, Department of Foreign Affairs, n.d. 1973, NAA: A1838, 759/1/9 PART 9.
52   Minute from Flood to Waller, 27 September 1973, NAA: A1838, 759/1/9 PART 9.
53   Letter from Flood to Crawford, 3 August 1973, NAA: A1838, 759/1/9 PART 9.
54   Letter from Crawford to Flood, 17 August 1973, NAA: A1838, 759/1/9 PART 9.
55   Ibid.

Whitlam was pleased with the draft so much so that, without consultation with other ministers or departmental heads, he announced to the press on 11 September 1973:

> I am myself very much attracted to … a treaty … I do believe … that it would be very appropriate for Japan and Australia, in a formal context, to acknowledge the very great interdependence they have on each other … Australia should be assured that as Japan's prosperity continues … our prosperity rises with hers.[56]

The statement was well received in Japan, which Whitlam visited in October. There, Japanese prime minister Tanaka Kakuei approved a recommendation from Whitlam that the treaty might be called the 'Treaty of Nara' after the city of Nara, the ancient capital and cultural centre of Japan and standing for Nippon Australia Relations Agreement.[57] Whitlam had earlier joked to the Japanese ambassador, Yoshida Kenzo, that 'he had not discussed this with the Department, whom he thought would not favour it'.[58] The two prime ministers, Whitlam and Tanaka, agreed on 31 October 1973 to 'begin discussions on a broad bilateral treaty which would help to formalise, stabilise and broaden relations between Australia and Japan in the economic and related fields'.[59]

At the beginning of January 1974, Alan Renouf, Waller's replacement as secretary of the Department of Foreign Affairs, delegated the task of negotiating the treaty with the Japanese to deputy secretary Lewis Border, with the instruction: 'This is a political question and we must have a Treaty.' Border, in turn, set up a small departmental working group headed by Michael Cook, head of the department's North and West Asia Division. Department of Foreign Affairs official W.P.J. Handmer suggested to Border designing a role for Crawford in the operations of the group, given Crawford's involvement in developing the concept of the treaty.[60] This, Handmer thought, would recognise his past role, give the department access to his experience, show that the department was taking the negotiations seriously, and 'give us important assistance should the negotiations run into serious difficulties with the Japanese

56   Cablegram from Australian embassy in Tokyo to Department of Foreign Affairs, 11 September 1973, NAA: A1838, 759/1/9 PART 9.
57   Letter from Whitlam to Tanaka, 'Nara', 28 October 1973, NAA: A1838, 759/1/9 PART 10.
58   File note by T.D. Wilson, 16 October 1973, NAA: A1838, 3103/10/20/1 PART 1.
59   'Whitlam/Tanaka Joint Communique', Tokyo, 31 October 1973, NAA: A1209, 1975/42.
60   Minute from Handmer to Border, 9 January 1974, NAA: A1838, 3103/10/20/1 PART 1.

or in Canberra'. Handmer recommended that Crawford be a consultant rather than an active member of the working group because 'apart from my doubts whether Sir John would have the time needed for active membership, he is getting pretty deaf'.[61]

The Japanese presented a revised draft treaty in May 1974 and, following further discussions between officials in Tokyo in July, on 6 September 1974 they presented a revised text. There were significant differences between the Australian and Japanese positions, differences which the Australian negotiators tried to address. From Japan, Shann, now the ambassador, cabled:

> I have read the latest draft from our side with some dismay. The document is becoming so anodyne and so hedged around with qualifications as almost to invite ridicule as something with no real substance.[62]

Shann recommended the involvement of ministers in the negotiations. Once again, Crawford's advice was sought, and he was given copies of the drafts of the Japanese and Australian delegations in September 1974. Crawford assured Whitlam:

> The drafts were closer together than I had expected and, in my judgment, a firm ministerial decision in support of the Australian draft would produce worthwhile results. As the drafts stand now, they do have value.[63]

In the event, after the dismissal and defeat of the Whitlam government in 1975 and intensive negotiations between Australia and Japan in 1975 and 1976, the NARA Treaty was signed by the Fraser government in June 1976. While less important than the landmark Commerce Agreement of 1957, it was nonetheless a valuable instrument for implementing long-term policy and served as a positive influence and constraint on both countries in the 1970s and 1980s.

---

61 Ibid.
62 Cablegram from Shann to Acting Secretary, Department of Foreign Affairs, 12 July 1974, NAA: A1838, 3103/10/20/1 PART 3.
63 Letter from Crawford to Whitlam, 11 October 1974, NAA: A1209, 1974/7435.

The Australia–Japan Foundation

In the meantime, one of the recommendations coming out of the Crawford–Ōkita research project on Australia, Japan and the Western Pacific was an idea of Crawford's for the government to establish an institution to foster a broad range of exchanges between Australia and Japan. The result of lobbying by senior public servant and Whitlam adviser H.C. Coombs at the beginning of 1974 for a more formal advisory role for Crawford to the Whitlam government had resulted in an interested response from Whitlam 'but more in the direction of special assignments than of a continuing consultancy at this stage'.[64] At the end of 1974, Whitlam gave Crawford another ad hoc assignment. He took up Crawford's idea for a new Australia–Japan institution with alacrity and foreshadowed it being discussed at heads of government level during the visit to Australia of Japanese prime minister Tanaka Kakuei in November 1974, at which Whitlam and Tanaka signed an Australia–Japan Cultural Agreement. After Tanaka's visit, Whitlam asked Crawford to chair a committee to:

> prepare a basic outline report on the arrangements needed to advance a wider spectrum of relations between the people of Australia and Japan through the establishment of a foundation or similar institution.[65]

The committee consisted of a colleague on the Vernon Enquiry, Kenneth Myer, E.S. Crawcour, professor and head of the Department of Japanese Studies at ANU, and two officials, D.J. Munro of the Department of the Prime Minister and Cabinet and John Rowland of the Department of Foreign Affairs. The Crawford Committee completed its report in March 1975 recommending the establishment of an independent non-governmental statutory body to be called the Australia–Japan Foundation with an invited national council of not more than 15 members.[66] It thought that the national council should be drawn from the key elements of Australian society to make it properly representative of Australian society as a whole and to 'give it as much stature as possible in Japanese and

---

64   Letter from Bunting to Coombs, 22 February 1974, NAA: A6385, 270.
65   Submission from Whitlam to cabinet, 'The Australia Japan Foundation', 4 July 1975, NAA: A5915, 1918.
66   'Australia–Japan Foundation', *Australian Foreign Affairs Record* 46 (August 1975): 460–61.

Australian eyes'.[67] The Australia–Japan Foundation was another initiative started by Whitlam but implemented by Fraser. The latter announced on 30 January 1976 that he would introduce legislation to establish the foundation that would:

> deepen and broaden contacts between Australia and Japan in all fields, including business, academic, cultural, scientific and the trade unions and thereby foster an understanding of each other's problems and cultures.[68]

The Australia-Japan Foundation Act 1976 (Cth) was proclaimed on 27 April 1976 and came into effect on 10 May with an initial budget of A$250,000 and a further A$100,000 held over from 1975. In accordance with the Crawford Committee's recommendations, the first council reflected a diverse range of interests and backgrounds.

Chaired by one of Australia's leading mining executives, Russel Madigan, chairman of Hamersley Holdings, it also included ANU academics Crawcour and Crawford; public servants John Menadue (Whitlam's permanent secretary of the Department of the Prime Minister and Cabinet) and John Rowland; businessmen Sir Kenneth Humphreys and S. Baillieu Myer; Peter Nolan from the ACTU; Milton Moon, an artist; and Rosemary Trott, an honours student studying Japanese at ANU. Also on the committee was Owen Harries, an academic from the University of New South Wales seconded to the Department of Foreign Affairs to work for the young Liberal foreign minister, Andrew Peacock.[69] The establishment of the Australia–Japan Foundation in 1976 coincided with the signing by Crawford and Ōkita of their massive report of the Australian and Japanese governments on Australia, Japan and Western Pacific Economic Relations, work which would help lay the basis for the Asia-Pacific Economic Cooperation group (APEC) in the 1980s.

67 Main conclusions of Crawford Committee report, submission from Whitlam to cabinet, 'The Australia Japan Foundation', 4 July 1975, NAA: A5915, 1918.
68 'Australia–Japan Foundation', *Australian Foreign Affairs Record* 47 (January 1976): 47.
69 'Australia–Japan Foundation', *Australian Foreign Affairs Record* 47 (November 1976): 610–11.

Conclusion

Crawford's key role in the development of the Australia–Japan relationship after World War II underlines the way in which that relationship differed from other key bilateral relationships. Although the Department of External Affairs was responsible for the post in Tokyo from 1940, the department that drove the most important postwar aspects of policy with Japan, namely economic policy and trade, was the Department of Commerce and Agriculture and its successor, the Department of Trade. It was the dynamic head of this department, Crawford, and its powerful minister, John McEwen, who initiated and sponsored the 1957 Commerce Agreement with Japan. In the concurrent years of the Japanese Economic Miracle, it was the Department of Trade (supported by the Department of National Development) that was bureaucratically responsible for the flourishing resources trade from the 1960s onward. Moreover, it was Crawford, more so than any bureaucrat, who persuaded Whitlam of the necessity for the NARA Treaty of 1976 and who championed the establishment of Australia's first and perhaps most important cultural council supporting people-to-people links, the Australia–Japan Foundation. In doing so, Sir John Crawford was one of the key architects of the postwar Australia–Japan relationship. This chapter has demonstrated the extraordinary role that one individual made to the development of Australia's postwar relations with Japan. His role was never as a member of Australia's diplomatic mission in Tokyo but as a senior bureaucrat and academic working in concert with it.

6

Creation, Destruction and Re-creation: The Australian Embassy in Tokyo

Alison Broinowski and Rachel Miller

Edo in 1590 was a small castle town on the Sumida River when Tokugawa Ieyasu, the first *shōgun* of the period, surprisingly chose it as the site for his capital. It remained so for 265 years while the Tokugawas were the de facto rulers, with the imperial line continuing in Kyoto.[1] After the restoration of Emperor Meiji in 1868, the last two *shōguns* retired to Kyoto, and Edo was renamed Tokyo (Eastern capital). The castle became the Imperial Palace, wealthy merchants bought land and the new nobility were granted properties and built Western-style mansions.

A modern city rose, with buildings for government in Kyobashi, for business in Marunouchi, and for entertainment in Asakusa. 'Tokio [*sic*] looks like a series of villages', said an American observer in 1879, 'with bits of green and open spaces and inclosed [*sic*] grounds breaking up the continuity of the town'.[2] It quickly became a wheeled city. Many canals and rivers were confined or paved over for the roads and railways that shrivelled the distance between the old localities. Successive Imperial

---

1   For personal names, the Japanese order is used: family name then given name; Hiroshige Utagawa, *One Hundred Famous Views of Edo* (Nagoya: Tokai Bank Foundation, 1987).
2   Edward Seidensticker, *Low City, High City: Tokyo from Edo to the Earthquake: How the Shogun's Ancient Capital Became a Great Modern City, 1867–1923* (Cambridge, MA: Harvard University Press, 1991), 34.

Hotels rose and fell, often with a new one under construction to replace its predecessor, just as the Imperial Shrine at Ise is rebuilt every 20 years. In 1867 foreign living quarters, including St Luke's Anglican church and hospital, were established in Tsukiji, which kept *gaijin* (foreigners) and most of the Japanese population at a mutually safe distance. Eleven legations were opened in Ichibancho, Akasaka and Azabu—the 'ward of singing insects', near Mita.[3]

European architecture reached Mita in 1877, when Keio University was founded by a pioneer proponent of Westernisation, Fukuzawa Yukichi. The Mitsui Club followed, designed by the British architect Josiah Conder in 1913. Its neighbour, the next Western mansion in Mita-Tsunamachi, would eventually become the Australian embassy. This chapter draws upon historical records and personal memoirs to provide an account of the origins of the embassy's physical presence, and the creation, destruction and re-creation of its buildings. The property in Mita was occupied by Australian diplomats just before the outbreak of the Pacific War, and again from 1946 to the present. We trace its history as far as 1990, when a new building by the architectural firm Denton Corker Marshall (DCM) was erected on the site of the historic mansion and gardens.

Mita: Farming, Fishing and Feudal Seat

In 1884, 50,000 *tsubo* (40 acres) of rice-land in the fishing village of Mita were transferred to the last *daimyō* (feudal lord) of Awa, Hachisuka Mochiaki, making the site the fifth of the Hachisuka family's estates in and around the city. As one of the five richest noble families in Japan, they also had two land holdings in Tokushima on the island of Shikoku, and another on the northern island of Hokkaido.[4] The Mita property remained in the names of Hachisuka Mochiaki's son Masaaki and grandson Masauji until 1951.

In the new Meiji order of nobility, Hachisuka Mochiaki (1846–1918), the sixteenth *daimyō,* was made a marquis (*kōshaku*). Educated at Oxford, he served as minister in the Japanese embassy in Paris, and returned to

---

3   Ibid., 36, 247.
4   E.M. Weatherstone, 'The Australian Embassy Tokyo: A Brief History of the Property and Families from Whom It Was Purchased by the Commonwealth Government', typescript, Tokyo, 1958–60, in possession of authors.

become minister of education, governor of Tokyo and president of the House of Peers. He married Tokugawa Yoriko, who asserted her *noblesse* by demanding that he dismiss his 11 concubines (the Tokugawa Shogunate had permitted *daimyō* to have 10) and should instead have only one proxy wife. The young Okyo, Yoriko's choice, went with them everywhere, including to Paris, as Yoriko's maid.[5]

The next marquis, Masaaki (1871–1932) studied at Cambridge and later became vice-president of the House of Peers. A stern supporter of Japanese tradition, he married Tokugawa Hitsuko, a daughter of the last *shōgun*: an invalid, but very beautiful, she died young.[6] Their son Masauji (1903–53) spent eight years at Cambridge and succeeded his father in the House of Peers, but declared the Hachisuka line would end with him, as their peerage indeed did in 1945. A capable pilot and ornithologist, if eccentric and a spendthrift, Masauji travelled to Asian countries and the United States to research exotic birds, including the dodo, which particularly fascinated him.[7] To his father's chagrin he refused an arranged marriage into the Tokugawa family, and married Nagamine Chiye, a *nisei* ('foreign-born Japanese') divorcée, in California in 1939. They had one daughter.

The Mansion and the Garden

The large single-storey villa which Hachisuka Mochiaki occupied in Mita-Tsunamachi from 1886, and the annex he had built for his son's return, were destroyed by fire between 1923 and 1926.[8] Most of the Hachisukas' Mita estate was sold, and on the remaining four acres Masaaki, in 1927–28, built an English Regency Gothic-revival manor house with Japanese and Chinese elements. Records differ as to the architect and builder, Hachisuka Chiye recalling that they were Seichiro Chujo and Kobayashi Shirosaku, respectively, while photographer Akahisa Masuda and Geraldine Currie, whose husband Sir Neil Currie was ambassador in Tokyo in 1982–86, credit Moriyama Morisuke with the design of the ivy-covered mansion. Lady Currie writes:

---

5   Weatherstone, 'The Australian Embassy Tokyo'.
6   Geraldine Currie, 'A History of the Australian Embassy Gardens and Buildings, Tokyo, to 1986', typescript, c. 1999–2009, in possession of authors.
7   Hachisuka Chiye, personal communication to Geraldine Currie, n.d., in possession of authors.
8   Paul Molloy, 'A Short History of the Australian Embassy Property in Tokyo', typescript, n.d., in possession of authors; Weatherstone, 'The Australian Embassy Tokyo'.

> The outer walls looked as if made of stone but were actually made of concrete and brick, with random steel rods threaded through to make the building as earthquake-proof as possible and, throughout all the subsequent years until it was demolished, there was never any earthquake damage to the structure or cracks in the walls despite many tremors of varying degrees of severity. Unfortunately, drawings of Moriyama's designs were destroyed in air raids during the war, just after his death in 1941.[9]

Approached through an imposing porte-cochère, the entrance included a pair of cast-iron gates with foliage design surrounding a small Peter Pan figure. The interior walls were panelled with *keyaki* (*Zelkova serrata*), and the plaster ceilings were crisscrossed with ribs carved from the same fine-grained wood, as were the bannisters of the staircase. Set in the stair wall was a stained-glass triptych depicting Awaji, one of the two Hachisuka properties in Shikoku. Small, square, stained-glass windows high in the dining room wall illustrated the Chinese zodiac (*junishi*), one creature representing the birth year of each member of the family. These, and the windows in the southern sun porch, were the work of Japan's first stained glass artisan, Ogawa Sanchi, who had learned his craft in the United States.[10]

Combining British and Japanese traditions, function also determined the design of the house. Upstairs were two Japanese *tatami* rooms, with *shōji* and *fusuma* (sliding doors) decorated with peonies, peach trees and peacocks by Ikegami Shuhō and Araki Kanpō. Together with three Western-style bedrooms, they were intended to provide for marital flexibility on the part of the *daimyō*.[11] Two stone *kura* (warehouses) in the grounds provided storage for the family's documents and treasures. In the stone-floored basement were *tatami* rooms for the servants, with other servants' quarters upstairs in the north wing, and still more in detached annexes. The large kitchen had a water tank sunk into the floor to keep fish alive for the household's *sashimi*.[12] Also under the house was 'a large sunken space full of very hot water, where the domestic staff and their families had their evening bath', the first resident ambassador's wife,

---

9   Currie, 'A History of the Australian Embassy Gardens'.
10   Masuda Akihisa, 'Lost Modern Architecture—the Old Ambassador's Residence (Marquis Masaaki Hachisuka Residence)', n.d., printed pamphlet, held at the Australian embassy, Tokyo.
11   Ibid.
12   Currie, 'A History of the Australian Embassy Gardens'.

Louise Walker, recalled.[13] Underground and leading into the house were 'secret passageways for the movement in and out of mistresses and an emergency escape route … to a nearby canal', wrote a later diplomat, Howard Debenham.[14]

The outdoor surroundings of Hachisuka Masaaki's Mita residence were designed in 1931 by Aoki Seitarō, who had created gardens for the Imperial Household.[15] He combined four of Japan's traditional garden styles with English landscape taste. Screened from the entrance drive by an iron fence and gate, a large level lawn below the terrace was surrounded with cherry, peach and plum trees and hedged with banks of azalea, box, elm, holly, laurel, privet and quince, which Louise Walker described as a multicoloured mosaic. A 'forest' of pines, maples and, later, Australian eucalypts defined the boundaries. The design followed the *shakkei* (borrowed) landscape style of the Shugakuin Rikyu (Detached Palace) in Kyoto, where a distant scene is viewed as if a part of the immediate garden. To allow this view, mature trees were successively thinned, and their stumps remained in the surrounding forest.[16] Overlooking the lawn was a *tsukimi-na-oka* (moon-viewing hill), exemplifying the 'hill-style' of Japanese garden design.[17] A gnarled pine tree (*Pinus pentafolia*) said to be over 400 years old was wrapped in straw for the winter. A nearby group of cycads could be 300 years old, garden experts Harvey and Bayliss thought:[18]

> On the slope below the lawn were bridges, large stone lanterns, a stone waterfall and watercourse, reflecting the *karesansui* (dry rock and pebble) style, which originated with Muso in the thirteenth century Muromachi period. The 'river' of *Ogawa-ishi*— stones which glow deep blue with white markings when wet—led to a well, which may in ancient times have supplied the farming and fishing families of Mita with fresh water. A commemorative stone dated 1817 described the well as the first natal bathing place of Watanabe-no-Tsuna (953–1024), a warrior of the Imperial Guard in Kyoto and retainer of Yoritomo Minamoto,

13   Louise Walker, *But I Digress*, ed. Ron Walker (Canberra: R.A. Walker, 2009), 119.
14   Howard Debenham, *Waiting 'Round the Bend: A Life in Australia's Foreign Service* (Griffith, ACT: Barrallier Books, 2017), 203.
15   Weatherstone, 'The Australian Embassy Tokyo'.
16   Harvey and Bayliss, 'Australian Embassy Garden Report', typescript, n.d., in possession of authors.
17   Molloy, 'A Short History of the Australian Embassy'.
18   Harvey and Bayliss, 'Australian Embassy Garden Report'.

who is commemorated in the name Mita-Tsunamachi. Close by was a *kujo no to* (nine-tiered pagoda) from the Kamakura period (about 1320 CE), brought from Kansai.[19]

Japan's 'teahouse' (*chashitsu*) garden style was represented by a thatched tea ceremony building, which would typically have been three metres square and approached by a stepping stone path.[20] Built to harmonise with its natural surroundings, the hut was 'simple, small and humble', a deliberate contrast with the wealth and power of the military and warrior class to which the Hachisuka clan belonged.[21] It was close to a field once used for archery and later as a vegetable garden.[22]

The 'stroll' (*kwaiyu*) style favoured in the Edo period was represented by the upper garden's semicircular path. Following it traditionally anticlockwise from the terrace past the *tsukimi* hill, a strolling visitor could see a dozen or more carefully placed stone lanterns. Several were from remote parts of Japan, some over 500 years old, and others from the Meiji period. In the lower garden was a tortoise-shaped stone basin for washing before the tea ceremony, and in the azalea hedge below the terrace another large stone water-basin was placed on a mill stone for its base. Writing to Ambassador John Menadue, the American consultants Harvey and Bayliss confirmed 'what an excellent garden you've got'.[23]

Australians in Mita

Hachisuka Masauji and his wife preferred their American-designed Spanish-style house in Atami to the residence in Mita, and in the 1930s the Tokyo property was leased to the Polish legation, as a map of that period shows, and possibly also to the neutral government of Sweden.[24] After Poland fell to German invasion, the Australian government rented the house in 1939. Lieutenant-Commander Eric Longfield Lloyd had been in Tokyo since 1935, first as Australia's trade commissioner and then 'government commissioner'. He presciently left for Melbourne in 1940 and resumed work in the Investigation Branch of the Attorney-General's

---

19 Ibid.
20 Liza Dalby, *All-Japan: The Catalogue of Everything Japanese* (New York: Quill, 1984), 96.
21 Harvey and Bayliss, 'Australian Embassy Garden Report'.
22 Currie, 'A History of the Australian Embassy Gardens'.
23 Harvey and Bayliss, 'Australian Embassy Garden Report'.
24 Weatherstone, letter to John Menadue, n.d., copy in possession of authors.

Department.[25] Sir John Latham arrived in Tokyo as minister in 1940, but in less than a year he too returned to Australia, in ill health. Into the vacuum, Canberra's fledgling foreign service sent Keith Officer as chargé d'affaires to establish Australia's first diplomatic mission in Japan in November 1940.

With the outbreak of the Pacific War in December 1941, the three remaining diplomats (Keith Officer, Patrick Shaw and Ted Eckersley), with Helen Shaw and the Shaws' baby daughter and four other Australians, were interned in the residence under armed guard.[26] This they endured until September 1942, reportedly rationing their supply of gin and cigarettes. Eventually a bilateral exchange was arranged in Mozambique and with more than 40 other Australians, they returned to Australia by sea in November.[27] During the war the Mita premises were under the control of the Japanese Navy, and after that, the property was requisitioned by the occupation—the supreme commander for the Allied powers (SCAP)—and the United States Marines moved in.

In 1946 Professor William Macmahon Ball was appointed by Prime Minister Chifley and External Affairs Minister Evatt to represent the British Commonwealth on the Allied Council for Japan, his counterparts being American, Russian and Nationalist Chinese diplomats. When he arrived in war-ravaged Tokyo to take over from B.C. Ballard in 1946, housing was scarce. Ball lived temporarily in Azabu, while his secretary had to share a room at the YWCA with five or six other women.[28] Ball complained that the 'Oda house' rented for him was poorly furnished, and requested instead 'one of the best houses irrespective of who was now occupying it'.[29] Australian lieutenant-general H.C.H. Robertson, as commander of the British Commonwealth Occupation Force (BCOF), succeeded in retrieving the Mita premises from SCAP, first for the Australian military contingent which guarded the Imperial Palace, and then for Ball and the Australian diplomats. From 1947 and until the occupation ended in

25   David Sadleir, 'Lloyd, Eric Edwin Longfield (1890–1957)', *Australian Dictionary of Biography*, vol. 15, 2000, adb.anu.edu.au/biography/lloyd-eric-edwin-longfield-10840/text19235, accessed 5 June 2018.

26   Currie, 'A History of the Australian Embassy Gardens'.

27   Rachel Miller, *Wife and Baggage to Follow* (Canberra: Halstead Press, 2013), 36; Rowena Ward, 'The Asia-Pacific War and the Failed Second Anglo-Japanese Civilian Exchange, 1942–45', *The Asia-Pacific Journal: Japan Focus* 13, no. 4 (23 March 2015): apjjf.org/2015/13/11/Rowena-Ward/4301.html.

28   Alan Rix, ed., *Intermittent Diplomat: The Japan and Batavia Diaries of W. Macmahon Ball* (Carlton: Melbourne University Press, 1988), 20.

29   Rix, *Intermittent Diplomat*, 21.

1952, it was known as 'Commonwealth House'. Ball, his wife Katrine and daughter Jenny shared it with his economic adviser Eric Ward; David McNicoll from External Affairs; journalist Harry Plumridge and his wife; and Lloyd, who had returned to Tokyo. Some of their successors lent their names to their quarters: the 'Border flat' (diplomat Lew Border) and the 'Hocking cottage' (journalist Norman Hocking). The flat roof provided the residents with a space for games. The BCOF imported supplies which occupation personnel bought from a storage facility in Ebisu. Meanwhile at Allied Council meetings the victors regularly discussed postwar Japan's dire food shortage.

Australia led the BCOF from 1945 until the peace treaty was signed in 1952. Under three successive Australian lieutenants-general, including Robertson, BCOF supervised demilitarisation and the disposal of Japan's war industries. Australia played a prominent part in the Tokyo war crimes trials, at which the president of the International Military Tribunal for the Far East was Sir William Webb. Both Robertson and Webb were regular visitors at Commonwealth House.[30]

Like Ball, Webb had to contend with General MacArthur's desire to end the occupation early and to make many concessions to Japan. These were unpopular in Australia where Japan was regarded more as enemy than ally. But Minister Evatt, visiting in 1947, supported MacArthur and they had a cordial exchange. Ball's advice was ignored and, feeling marginalised by Evatt, he resigned, returned to Australia and in 1949 published a book about the Japan question.[31] Patrick Shaw, one of the prewar internees, returned in 1947 to take over at the Allied Council.

The Shaws and their daughters had the residence to themselves, apart from the occupant of the 'Border flat' and the servants.[32] Colonel W.R. Hodgson followed in 1949 and began negotiations in 1950–51 to buy the Mita property of 18,000 square metres for A£93,350 from Hachisuka Masauji. The contract with the government of the Commonwealth of Australia was eventually approved by Japan's Foreign Investment Commission, validated by SCAP and concluded in 1952 through Japan's Ministry of Finance.[33] 'Even back then, it was a steal',

30   Rix, *Intermittent Diplomat*, 131–33, 185.
31   Ibid., 278; see W. Macmahon Ball, *Japan: Enemy or Ally?* (Melbourne: Franklin Classics, 2018).
32   Miller, *Wife and Baggage to Follow*, 30–41.
33   Weatherstone, 'The Australian Embassy Tokyo'.

a later diplomat recalled.[34] After the San Francisco peace treaty was signed, three parcels of adjoining land were bought in 1952 and 1953: the 'Asano block', the 'Negoro block', and the 'Ministry of Finance block'. Payments were made from the A£330,000 which was Australia's share of funds 'held in Japan as a result of [unspecified] equipment disposed of by the BCOF'.[35] The money had to be spent in Japan: it was, in effect, a reparations payment. Australia also bought the 'Itō house' opposite the residence for the commercial counsellor.[36]

A succession of distinguished Australians took up residence in Mita, the first ambassador being Dr E. Ronald Walker in 1952. As circumstances changed, various outbuildings were removed or relocated, and the large common refrigerator was replaced. The two *kura* were made into staff flats. The contents of the septic tank were collected and paid for by companies needing fertiliser.[37] In Sir Alan Watt's time (1956–59), Lady Watt added a rose garden in the north-west corner.[38] A new chancery and staff residences were built in the tenure of Sir Laurence McIntyre (1960–65) and a tennis court was laid at a cost of A£100 over the original archery field. Sir Allen and Lady Brown (1965–68) installed air conditioning and a west-facing, Fuji-viewing window, shaped like the sacred mountain, which provided a fine vista on a clear day.[39] Sir Gordon and Lady Freeth (1970–73) preferred lighter internal surroundings, and had the beautiful wood panelling in the downstairs rooms painted white. The Steinway grand, which had appeared during the occupation, was sold and replaced by a smaller Kawai piano.

The sporadic debate about whether to keep the residence was temporarily resolved when Sir Keith Shann was ambassador (1974–79), and more improvements to plumbing, wiring, water supply, air conditioning, and guest and staff accommodation were made. Grey carpet from the Australian Pavilion at the Okinawa Expo '75, 'dull but serviceable' according to Lady Currie, was laid in all the public rooms. A large wine cellar took the place of what had been an air raid shelter, and the 'Bunker Bar' nearby continued to provide for Friday night relaxation. The upstairs bedrooms were modified in readiness for the next incumbent, John

---

34 Debenham, *Waiting 'Round the Bend*, 273.
35 Weatherstone, 'The Australian Embassy Tokyo'.
36 Currie, 'A History of the Australian Embassy Gardens'.
37 Walker, *But I Digress*, 111–67.
38 Mildred Watt, *Land of Sun and Storm* (Melbourne: F. W. Cheshire, 1966), 10.
39 Currie, 'A History of the Australian Embassy Gardens'.

Menadue, his wife Cynthia and their five children (1977–81).[40] The Menadues were Japan-enthusiasts like most of their predecessors. The kitchen in the basement, Cynthia Menadue recalled, was connected to the living quarters on the first floor by a dumb waiter, in which the children took rides.[41] The residence was quieter when Sir James Plimsoll, a bachelor, took over in 1981. He left to become governor of Tasmania the following year.

Sir Neil and Lady Currie returned to Tokyo in 1982, having married and lived there during his first posting as third secretary in 1951–53. Like many other Australians who were married in the residence over the years, they remembered it fondly. Determined to preserve the building, the Curries had the white paint stripped and the panelling refinished. They replaced the grey carpet with the previous Persian (Pakistani) rugs and restored the parquet floor. The kitchen was also upgraded. What remained of the teahouse was rebuilt as a tennis pavilion in 1985, complete with a drinks machine. To provide funds for the renovations, Sir Neil sold the embassy's holiday cottage at Karuizawa, which had been bought during the occupation and was deteriorating. John Menadue had moved Australia Day to April so guests on the lawn could admire the cherry blossom, and Geraldine Currie introduced Japanese folk-dancing there in the summer. She spoke often with the priests at the nearby shrine and assured them that Australia would look after its heritage site. She researched the history of the residence and garden in great detail.[42]

Building a New Embassy

At the time when Sir James Plimsoll departed for Tasmania, the Australian government was concerned about the cost of leasing accommodation for staff in overseas posts. The government occupied 1,567 offices and houses overseas, 67 per cent of which were leased (in 1985 and 1986) at a cost of A$40 million.[43] The property in Tokyo on Mita Avenue was an attractive and obvious source of potential revenue. On the large original estate were

---

40 Ibid.
41 Cynthia Menadue, *Shadows on the Shoji: A Personal View of Japan* (Sydney: John Ferguson, 1985), 22.
42 Currie, 'A History of the Australian Embassy Gardens'.
43 Cabinet Submission 3268—Strategy for Australian government property in Tokyo, 18 September 1985, National Archives of Australia (NAA): A14039, 3268.

the chancery and the residence, three houses for senior officers, a small block of apartments for junior personnel, and on the other side of the road, a block of spacious apartments built in the 1970s for other staff.

Australian government architects consulted Japanese authorities about the value of the residence, including the son and grandson of the original architect, Moriyama Matsunosuke (K. and O. Moriyama), the Social and Education Section of Minato-ku, and the Japan National Trust. Neil Currie recalled:

> There were as many opinions as there were representatives but, overall, the general opinion was that, as the property belonged to Australia, it was the Australian Government's business and few Japanese would be fussed one way or the other should the building be demolished. Some considered the building and its contents of value, others felt its historical value was 'medium to low,' but all agreed that it had been meticulously cared for. It was listed as a 'significant building built between 1870 and 1940' in a book published in Japanese in 1980 by the Japan Institute of Architects, but was not listed under the Cultural Property Protection Department of the Agency for Cultural Affairs, nor by the local Ward office. Tsuna's Well was included on a list of places of historical interest in Minato-ku. The Japan National Trust had the last word and I quote from their report: 'not only in the outside structure, but also in the interior design, they are very worthy to conserve …'[44]

The perennial question of savings arose in 1982, again in 1983, and in 1985, when Tom Uren, minister for the Department of Local Government and Administrative Services (DOLGAS), set out to 'seek agreement to advertising in Australia and Japan for expressions of interest' to construct accommodation on the existing site and thereby reduce accommodation costs in Japan.[45] This, the brief stated, would produce security, reliable and adequate facilities as well as recreational facilities in a 'difficult cultural environment'. One suggestion was that the trade office needed a separate 'shop-front' in the commercial district, as much of the work of the embassy—as for most other embassies in Tokyo—was focused on

---

44   Currie, quoted by Trevor Wilson, personal communication with Alison Broinowski, 2018. Because the property was owned by a foreign country, by 1980 Japanese agencies did not list it for protection.

45   Cabinet Memorandum 4692—Savings option—1987–1988 Budget—sales and redevelopment of Tokyo Embassy site (Mita Avenue), 18 September 1985, NAA: A14039, 3268.

trade with Japan. Australia's exports were mainly coal and beef, making the United States with its strong postwar relationship with Japan a major competitor. Another suggestion was that existing staff accommodation on the site should be demolished and replaced by 33 staff apartments, but that the Japanese garden and the formal gardens should be preserved— 'integrated with the present Chancery and the Official Residence' and 'with no detriment to the site'. Asked for its views, the Trade Department reported that the Australian Department of Housing and Construction 'considered it unlikely that Australian construction firms would work in Japan or in a co-operative arrangement with a Japanese firm'.[46]

As late as March 1987, DOLGAS stated that 'the main Embassy site, the HOM [head of mission] residence and the traditional garden should, for historic and representational reasons, be retained'.

However, Japan's economy was booming, the exchange rate was climbing rapidly, and a large profit could confidently be expected from the sale of land in one of the best parts of Tokyo. A square metre could command A$110,000 and Australia had 600 square metres and a budget deficit. As Geoff Miller (ambassador, 1986–89) recalled:

> Australia was in recession, and Japan was in a land and housing bubble. Someone in Canberra put the two together and with pressures on the national Budget very much in mind the decision was taken to sell part of the Embassy land, rebuild on the retained portion and use the rest of the proceeds to save the Budget. Two officials from Canberra, Harold Heinrich from the Treasury and a senior administrative officer, came to Tokyo to make the arrangement for the partial sale. I argued strongly against aspects of the proposal, and in a series of unavailing telegrams to Canberra tried to limit the amount of land to be sold, to keep a reasonable amount of the historic garden in Embassy hands. But the land was just too valuable, and I failed.[47]

Discussions and consultations continued until a task force was set up to look into all aspects of the development. It included DOLGAS and Finance, with a representative of the Melbourne-based architectural firm DCM, which was hired as a 'consultant'.

---

46   Cabinet Memorandum 4692—Tokyo—consolidation of the Australian government's property holdings and disposal of land surplus to requirements, 17 February 1986, NAA: A14039, 3268.
47   W.G.T. Miller, personal communication with Alison Broinowski, 2017.

Unsurprisingly, the task force found that embassy design was complex and involved 'specialist user and security requirements'. Equally unsurprising was the observation that the design scheme being developed was 'intended to reflect requirements for a functional and appropriate building in which size and costs are contained'. However, a warning that both political and media criticism could be expected if the embassy complex were to be designed by a Japanese architectural firm, appeared to reveal the interests of the task force members more than an appreciation of the capacities of Japanese architects, several of whom were better known around the world than their Australian counterparts.

In June 1987, as Geoff Miller remembers, DOLGAS advertised for expressions of interest for the development of the site based on the existing redevelopment concept:

> I think a number of major Japanese companies, including Shimizu Constructions, a very leading firm, submitted designs, but in a process which I neither understood nor uncovered, Denton Corker Marshall's role was changed from supervising the design competition to becoming the designers themselves … Anyway, in their new role they conducted extensive consultations with staff members and families about the new office and living quarters, but we eventually concluded that they had really arrived with their minds made up.[48]

Finally, in an undated attachment to the Amended Decision, the task force outlined several ideas for selling or disposing of the land. This included proposals that a new head of mission residence be included in the redevelopment and that 'restraint in the provision of accommodation is appropriate'.[49] In a 1991 publication by a London firm, the DCM architects dismissed the 'small village' approach. This would have separated the chancery, the apartment building, and the ambassador's residence, which, 'used for the brandy and cigars aspect of diplomacy', would have stood alone surrounded by lawns'. For DCM, which had designed the Australian embassy in Beijing, both projects demonstrated 'commitment to the public patronage of architecture'. In Tokyo, the bold modern design was 'rooted in a European tradition', according to the architects.[50]

---

48   Ibid.
49   Cabinet Decision 9333/ER(Amended)—Possible sale of Tokyo Embassy—Without Submission, 27 April 1987, NAA: A13979, 9333/ER.
50   Deyan Sudjic, *Australian Embassy Tokyo, Architects Denton Corker Marshall* (London: Wordsearch, 1991), no page numbers.

The residence was demolished in 1987 and the Japanese-style half of the garden (1.2 hectares) was sold for A$640 million to the construction company C. Itoh (*Itō-chu*). By the time the proceeds arrived, Australia's budget deficit had already been wiped out. The 400-year-old pine tree died and Tsuna's Well dried up, both literally and figuratively. Trevor Wilson used wood from the tree to frame a small stained-glass window. The Millers and the Curries each received a 'gargoyle' from the residence roof as souvenirs. Some stained glass, a screen and the Hachisuka propeller went into the new residence, but Tsuna's inscribed stone and most of the stone lanterns were sold, as was the stone turtle, which Rachel Miller had tried to save by hiding it in the garden. We have seen no record of who bought them, the prices they fetched, or the fate of other contents of the residence.

For *Itō-chu* the result was not so profitable. The company had agreed that they would not build on the part of the land where Tsuna's Well was situated, and they planned a high-rise development of a residential and office building of 110 floors—as high as Tokyo Tower and higher than the Eiffel. But the Mita authorities refused to grant *Itō-chu* permission to build anything higher than four storeys on the site (in the tennis court area) and it remained unused for 30 years, losing the company A$600 million.[51] The people in *Itō-chu* responsible for the purchase lost their jobs and the company's aspirations for a high-rise development were not realised until this advertisement for apartments appeared in 2018:

> Park Mansion Mita Tsunamachi. 'The Forest' is a brand-new, 11-storey condominium located on a large 6,100 sqm site directly south of the Australian Embassy. It is directly across the street from the gardens of the historic members-only Tsunamachi Mitsui Club as well as Mitsui's very first Park Mansion building— Mita Tsunamachi Park Mansion (1971) … The building will be surrounded by carefully landscaped gardens designed by California-based Daniel Garness. The gardens will feature a number of traditional Japanese lanterns and stonework and will blend seamlessly with the adjoining embassy … The most desirable apartments are those facing north and east as they overlook the embassy and Mitsui Club grounds.[52]

51 Debenham, *Waiting 'Round the Bend*, 207.
52 'Mita Tsunamachi Park Mansion', Japan Property Central, japanpropertycentral.com/mita-tsunamachi-park-mansion/2018, accessed 17 May 2021.

Under the supervision of the Melbourne architects, redevelopment of the remaining site took place in 1988–90. In DCM's view, the financing and completion of the project in three years was 'a remarkable entrepreneurial and architectural success story', and the embassy is 'a building of great presence and subtlety' which presents Australia 'in a forceful, confident manner'. Internally, DCM added, a 'high degree of prefabrication' allowed for fast construction.[53] A diplomat present at the time saw it differently: DCM delivered 'a brutishly cluttered design and functional outcome and the Hachisuka mansion hit the dust'.[54] Elevated on turrets on each side of the entrance, two coats of arms displayed Australia's native symbols— enclosed in stainless steel cages. In what remained of the garden, the lawn and the cherry, pine, maple and eucalyptus trees were retained, as were the wrought iron gates. The beautiful old porte-cochère was installed as a non-functional, separate structure. The Kawai grand piano and the Pakistani rugs reappeared in Shanghai, to the surprise of Murray McLean, the consul-general, who later became ambassador in Tokyo.[55]

DCM asked those who would live in the new apartments for their views, but they were not reflected in the design. The kitchen proposed for the ambassador's apartment was unsuitable for entertaining large numbers of guests. In the architects' view, it would be more democratic to install a large kitchen and entertainment area in the chancery for common use. They were eventually persuaded that this was impractical, but due to restrictions of space, the ambassador's expanded kitchen was divided between two floors, inconveniently connected by an open staircase. Uehara-san, who had been major-domo for successive ambassadors, found himself working in a dark basement room. On the day the first occupants of the ambassador's apartment, Rawdon and Ross Dalrymple, moved in, they were to host a formal dinner for Japanese and other guests. For the cook, who like his predecessors and colleagues had dedicatedly served the embassy for many years, the transition proved too much. Ross and her daughter took over, producing the dinner on their own and trying to make a pavlova while the butler plied the waiting guests with Scotch.[56]

---

53   Sudjic, *Australian Embassy Tokyo*.
54   Debenham, *Waiting 'Round the Bend*, 204.
55   Murray McLean, personal communication with Alison Broinowski, 2017.
56   Ross Dalrymple, personal communication with Alison Broinowski, 2018.

THE AUSTRALIAN EMBASSY IN TOKYO AND AUSTRALIA–JAPAN RELATIONS

The upstairs living quarters for the ambassador and his family were very cramped. A later ambassador, John McCarthy, said that the formal downstairs area was quite dark despite looking out onto the garden, and the lobby opened directly onto the dining table.

Fortunately, funds became available to extend that area further out into the garden, giving it more light and space.[57] The largest apartments were allocated to the most senior staff members (the minister, the trade commissioner and others), and the rest of the apartments went to those already in Tokyo, based first on family considerations and then on a ballot system. An occupant of the minister's apartment objected that the narrow entrance lacked a *geta bako* (shoe cupboard) and guest toilet. Two other early occupants of the embassy apartments were Michelle and Geoff Marginson, both officers in the embassy, who arrived with two children and a nanny. The Marginsons were given a three-bedroom apartment with access from the street and small rooms, half of which were subterranean, with used furniture that took up too much space. Although the larger apartments could accommodate receptions for about 50 people, the smaller ones were not suitable for entertaining and most people at junior levels, including the Marginsons, held such events elsewhere.[58]

It was rumoured that some of the bathroom fittings had been intended for a primary or middle school, as the general height of the fittings was so low.[59] Michelle Marginson commented that her 6'5" (1.9 m) husband had to kneel on the floor to clean his teeth![60] Design problems also affected other apartments—a married couple were forced to have their small child sleep in their bedroom because there was no other suitable room on that floor. Other design factors generated a degree of rivalry among the residents, particularly those in small apartments who felt they could be scrutinised by passers-by.

The recreational facilities, however, were good and included a swimming pool and a recreation room with bar and club facilities, topped with a tennis court. The chancery foyer has been described as beautiful, with views of the garden from waist-high windows, although others find it rather dark. The offices are spacious and well interrelated. Nonetheless,

---

as has happened in other posts, by the time the chancery was completed it was not big enough. Some of the integrated departments, such as Immigration, felt they needed more room.

The Australian embassy in Tokyo, DCM stated, would have 'the visual and architectural staying power' to make its presence lastingly felt in the city.[61] Since the 1990s its occupants and visitors have known only the new building. But the old Hachisuka residence and its gardens will always be missed by those who knew and loved them. As Louise Walker said, the sale and demolition saddened her 'as it would the loss of a friend'.[62] Nothing in Tokyo is really permanent—including, unfortunately, the old Australian embassy residence and its garden.

61   Sudjic, *Australian Embassy Tokyo*.
62   Walker, *But I Digress*, 167.

7

Building Diplomacy: The Architecture of the Australian Embassy in Tokyo

Philip Goad

Buildings that represent nations—embassies—can be potent cultural diplomats. In addition to satisfying the functional requirements of diplomatic business and housing embassy staff, one of the most valuable attributes of an embassy or foreign mission building is its symbolic capital. An embassy can signal international neutrality. It can signal political ties. It can tell national stories—some selective, some inclusive—but rarely, of course, will it relate unwanted ones. There is also the necessary measure of welcome expected in any embassy complex. That is part of an embassy's role: to assume in physical form the role of the diplomat; crucially a position that has to withstand shifts in foreign policy over time. An embassy is also about selective presence: it is important to know where to choose to build, for whom and how much to spend. As an edifice, therefore, an embassy ought to be resilient in terms of its message. If this is a measure of success, then the Australian embassy in Tokyo, in its design and construction between 1986 and 1990, can be regarded as an exemplary signifier of cultural diplomacy, its completion an assured and, in this especial case, profitable act of building diplomacy.

This chapter examines the architectural history of the 'new' Australian embassy in Tokyo within its national and international contexts. What also gives this building significance is the way in which the architects,

Denton Corker Marshall (DCM), negotiated cultural understandings through a subtle and deliberate interplay of Japanese and non-Japanese formal gestures and at the same time, through its design, made Australia's presence appear physically greater, an impression clearly intended to strengthen and make more visible the nation's diplomatic role within the region more generally.

Embassy-building across the globe after World War II saw architectural modernism triumphant and the commissioning, often, of a distinguished architectural practice to represent the nation—though not always with success. With any embassy, there is the risk of no impact or a misplaced gesture. Architect Macy DuBois's Canadian embassy in Beijing (1989), for example, must rate as one of his least successful buildings: a series of respectfully dull, unprepossessing brick and concrete forms that say virtually nothing about the nation of its occupants or its place on foreign soil. By contrast, Finnish-American architect Eero Saarinen's US embassy in London, in Grosvenor Square (1956–60), while heavily criticised at the time of its completion for its overtly decorative precast concrete panelled façade and the oversized gilded aluminium American eagle perched above the entrance, can now be seen to have been not just prescient of but also highly original in its forging of an imperial impression of America's power and global influence in the 1950s and 1960s.[1] Indeed, the ambition and extent of the US embassy-building program after World War II was matched by no other country across the globe in terms of scale and expense.[2] Because of this, Ron Theodore Robin's *Enclaves of America: The Rhetoric of American Political Architecture Abroad, 1900–1965* (1992) and Jane Loeffler's *The Architecture of Diplomacy: Building America's Embassies* (1998) remain the benchmark studies in this area, complemented by Fredie Floré and Cammie McAtee's *The Politics of Furniture: Identity, Diplomacy and Persuasion in Post-War Interiors*

---

1   Harsh criticism, expressed especially by British architects, appeared in 'Controversial Building in London', *Architectural Forum*, no. 114 (March 1961): 81–85. See also 'Critical Appraisal of the New American Embassy', *Times* (London), 28 October 1960.

2   Prior to World War II, the embassy-building exploits of Great Britain rated as the most lavish and extensive. See Mark Bertram, *Room for Diplomacy: Britain's Diplomatic Buildings Overseas, 1800–2000* (Reading: Spire Books, 2011); James Stourton, *British Embassies: Their Diplomatic and Architectural History* (London: Quarto Publishing, 2017); J.E. Hoare, *Embassies in the East: The Story of the British Embassies in Japan, China and Korea from 1859 to the Present* (Richmond, Surrey: Curzon Press, 1999).

(2017).[3] Apart from a chapter on Australia's embassies in Washington, DC, and Paris in the latter edited volume, a small number of design review articles on individual embassies, and presentations and a doctoral thesis by Rowan Gower on Australian diplomatic building procurement in Asia,[4] critical literature focused on the architecture of Australia's diplomatic missions overseas is remarkably slight, especially given the high quality achieved and considerable finance expended by the Australian Commonwealth over the past 30 years on embassy buildings. Yet this is also understandable: it could be said quite simply that, as a world player, Australia came late to the embassy-building game. This chapter therefore adds to much-needed scholarship in this field. The Australian embassy in Tokyo exemplifies an aesthetic highpoint in one of the most active and expansionist phases (c. 1973–90) of Australian diplomatic building in the twentieth century.

As a building type, the embassy is rich with opportunity. It is both a public and a private building—a place of public ceremony and official reception as well as a secure and private retreat, and for some of its staff, a home literally away from 'home'. An embassy generally has three parts, each with a different level of public and private access, and each with a different level of aesthetic ambition in terms of representation: a chancery which houses administrative offices and public spaces for ceremonies and exhibition; an ambassador's residence; and, frequently (though not always), residential accommodation for diplomatic staff with sometimes ancillary recreation facilities depending on the so-called difficulty of the posting.

---

3   Ron Theodore Robin, *Enclaves of America: The Rhetoric of American Political Architecture Abroad, 1900–1965* (Princeton: Princeton University Press, 1992); Jane Loeffler, *The Architecture of Diplomacy: Building America's Embassies* (New York: Princeton Architecture Press, 1998); Fredie Floré and Cammie McAtee, eds, *The Politics of Furniture: Identity, Diplomacy and Persuasion in Post-War Interiors* (Abingdon: Routledge, 2017), doi.org/10.4324/9781315554389.

4   See, for example, Chris Abel, 'Embassies', in *The Encyclopedia of Australian Architecture*, ed. Philip Goad and Julie Willis (Port Melbourne: Cambridge University Press, 2012), 232–33; Philip Goad, 'Designed Diplomacy: Furniture, Furnishing and Art in Australian Embassies for Washington, DC, and Paris', in Floré and McAtee, *Politics of Furniture*, 179–97; Rowan Gower, 'Image Building: A Study of Australia's Domestic and Foreign Policy in Relation to Embassy Architecture', in *Proceedings of the Society of Architectural Historians of Australia and New Zealand* 34 (Canberra: University of Canberra, 2017), 193–203; Rowan Gower, 'Exporting Australian Architectural "Expertise" as a Matter of Policy', in *Proceedings of the Society of Architectural Historians of Australia and New Zealand* 36 (Sydney: Society of Architectural Historians of Australia and New Zealand, 2020), 196–204; Rowan Gower, 'Image Building: Examining Australia's Diplomatic Architecture in the Asian Region, 1960–1990' (PhD thesis, University of New South Wales, 2019).

Figure 7.1: Perspective drawing of Australian high commissioner's residence, New Delhi, India, 1955.
Architects: Joseph Allen Stein and Benjamin Polk.
Source: Environmental Design Archives, UC Berkeley.

Australia constructed its very first embassy in London between 1913 and 1918. Designed by Scottish architect Alexander Marshall Mackenzie, it was a suitably pompous example of Edwardian Baroque, a style much favoured in London at the time. As a grand classical pile, Australia House symbolised the nation as a faithful and prosperous servant of empire. It remains the oldest purpose-built chancery of any foreign mission in London. However, over the next five decades, Australian missions invariably occupied existing buildings. There appeared to be no need, apart from the hoisting of the Australian flag, to assert identity through any specially commissioned architecture. It was only after World War II that, given the strengthening of the Cold War alliance with the United States and Australia's increasing awareness of its role in the Asia-Pacific region, two significant mission buildings were constructed: the Australian high commissioner's residence at Chanakyapuri (1955–58) in New Delhi's diplomatic enclave and the Australian chancery in Washington, DC (1965–69).

The New Delhi residence, designed by American architects Joseph Allen Stein (1912–2001) and Benjamin Polk (1916–2001), who had both shifted to India in 1952, remains one of India's finest (though little known) examples of a regionally inspired modernism.[5] Combined with its embrace of local stone, arcades, floating eaves and the adaptation of the traditional *jali* (perforated stone or lattice screen), Stein's deep interests in climate and landscape conspired to produce a 'building that reflected India' and which, in many respects, transcended in terms of quality and ambience, the much better-known and controversial chancery design for the US embassy (1954–59), also nearby in Chanakyapuri, designed by Edward Durrell Stone.[6] This concept of a building that might reflect upon the aesthetic, historic and urban contexts of its setting was a theme that would find an echo in Tokyo. By contrast, Bates Smart & McCutcheon's white marble–clad design for the Australian chancery in Washington, DC, on Massachusetts Avenue at Scott Circle, with its corporate-styled public spaces at ground level and ambassadorial suites indicated by a loggia at mid-level, was modern but classical in mood— symptomatic not just of Washington's strict design controls but also of the replacement of the language of classicism by modernism as a language of international diplomacy, a pattern determined largely by the expansionist program of American embassies constructed across Europe, the Middle East, India and Brazil in the 1950s. National identity in Washington was subsumed beneath a new form of contemporary architectural manners: the studied neutrality of classical modernism. Australia was thus positioned as a most competent participant in the global conversation of architectural modernism.

In the late 1960s but especially after 1972, with the election of a federal Labor government under Gough Whitlam, there was further expansion and confidence in the need for overseas presence, first in France but more particularly and ever since, in Asia. Again, an assured internationalism held sway. The Australian embassy in Paris (1973–77), designed by Harry Seidler, was later described unkindly by Deyan Sudjic as 'an elegant iceberg'.[7] Yet Seidler's double crescent form design was brought into effective dialogue with the curving forms of the Champ de Mars, gaining

5   Stephen White, *Building in the Garden: The Architecture of Joseph Allen Stein in India and California* (Delhi, New York: Oxford University Press, 1993), 39–40, 107, 125.
6   For an account of the praise and controversy surrounding the aesthetics of Edward Durrell Stone's US embassy in New Delhi, see Mary Ann Hunting, *Edward Durrell Stone: Modernism's Populist Architect* (New York: W.W. Norton, 2013), 83–86, nn. 52, 53 and 55. Australian architect Robin Boyd also weighed in with criticism: see Robin Boyd, 'Decoration Rides Again', *Architectural Record* 122, no. 3 (September 1957): 183–86.
7   Deyan Sudjic, *Australian Embassy Tokyo, Architects Denton Corker Marshall*, Blueprint Extra 02 (London: Wordsearch Ltd, 1991).

for its users panoramic views of the Eiffel Tower.[8] The chancery bulged towards this prospect with the ambassador's apartment on the top having spectacular views from a rooftop terrace. While, at ground level, Italian engineer Pier Luigi Nervi, working with Seidler, designed two giant concrete legs on pointed toes that formed a porte-cochère and denoted a giant 'A' for Australia. The second crescent housed the staff apartments, all facing away from the street with views to the Eiffel Tower. Seidler's confident use of an abstract late modern language of concrete and granite presented Australia as a model modern *citoyen du monde*—citizen of the world.

In Southeast Asia, modernism also informed new chancery buildings in Kuala Lumpur (1973–78; architects: Joyce Nankivell) and Bangkok (1973–78; architects: Ancher Mortlock Murray & Woolley) but these were now modified by boldly accentuated *brises-soleil* (sun breakers/ baffles) and extensive water bodies to acknowledge each site's tropical climate—again, neutral gestures rather than overt symbolic references to Australia. In Bangkok, deep overhangs and expressed structure, like a house on stilts, accentuated cooling shadows and responsible deference to regional building traditions.[9] It was as if Australia, through its embassy buildings, was demonstrating that it knew how to behave in the tropics.

Figure 7.2: Street view. Australian embassy, Beijing, People's Republic of China, c. 1992.

Architects: Denton Corker Marshall Pty Ltd.

Source: Photograph by John Gollings.

---

8   See Harry Seidler and Associates, *Ambassade d'Australie, Quai Branly Paris 15* (Sydney: 1974); Harry Seidler, *Australian Embassy = Ambassade d'Australie, Paris* (Sydney: Horwitz Australia, 1979).
9   'Australian Embassy: Bangkok', *Architecture Australia* 74, no. 2 (March 1985): 42.

By the early 1980s, in an atmosphere of postmodern inclusion, this deference to local context became even more marked. At that time, the People's Republic of China had not yet opened up to the West. In Beijing, much of the distinctive spaces of the residential streetscapes surrounding the Forbidden City still retained many of the *hutong* (laneways) and traditional courtyard houses. In their design for a new Australian embassy (1982–92), DCM used the concept of the walled courtyard house compound, the familiar greys of stucco and cement render of the hutong, and a traditional north–south orientation as the basis for their design of chancery, ambassador's residence and diplomatic staff compound.[10] Inspiration for examining the local context had been partly influenced by DCM's regard for the Danish embassy in Beijing (1974), a soft-brown, brick-walled, low-rise compound designed by Gehrdt Bornebusch, replete with human-scaled courtyards and heavily planted with trees. However, what makes DCM's accomplished postmodern design acutely Australian, even provocative, are the 'open windows' set into the walls of each implied 'courtyard house' of the diplomatic residences facing Dongzhimenwai. It was a tactical critique of and counter to the traditional closed walled compound: the huge openings punched into the walls suggested openness and transparency. It was very un-Chinese.

The embrace of the local—in terms of empathy with local urban morphology, building typology, style, materiality and colour—was taken to its logical extreme in the Australian embassy in Riyadh, Saudi Arabia (1985–87). Daryl Jackson with Meldrum Burrows produced a design of closely packed flat-roofed blocks, massed like a casbah and spatially informed by multiple courtyards, shading privacy screens endemic to Islamic architecture and local desert colours.[11] The result was an utterly convincing piece of interpretive contemporary architecture but the reality is that no foreign embassy in Saudi Arabia is allowed to express national characteristics—all must accord with the 'Central Nadj' style—this is an official guideline. Australia, then, was simply following protocol.

---

10 'Beijing Embassy: Denton Corker Marshall', *Architecture Australia* 81, no. 7 (Nov–Dec 1992): 42–43; Deyan Sudjic, 'Life in the Forbidden City', *Blueprint*, no. 94 (Feb 1993): 32–34; Haig Beck and Jackie Cooper, *Denton Corker Marshall, Rule Playing and the Ratbag Element* (Basel: Birkhäuser, 2000), 86–87, 90–95; Jianfei Zhu, 'Denton Corker Marshall in China—Interactions', in *Denton Corker Marshall: Non-fictional Narratives*, ed. Leon van Schaik (Basel: Birkhäuser, 2008), 136–37, 142–44.

11 Daryl Jackson, 'Desert Diplomat', *World Architecture* 13 (1991): 58–61. See also Daryl Jackson, *Daryl Jackson: Selected and Current Works* (Mulgrave: Images Publishing Group, 1996), 106–09.

The careful balance of respect for context and respectful critique as a means of marking identity found full expression in the 1986 design of the Australian embassy in Tokyo, one of Australia's largest and most important foreign missions. The location of the embassy in central Tokyo's leafy Mita district was key not just to the eventual design of the new building but also to the status, even gravitas, that it bequeathed to the building. During the Edo period (1603–1867), the ruling Tokugawa Shogunate required the nation's wealthy aristocracy to maintain a residence in Edo (present-day Tokyo). The Hachisuka clan from Tokushima, on the island of Shikoku, obtained land atop a hill in central Mita. The location was a favourable one, and others of the Japanese elite had already built there. The Mitsui family, for example, owned land next door and built a huge neo-Italianate reception and guest house in 1913 to the designs of the British architect and so-called 'father of modern Japanese architecture' Josiah Conder (1852–1920).[12] That house, now the Tsuna-machi Mitsui Club, had—and still has—extensive and very beautiful landscaped gardens.

Mochiaki Hachisuka (1846–1918) was a grandson of *shōgun* Ienari Tokugawa. But leading up to and anticipating the dramatic political and societal changes that would accompany the Meiji Restoration from 1868, he shrewdly shifted his alliance to the Imperial throne. Newly relaxed laws on foreign travel during the Meiji Era (1868–1912) allowed Mochiaki to attend Oxford University in his late 1920s, before he returned to serve as second president of Japan's House of Peers (the upper house of the Imperial Diet).

Mochiaki's son, Marquis Masaaki Hachisuka (1871–1932), and his grandson, Masauji (1903–1953), also studied in England but at Cambridge University. Both returned to Japan with a fondness for British architecture and, following the Great Kanto earthquake of 1923, in 1927 they built on the Mita site a picturesque Western-style mansion that resembled a grand, rambling English country house with landscaped gardens on two levels. Over time, ivy engulfed the house and its porte-cochère. At the rear, also ivy-covered, the house was informally massed with generous timber-panelled entertaining rooms that gave directly onto the gardens. It was a relaxed house that spoke of its cultured owners—the younger

---

12 *Josiah Conder: A Victorian Architect in Japan*, exhibition catalogue (Tokyo: Higashi Nihon Tetsudo Bunka Zaidan, 1997); Jordan Sand, *House and Home in Modern Japan: Architecture, Domestic Space and Bourgeois Culture, 1880–1930* (Cambridge, MA: Harvard University Asia Center, 2003), doi.org/10.1163/9781684173846.

Hachisuka, for example, becoming in his early thirties an internationally acclaimed ornithologist, writing an important series of volumes on birds of the Philippines.[13]

The Hachisuka mansion was purchased by the Australian government in 1951 from the widow of the elder Hachisuka for what was then a very modest sum.[14] Over the years, the Tokyo embassy subsequently came to be a much-loved locale of not just diplomatic business but also entertaining: its attraction almost certainly was as a place and space that was intimately connected with physical reminders of 'home', despite its commissioning by a Japanese family intent on celebrating their connections with an outside, international world.

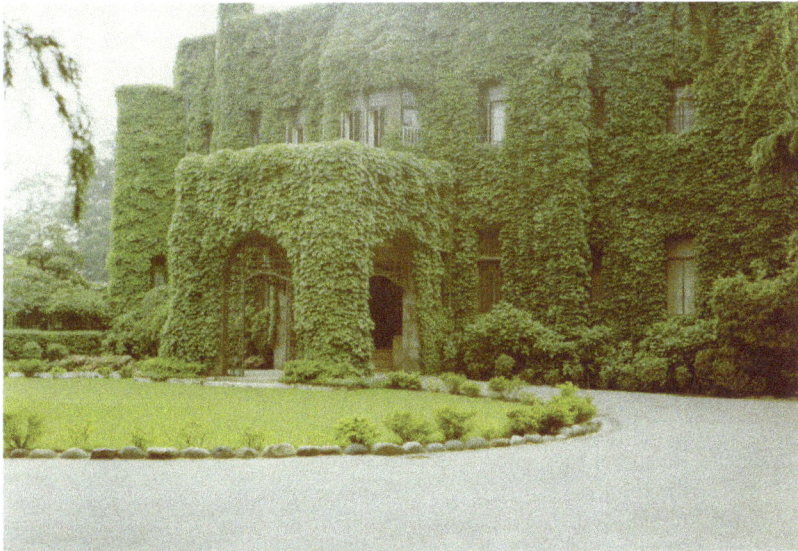

Figure 7.3: Front of the original Hachisuka mansion in Minato-ku, commissioned in 1927 by the Marquis Masaaki Hachisuka (1871–1932) and his grandson, Masauji (1903–1953).
Architect: Unknown.
Source: Australian embassy in Tokyo.

---

13   Masauji Hachisuka, *The Birds of the Philippine Islands, with Notes on the Mammal Fauna*, 4 vols (London: H.F. & G. Witherby, 1931–35). Another but later significant work by the Japanese scholar was Masauji Hachisuka, *The Dodo and Kindred Birds: Or, the Extinct Birds of the Mascarene Islands* (London: H.F. & G. Witherby, 1953).
14   There is an apocryphal story that the widow sent her major-domo to collect the sum of nearly A\$200,000 from Australian government representatives in Tokyo, who duly did so but absconded with the money. She was never paid but honoured the deal and handed over the mansion and land to the Australian government. John Denton, interviewed by Philip Goad, Melbourne, 28 August 2018.

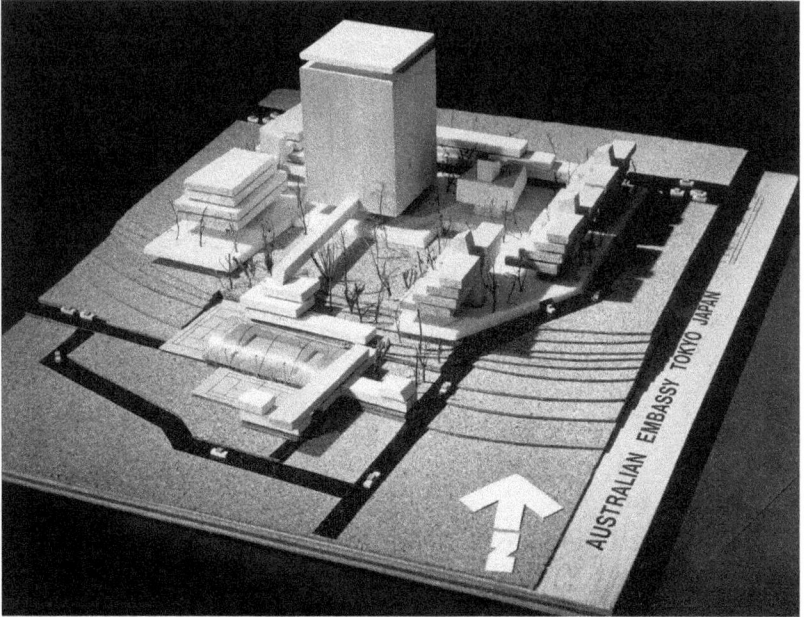

Figure 7.4: Model, proposed Australian embassy, Tokyo, 1974.

Architect: Commonwealth Department of Works.

Source: National Archives of Australia (NAA): B6295, 3639G, Item barcode: 9744384.

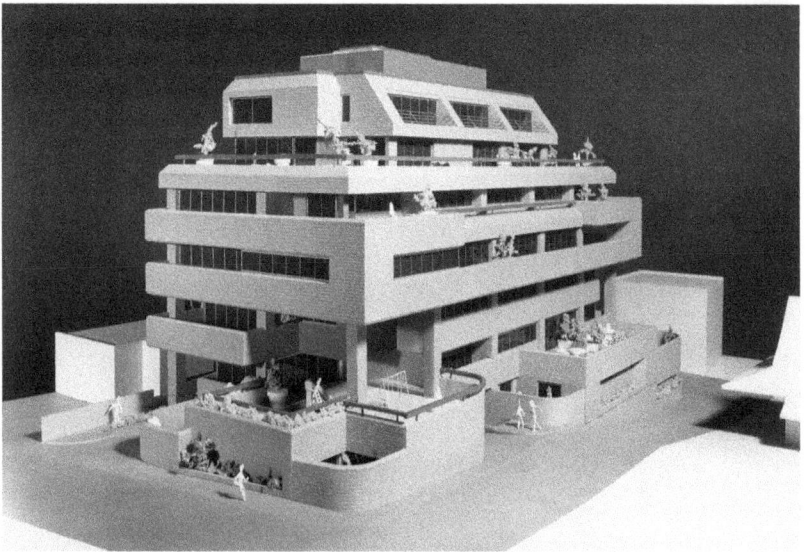

Figure 7.5: Model, proposed staff apartments for the Australian embassy, Tokyo, 1975.

Source: NAA: B6295, 4141H, Item barcode: 9737521.

However, development plans for the site, through force of circumstance, were put forward over the next decade as the embassy and its staff grew. In 1963, after just over a decade of occupation, plans were proposed for a detached multistorey chancery block to be built.[15] This did not proceed and other proposals were put forward in 1970 and again in 1974 when designs for redevelopment of the entire site by the Commonwealth Department of Works proposed the demolition of the Hachisuka mansion and the construction of a new chancery, ambassador's residence and staff apartments disposed across the site, removing the old garden and replacing it with a tennis court and recreation facilities.[16] This also did not proceed but what did occur was the 1975 design and eventual construction of a seven-storey, 16-unit block of flats directly across the street.[17] Despite some local resistance to the possibility of increased traffic, the blocking of sunlight and suggestions in the Australian parliament in 1976 that the Japanese storehouse on site that was to be demolished was of historic value, the Japanese Foreign Ministry and the Tokyo government raised no objection.[18]

By 1987, opinions had changed and there were thoughts of selling off the entire 1.7-hectare site. The problem was that only about half of the mission's staff of 51 could be housed on the embassy grounds and in the 16-unit apartment block across the street. Given the high costs of external rental accommodation, it was felt that all options should be investigated. At a time of spiralling real estate prices in Tokyo—the site was worth some A$600 million in 1987—it was even mooted at one stage that sale of the site would assist in reducing the government's budget deficit back in Australia.[19] But selling the site was controversial.

There was a sense that by selling off the site for a quick capital gain, the Australian government might deliver an affront to Japanese heritage and cause diplomatic embarrassment. As the *Canberra Times* reported in April 1987:

---

15   Artist's impression of new chancery for the Australian embassy, Tokyo, 1963. National Archives of Australia (NAA): A1200, L45137, Item barcode: 30673288.
16   Photographs of proposed Australian embassy, model, 1974, NAA: B6295, 6369F, Item barcode: 9744383, and B6295, 3639I, Item barcode: 30891508.
17   Photographs of proposed apartments for Australian embassy staff, Tokyo, model, 1975, NAA: B6295, 4141H, Item barcode: 9737521, B6295, 4141K, Item barcode: 30816121.
18   'Embassy Will Demolish Two Houses', *Canberra Times*, 14 September 1976, 12.
19   'Embassy Sale as Aid to Reduce Budget Deficit', *Canberra Times*, 6 April 1987, 9.

There is also the problem of historical value. Half of the embassy grounds are landscaped, the upper level of lawns and azalea beds descending to an old Japanese-style garden which is said to be among the loveliest in the capital.

Feelings run deep that redevelopment affecting the garden – with its reputedly 400-year-old pine tree and legendary moon-shaped rock from behind which a famous samurai is supposed to have leapt out and hacked off the arms of a demon would not have gone over well in Japan.[20]

Australian woman Josephine Soothill, who had been an exchange student at Daito Bunka University of Tokyo and had been married in the garden in December 1986, also contacted the *Canberra Times* to lodge a protest, suggesting that 'for international relations, to sell it off to land developers would be pretty slack'.[21]

What finally eventuated was that the Australian government did in fact sell off part of the grounds—the lower level of the gardens, just under half of the site—and the 1970s apartment block for A$640 million by March 1988 as part of a broader project of asset sales in 1988.[22] As part of the tender process, a new chancery, ambassador's residence and staff apartments were to be built for no cost by the successful MITA consortium of tenderers for the land.[23] It was an excellent deal. The Australian government had bought the site in 1951 for just A$196,000 (at 1988 estimates). Even with the excision of land, the remaining site was valued at A$500 million, and it was still Australia's most valuable offshore asset.

---

20 'Dismay in Tokyo over Plan to Sell Australian Embassy Site', *Canberra Times*, 8 April 1987, 13.
21 Keith Scott, 'Woman in Fight to Save Garden', *Canberra Times*, 11 April 1987, 11.
22 Another part of the deal was that one of the members of the purchasing consortium had also agreed to buy an additional 1.5 million tonnes of NSW coal over its normal coal purchases. See 'Confidence on Tokyo Package', *Canberra Times*, 9 April 1988, 3; Lenore Taylor, 'Tokyo Land Deal Settled', *Canberra Times*, 23 April 1988, 3. The final sale price as reported in October 1988 was A$607 million, though another A$50–$60 million was gained through the sale of a strip of land for road widening to a local city government. See Philip Hobbs, '$50m Sale of More Tokyo Land Expected', *Canberra Times*, 23 October 1988, 2.
23 The MITA consortium comprised C. Itoh and Co., Takenaka Komuten Co. Ltd, Hazami-Gumi Ltd, Pacific Real Estate Co. Ltd, and the Yasuda Trust and Banking Co. Ltd, along with Melbourne developers Lustig and Moar. See Andrew Fraser and Andree Coelli, 'Embassy Sale Nets $640m', *Canberra Times*, 12 March 1988, 1.

Conditions on the sale imposed by the Australian government included retention of most of the existing gardens that were thick with 400-year-old trees, and especially the famous historic areas that camouflage a cave and an ancient well some believe was the first bathing place of the renowned Heian-period samurai, Watanabe-no-Tsuna (953–1025). Suggestions were made that the preserved gardens might be made open to the public, but these came to nothing[24] and there was a last-ditch effort by Mrs Mary Kinney, an American resident of Tokyo, who organised a petition to try to save the old mansion-embassy from demolition but this too failed.[25]

The architect of the new Australian embassy in Tokyo was the Melbourne and Hong Kong–based practice of DCM, headed by its partners, John Denton (1945–), Bill Corker (1945–) and Barrie Marshall (1946–). At the time, the firm had designed a series of important urban-based public works, including Melbourne's City Square (1976–79, now demolished), additions to the Australian War Memorial in Canberra (1985), the office skyscraper at 101 Collins Street, Melbourne (1987–90), and the Australian embassy in Beijing, then still under construction and a commission gained largely due the expertise demonstrated in their final-placed design for Australia's Parliament House (1979–80) and a recommendation through Richard Johnson, then a principal architect within the Commonwealth Department of Works.[26] An additional attribute possessed by DCM was that it was familiar with working in the region and had an office in Hong Kong, which made supervision easier and potentially more affordable for the government.[27]

The commission for the Tokyo facility had arisen with some urgency. There were mounting concerns over lack of security at the existing facility: its openness, while endearing and relaxed for staff and visitors alike, meant that people could, quite literally, just walk in off the street. According to John Denton, concerns about the typically very high levels of security employed at any US embassy—and Tokyo was no exception, given attacks on US, Japanese and Canadian embassies by the Japanese Red Army in

---

24   Fraser and Coelli, 'Embassy Sale Nets $640m', 1.
25   Hobbs, '$50m Sale of More Tokyo Land Expected', 2.
26   In 1985, Richard Johnson joined DCM and worked directly on the Australian embassy in Beijing. Prior to 1985, his design works in Japan, on behalf of the Commonwealth Department of Works, included Australian Pavilions at Expo '75 at Okinawa and Expo '85, Tsukuba (both in collaboration with Yoshinobu Ashihara).
27   John Denton, interviewed by Philip Goad, Melbourne, 28 August 2018.

1986—prompted the client, the Overseas Property Group (OPG) within the Australian Government Department of Administrative Services, to act quickly and appoint architects directly, bypassing otherwise lengthy registrations of interest and interviews to select suitable architects.[28] DCM was appointed in 1986 and the building was completed by 1990, with a construction period of two years, as opposed to the five years it took to build the embassy in Beijing. Only one day was lost in the construction schedule: a day of mourning to commemorate the passing of Emperor Showa (Hirohito) on 7 January 1989.

In the design of an embassy, there is always an inevitable and necessary disconnect between the eventual users of the building and the architect. The architect does not deal directly with the ambassador or diplomatic staff who will be resident on site. The ambassador and diplomatic staff are itinerant—invariably short-term tenants liable to move with the next posting. Instead, the major client is the agency which represents government, in this case the OPG. DCM thus made presentations to the OPG, the Department of Foreign Affairs and Trade, the more than 10 government departments that were involved with the embassy's day-to-day workings, diplomatic staff representatives, and delegates from the Foreign Affairs Women's Association. As with any diplomatic commission for building works, DCM was removed from any negotiations with the allocation of named staff within the facility, instead relying largely on standardised government space allocations as an overall planning guide. As DCM director John Denton stated clearly, 'Canberra takes the decisions', an acknowledgement that feedback and evaluation of design is negotiated through bureaucratic rather than personal channels.[29] At one level, this is restrictive in relation to creating a perfect fit with concepts of 'home' and domesticity but at another, it enabled the architects to explore more fully issues of representation and national identity on the building's exterior and in the spaces of arrival, reception and ceremony.

In the late 1980s, DCM, in terms of aesthetics, was interested in the postmodern project of the recovery of the city and the recovery of an autonomous language that relied increasingly on the abstraction of architecture into aesthetically discrete elements. For DCM, this was a hybrid interest—which combined the work of Belgian urbanist and

---

28   Ibid.
29   Ibid.

architect Rob Krier[30] and the formal reveries of American architect John Hejduk[31]—and can be seen in Barrie Marshall's early conceptual sketches for the embassy.[32] So DCM's aim was to search for an appropriate urban typology and language of formal abstraction rather than deploy any direct representation of obviously 'Australian' forms and images, apart from obligatory text announcing the building's name and the Australian coat of arms.

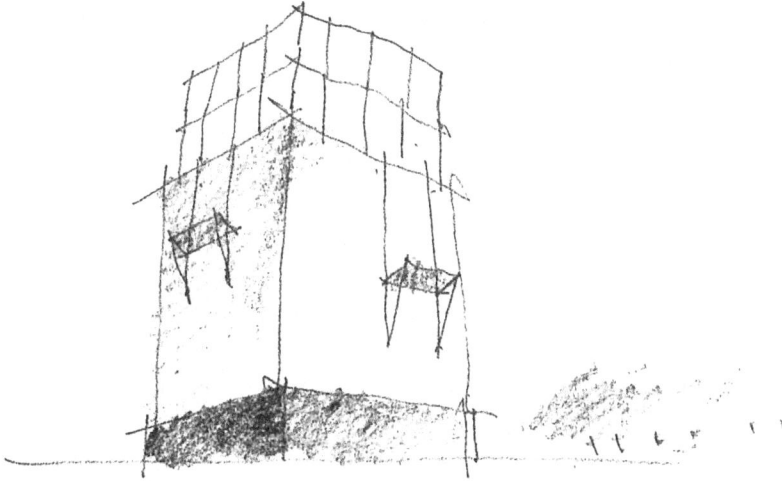

Figure 7.6: Preliminary sketch of residential block for Australian embassy, Tokyo, c. 1987.

Drawing: Barrie Marshall.

Source: Deyan Sudjic, *Australian Embassy Tokyo, Architects Denton Corker Marshall*, Blueprint Extra 02, (London: Wordsearch Ltd, 1991), no page numbers.

In many respects, then, DCM turned to a language of abstraction and an idea of generic urban and building typologies that echoed the contemporary ideas of European urbanists Rob Krier and also German urbanist O.M. Ungers. Within an urban context of small-scale subdivisions, as a way of creating a substantial presence, DCM inserted a large-scale symmetrical

---

30   For an explanation of Rob Krier's thinking on architecture and urban design, see Rob Krier, *Urban Space* (London: Academy Editions, 1979); Rob Krier, *Rob Krier on Architecture* (London: Academy Press, 1982); and Rob Krier, *Elements of Architecture* (London: AD Publications, 1983).

31   For an explanation of John Hejduk's design approach, see John Hejduk, *John Hejduk, 7 Houses* (New York: Institute for Architecture and Urban Studies, 1979); John Hejduk, *Victims* (London: Architectural Association, 1986); and John Hejduk, *John Hejduk: Mask of Medusa—Works 1947–1983* (New York: Rizzoli International, 1989).

32   Sudjic, *Australian Embassy Tokyo*, n.p.

form based on flanking the chancery with the residential apartments and orienting the ambassador's residence and the recreation block to the existing garden behind. A refined language of muted abstraction—metallic panels, glass and stone—applied to the building's exterior became an architectural suit and tie with only the Australian coat of arms celebrated, held aloft in a three-dimensional gridded metal cage. From the street, the new embassy appeared to signal the return of Australia as an international citizen, as had been expressed in Washington and Paris, as opposed to the good neighbour approach developed at Beijing, Riyadh and Bangkok.

However, at the same time, what distinguished DCM's design in Tokyo was its response to context, movement, landscape and memory. Once beyond the front gates, a different form of dialogue—architecturally—was engaged, one that dealt directly with the site, its context and aspects of spatial experience that are typically Japanese. Key is the experience of arrival and discovery of the beautiful, preserved gardens beyond. From the outset, the building's symmetrical form and looming grandeur is non-Japanese. The idea of axiality is not generally a principle adopted in traditional Japanese architecture, even in larger buildings. Here, one enters from Mita Avenue on axis, into an open forecourt, then proceeding forward—again on axis—underneath a portal-like undercroft and into a square courtyard. The feeling is European, rather like entering a palazzo, or an echo closer to home, the square courtyard of Roy Grounds's National Gallery of Victoria in Melbourne (before its 2006 refurbishment). Beyond, again on axis, is the chancery foyer, which is glazed on either side. Once inside, there is a view beyond to the beautiful, asymmetrical profile and elegant calm of the historic gardens. The move one has made as a visitor has been from public (street and forecourt) to semipublic (central court and foyer), and thence to private (foyer and garden), a progression that is typically Japanese, but in this case wholly Western in its emphasis on axis, a point architect John Denton was careful to emphasise when interviewed.[33]

---

33   John Denton, interviewed by Philip Goad, Melbourne, 28 August 2018. See also Veronica Pease, 'Australian Synthesis', *Architectural Review* 189, no. 1137 (Nov. 1991): 42–45; Beck and Cooper, *Denton Corker Marshall*, 88–89, 96–107.

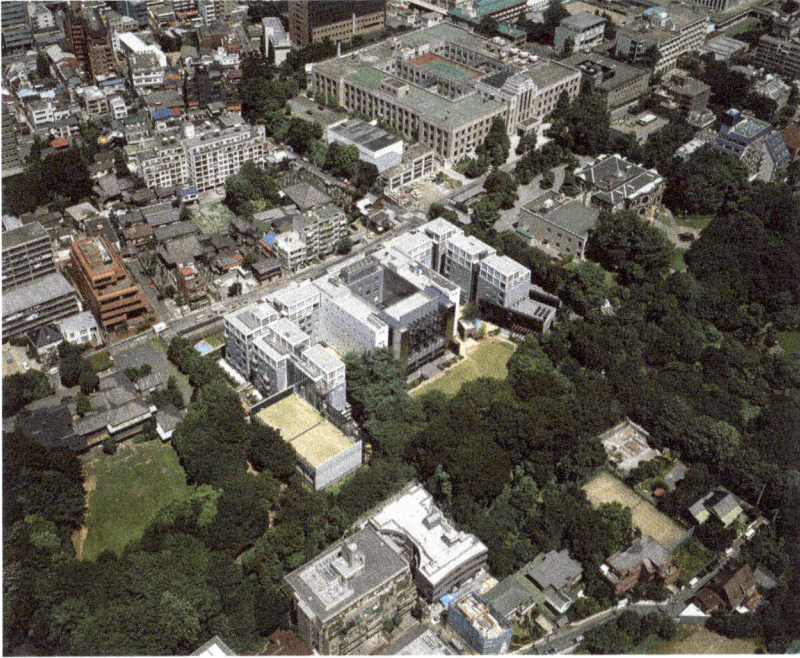

Figure 7.7: Aerial view. Australian embassy, Tokyo, c. 1990.
Architects: Denton Corker Marshall Pty Ltd.
Source: Photograph by John Gollings.

Flanking the chancery are two L-shaped wings, each comprising three near-square, planned residential blocks. The addition of these blocks, effectively pavilion wings, resembling in many ways a large eighteenth-century Palladian country seat, had a twofold aim: first, it referenced and alluded to the context of the Western-influenced mansions erected nearby by the Japanese in the late nineteenth and early twentieth centuries; and second, it effectively enlarged the embassy's visual presence, through each block's repetitive façade, creating the impression of a large and formidable institution.[34] So in addition to, as John Denton remarks, the embassy being 'another house on the hill',[35] it was also a deliberate and clear diplomatic ploy. Australia's embassy in Tokyo was to state its significant presence in no uncertain terms. Its local marking of great scale was to reinforce its enhanced presence within the great Asian region.

---

34   John Denton, interviewed by Philip Goad, Melbourne, 28 August 2018. This grand pavilion planning for an embassy also has a precedent in Tokyo with the construction of the British embassy in Chiyoda in 1929 to the designs of Richard Allison, chief architect of the Office of Works, London.
35   Ibid.

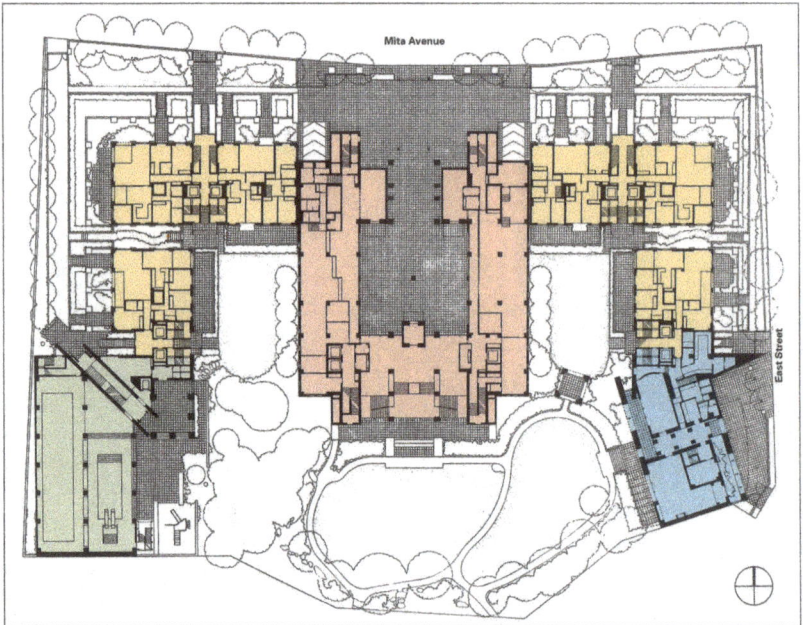

Figure 7.8: Ground-floor plan. Australian embassy, Tokyo.
Architects: Denton Corker Marshall Pty Ltd.
Source: Sudjic, *Australian Embassy Tokyo.*

Behind the imposing front façade to Mita Avenue, and at the end of each of the L-shaped wings flanking the chancery, were two further elements, each offset and individually different in form. As a design tactic, the building now became informal and relaxed. This was the 'garden' side of the 'palace', so to speak, where, traditionally in a Western sense, formality gave way to informality. To the west was the diplomatic residents' recreation block containing a gymnasium, lap pool and children's pool, and which gave onto a barbecue terrace. While on the east, angled to capture and maximise distant views of the garden and an asymmetric view of the chancery, was the black South Australian granite–clad ambassador's residence. Viewed from the garden, the embassy now appeared to comprise three distinctly different buildings, each scaled harmoniously with the mature trees of the garden and complemented further by the placement of the reconstructed arched brick porte-cochère of the original Hachisuka mansion as a folly fragment in the courtyard between the chancery and the ambassador's residence.

Figure 7.9: Ambassador's residence, view from garden. Australian embassy, Tokyo, c. 1990.
Architects: Denton Corker Marshall Pty Ltd.
Source: Photograph by John Gollings.

The material choices for the new embassy reflected not only upgraded practical requirements but also deliberate aesthetic choices. Special glass was specified to deflect bullets and laser eavesdropping. For earthquake and fire precaution, the building's construction was heavier than Australian conditions; windows had the Japanese standard 'red triangles' to indicate where escape ladders might go; and escape stairs were broader for emergency egress. But externally and in the main public spaces internally, material choices had a more symbolic role.

DCM looked to the way in which the Japanese were building at the time, and the enjoyment with which they constructed buildings, large and small. While the embassy's overall substructure is reinforced concrete, the exterior of the building is essentially high-precision panellised cladding, a technique that was also being explored by the most progressive Japanese architects of the time such as Fumihiko Maki, Arata Isozaki and Toyō Itō. In this way, DCM's building could be seen alongside the best of contemporary Japanese architecture in terms of construction technique. The chancery was thus framed by two thickened blades clad in stainless steel that ran from front to back. From the front, these blades appear as two tall silver pylons, which support on angled propped platforms two gridded cubes each containing within them a three-dimensional cast aluminium Australian coat of arms—a radical proposition which, remarkably, went through approval unscathed as a proposition. Between the two pylons, each of the chancery windows are shaded and protected by angled metal screens painted with a black micaceous iron oxide and supported off a slender grid metal frame that sits proud of the building face, while at the uppermost level, the windows are shielded by a single giant screen that thrusts forward, like a flaring visor. The screens serve a practical, protective purpose but in their lightness and semitransparency, there seems an echo of the Japanese *shōji* screen but inverted and 'dropped' outside. The overall composition is neither overtly Japanese nor Western but a new contemporary hybrid that seems to echo both cultures, an aesthetic exchange that characterised the equally mysterious exotic symbolism of Frank Lloyd Wright's Imperial Hotel (1923) with its capped piers, perforated eaves and insistent symmetry.

Figure 7.10: Night view of entry. Australian embassy, Tokyo, c. 1990.
Architects: Denton Corker Marshall Pty Ltd.
Source: Photograph by John Gollings.

To either side of the chancery, the cladding of the pavilion-like seven-storey residential blocks is appropriately prosaic. Grey PVF2-coated square-panelled and glazed cubes with angle propped balconies in grey steel, each topped by a receding two-storey grid crown of white panels and glass, and sitting on massive black concrete square columns reinforce the tripartite composition (base, middle and top), which reverberates through the annals of Western architectural history. Between each cube is a glazed stairwell, each with an entry canopy supported by jaunty, differently coloured 'sticks'. The repetitive language of panels, rivets and projecting bolt covers is relentlessly consistent. Again, the linguistic echoes are cross-cultural—is one seeing the tectonic 'bolts' of Otto Wagner's Secessionist work in Vienna or Japanese architect Tadao Ando's trademark concrete formwork holes but realised in reverse: as a rigorous aesthetic system for applying lightweight cladding?

A radical difference between the Tokyo and Beijing embassies was the construction capacity in Japan: it was infinitely superior to China at the time. Everything was made to precision: there was virtually no difference between shop drawings and constructed artefact. The construction was undertaken as a joint venture between the Takenaka Corporation and Hazama Corporation and local architectural support was given by Taro Ashihara (1950–) of Ashihara International & Associates, the son of noted local architect Yoshinobu Ashihara (1918–2003), who had been the architect in association with the Commonwealth Department of Works for the Australian Pavilion at Expo '70 in Osaka and who had worked closely with Robin Boyd on the exhibit's installations there.[36]

Complementing the building was the elegant typography and graphic palette developed by Garry Emery of Emery Vincent. This is evident from the street: on two black concrete squares that symmetrically flank the front gate, the words 'AUSTRALIAN EMBASSY' are matched in line, size and width by Japanese script. The gesture is at once formal and restrained, monumental just as are the shaking of hands and the traditional bow. Elsewhere, signage, often on brushed aluminium 3D easels is asymmetrical and again, understated and discreet. This restraint, so typically Japanese, is part of the overall strategy at the small scale—not to shout 'Australia'

---

36   DCM also had full-time staff based in Tokyo during the construction process—notably Frank Marioli, who had been initially based in Beijing as project architect to supervise construction of the Australian embassy, before moving to Tokyo to take over as DCM's on-site representative. He is now the director of Arkhe Techne Pty Ltd.

but to 'speak' as the Japanese speak, with deference and grace. At the same time, the major commissioned artworks[37] for the embassy—Japanese-Australian sculptor Akio Makigawa's (1948–1999) two garden sculptures, 'The Sun' and 'The Moon', two pieces for the central court, and foyer sculpture, where a perfect polished form seems to be emerging, birth-like, from a rough rock base—all executed in marble and all located on the central axis, suggest an inner, primary, almost visceral energy that lies at the heart of Japanese culture.

International commentary described the building as possessing 'some panache' and Peter Davey, editor of the *Architectural Review*, may have been alluding to DCM's black-clad ambassador's residence, when he stated, in architectural terms in 1991, that 'since Perry's black ships arrived in 1853, the cultural interaction between the West and Japan has always been enriching to both parties. It has never been more so than now'.[38] Indeed DCM's shiny black box ambassador's residence, accessible by a side street to the embassy's east, appears moored to the building's larger form. Like the Portuguese ships that arrived in 1543 and which had their hulls painted with black pitch, giving rise to the term 'black ship' (*kurofune*) to refer to any arriving Western vessel (especially Commodore Matthew Perry's expeditions of 1852–54, with their black smoking steamers), so too here in Tokyo, DCM openly signal Australia's *kurofune*—the ambassador's residence—as necessarily a foreign arrival on Japanese soil.

However, not everyone approved of the design. In October 1991, soon after staff had moved in, there were reports of complaints by embassy people living in the new complex: 'They all decry the misuse of space, lack of storage space, lack of drainage in wet areas, lack of natural light and sound intrusion problems.'[39]

---

37 In addition to the five Makigawa sculptures were two naïve paintings depicting the Melbourne Cup and surf lifesaving at Bondi Beach (artist unknown and since removed) and a silk artwork in the ambassador's dining room (artist unknown). John Denton, interviewed by Philip Goad, Melbourne, 28 August 2018.

38 Peter Davey, 'Into Japan', *Architectural Review* 189, no. 1137 (Nov 1991): 26.

39 'The Australian Embassy, Tokyo. Architect: Denton Corker Marshall Pty Ltd', *Canberra Times*, 23 October 1991, 15. A response to these claims was made in a letter to the editor by Denis Wilson, assistant general manager, OPG, 'Errors of Fact in Article', *Canberra Times*, 25 October 1991, 8. Wilson admitted to 'some teething problems with the Tokyo Embassy but no more than usual with a new building: The soundproofing inadequacies referred to have been addressed'.

Figure 7.11: View of foyer sculpture and, outside, 'The Sun' and 'The Moon', c. 1990. Australian embassy, Tokyo.

Sculptor: Akio Makigawa.

Source: Photograph by John Gollings.

Figure 7.12: View from the garden door of the ambassador's residence, showing garden, mansion fragment, chancery and sculptures (far left). Australian embassy, Tokyo, c. 1990.

Architects: Denton Corker Marshall Pty Ltd.

Source: Photograph by John Gollings.

The lack of linen cupboards and the complex appearing 'factory-like' were just some of the complaints. At the same time, it should be noted, none of the criticisms were directed at the retention of the garden or at the public spaces within the new embassy. As with any new building, teething problems were small but significant issues to some, but the overall impression was positive and nearly 20 years later, the building—virtually unchanged—has proved its resilience.

The success of DCM's designs for Tokyo and Beijing ensured for the firm more design work related to embassies and foreign missions in the Asian region, and not just for the Australian government.[40] These more recent projects, unlike the Tokyo embassy, pursued even greater abstraction and addressed substantially increased security as a defining and, arguably, limiting design determinant. DCM's London office, for example, completed the British embassy in Manila in 2008 as two giant (and mute) grey stone-clad walls surrounded by tall black concrete walls, a sort of contemporary linear 'keep'.[41] A similarly recessive language in form and layout was repeated in DCM's latest embassy design for Jakarta (2010–16): a hybrid of Beijing and Tokyo—a series of again mute box forms for the chancery (but with differentiated material cladding) with the ambassador's residence beside, and beside that again a low-rise complex of diplomatic staff quarters with recreational facilities at the site's perimeter. In both cases, the dialogue with the existing site does not, in this author's opinion, resonate with the contextual empathy of the Tokyo commission. In Jakarta, for example, the whole complex had to be surrounded by the now regular requirement of a three-metre-high impenetrable concrete wall. The architecture of the modern embassy has been, one might argue, from the position of the city and the street, reduced in its ability to 'speak'. With all of these embassies, even those that defer to local context as in Tokyo, there is a consistent, one might argue, lack of nationalistic expression—a sort of appropriate invisibility, a universalism of diplomacy that renders identity appropriately invisible. National pride is put aside. Architecture does not have to 'work': only the flag, almost always the coat of arms, and a program of art that hangs on the walls or adorns the major

---

40   Embassy-related work completed by Denton Corker Marshall since the Australian embassy in Tokyo includes the British embassy refurbishment, Budapest, Hungary, 1994–95; British ambassador's residence, Jakarta, Indonesia, 1996; consulate of the People's Republic of China, Melbourne, Australia, 2000–02; British embassy, Manila, Philippines, 2004–09; and Australian embassy, Jakarta, Indonesia, 2009–16.

41   Richard Vaughan, 'Denton Corker Marshall's Embassy in Manila', *Architect's Journal* 228, no. 9 (11 September 2008): 8–9.

public spaces are doing the work of direct symbolic representation. These are the vicissitudes of architectural diplomacy. In the Australian embassy in Tokyo, there is clear evidence that Australia knows how to play this necessarily repressed game but with a grace, critique and élan, and a direct engagement with the city that may now, with today's heightened and limiting security requirements, be a luxury of the recent past.

8

Working at the Australian Embassy in Tokyo: The Experiences of Locally Engaged Staff

Kate Darian-Smith and David Lowe

The multiple roles played by locally engaged staff (LES) in overseas missions are a field of diplomatic activity that invites deeper and more serious attention from scholars of international history. Beyond some admiring glances at the distinctive knowledge, including language skills, that local staff bring to bear on all aspects of diplomatic work, and the provision by longstanding LES of an institutional memory, there is surprisingly little research that interrogates their role more deeply.[1] Yet, local staff have always been crucial for diplomatic postings, and in the case of Japan their contribution extends back to the occupation period and remains crucial to the everyday operations and diplomatic work of the Australian embassy.

---

1   Some commentary based on the US experience of LES makes a start in this research direction—for example, Shawn Dorman, 'Profiles: Who Works in an Embassy', in *Inside a U.S. Embassy: Diplomacy at Work, All-New Third Edition of the Essential Guide to the Foreign Service*, ed. Shawn Dorman (Lincoln: University of Nebraska Press, 2011), 65, doi.org/10.2307/j.ctt1djmhxq.8; and the US *Foreign Service Journal* has featured views from LES on 'What Local Staff Want You [US diplomats] to Know', *The Foreign Service Journal*, December 2018, www.afsa.org/what-local-staff-want-you-know, accessed 3 June 2020. See also David A. Malone, 'The Modern Diplomatic Mission', in *The Oxford Handbook of Modern Diplomacy*, ed. Andrew F. Cooper, Jorge Heine and Ramesh Thakur (Oxford: Oxford University Press, 2013), 123–24.

The absence of scholarly research on LES is particularly striking in relation to their numerical strength. Over the past decade, LES have composed between two-thirds and three-quarters of the total count of Department of Foreign Affairs and Trade (DFAT) employees in Australia's international posts. These proportions have been even higher when it comes to the workforce of Austrade and Immigration offices overseas.[2] The gender ratios of LES are also of interest: slightly more women than men have been employed in recent years.[3] Since the 1990s, the expansion of the numbers, roles and levels of responsibilities of LES in Australia's embassies around the world has partly been a response to the rising costs of overseas representation: local employees are usually paid less than Australian-based staff (known as A-based), and do not receive the same range of benefits. However, there are also limitations on the work that LES staff may do, and embassies need to strike a balance between their local and Australian workforce in term of efficacy and the expectations of diplomatic representation both abroad and at home. Since 2001 DFAT policy has been to employ all LES on fixed-term contracts, where local labour laws allow this, although these may be extended for multiple terms.[4]

LES are active in a broad spectrum of roles in overseas posts, including household services, such as cleaning and cooking, but also immigration management, accounting, security, trade, cultural activities, education and chauffeuring. It is within this wider context that this chapter considers the experiences of LES employed at the embassy in Tokyo—the vast majority being Japanese nationals, with a small number of Australians living in Japan and employed on local rates—and the important contribution they make to Australia's international presence and diplomatic efforts.

---

2   Figures taken from Joint Standing Committee on Foreign Affairs and Trade, *Australia's Overseas Representation–Punching below Our Weight?*, report (Canberra: Parliament of the Commonwealth of Australia, 29 October 2012), www.aph.gov.au/Parliamentary_Business/Committees/Joint/Completed_Inquiries/jfadt/Overseas_Representation/report, accessed 3 June 2020; Australian Department of Foreign Affairs and Trade (DFAT), 'Department of Foreign Affairs and Trade Annual Report 2017/2018', DFAT at a Glance, Australian Government Transparency Portal, www.transparency.gov.au/annual-reports/department-foreign-affairs-and-trade/2018/dfat-glance/our-staff, accessed 3 June 2020. Except for those employed by Austrade, DFAT is the employer of all LES at overseas posts.

3   DFAT, 'Annual Report 2017/2018', Appendix 1: Locally engaged staff by location and gender, www.transparency.gov.au/annual-reports/department-foreign-affairs-and-trade/2018/appendix-1-staffing-overview/locally, accessed 3 June 2020.

4   Australian National Audit Office, Performance Audit, 'Employment and Management of Locally Engaged Staff', Australian National Audit Office, 5 August 2008, www.anao.gov.au/work/performance-audit/employment-and-management-locally-engaged-staff, accessed 2 December 2021.

In researching the inner life of Australia's embassy in Tokyo, we consulted with Australian staff based now or in the past in Tokyo and stationed at DFAT's Japan desk in Canberra. They were unanimous in acknowledging the crucial role undertaken by their Japanese colleagues. At a basic level, this is not surprising, given that the number of LES is more than double the number of Australian staff at the Tokyo embassy. In 2017, this amounted to the employment of 98 LES and 40 Australian staff.[5] In the Public Diplomacy section, for example, the team was led by an Australian diplomat who was supported by 10 local staff who were focused on cultural projects, including support for the Australia–Japan Foundation, and communications and translation.[6]

But beyond the numerical presence of LES, Australian diplomats at all levels have consistently enthused about the personal, as well as professional, qualities of Japanese colleagues—some of whom they have worked with very closely and across several years and regard with warmth and affection. Australians also recognise that the ongoing employment of LES staff has been crucial, given the fixed terms of ambassadors and other diplomats at the Tokyo embassy, in ensuring continuity in Australian negotiations with Japanese government departments and ministers. LES are often described by the career diplomats they work alongside as 'loyal' and dedicated to the embassy and to Australia's interests in Japan, and 'going the extra mile' in all aspects of their service. Many LES have lived, studied and travelled in Australia and 'have a personal commitment' to the bilateral relationship.[7]

This chapter contributes to one part of an ongoing inquiry by the federal government into the direct and indirect benefits to Australia's foreign relations through the employment of LES in missions abroad. There are several advantages in this practice. As mentioned, one is financial, with LES employment costs lower because they do not require relocation costs and allowances, and their salaries are tied to local, rather than Australian, conditions. Another is local language proficiency, which has been particularly important in earlier decades when fewer Australians in the diplomatic branch were fluent in Japanese. The most significant benefit, however, is the continuity of service by local staff, thus preserving relationships with key Japanese officials, which, amid the careful practices

---

5   DFAT Interviewee B, interviewed by Kate Darian-Smith and David Lowe, 24 January 2017.
6   LES Interviewee X, LES Interviewee Y, LES Interviewee Z, interviewed by David Carter, 22 June 2017.
7   Ibid.

THE AUSTRALIAN EMBASSY IN TOKYO AND AUSTRALIA–JAPAN RELATIONS

of embassy work, can also demonstrate proactivity towards achieving Australian goals. In some areas such as public or cultural diplomacy, the external perspectives of LES staff have proved invaluable in the 'discovery' of features of Australia, bringing sensitive insights as to how these may be encountered by or promoted to a wider Japanese audience.

Some of the experiences of LES in Japan are generic: they will be similar to those of their counterparts working in Australian embassies around the world. There are unique circumstances in Japan, however, requiring LES to play a culturally specific role in the layered form of engagement that is needed in negotiations with the Japanese government and bureaucracy. For instance, a meeting of minds between an Australian diplomat and a Japanese minister or head of a government department does not guarantee action. It is equally important for there to be resulting interactions with middle management in Japan, and for initiatives to be taken through a very structured system of responsibility. This is where LES can excel in advancing Australian interests.[8]

Despite their importance to diplomatic efforts, the voices of LES who have worked at the Australian embassy in Tokyo are generally absent in accounts of the mission (as is the case in posts elsewhere). In the course of our research into the embassy, we have deliberately sought out long-serving LES staff during fieldwork in Japan and conducted, where possible, oral interviews to better understand their experiences. We were interested in how LES assess their job satisfaction and balance of work and life, and how employment in the Australian embassy has been situated within their career more widely. While the majority of Japanese staff who participated in those conversations have chosen to remain anonymous, we have drawn upon their collective perspectives in this brief overview of the embassy as a place where cross-cultural interactions between Australian and Japanese staff are always in play.[9]

---

8   Ibid.
9   In drawing on oral recollections by LES and Australian diplomats in this chapter, we have identified, with their permission, those members who have retired from service, and we have made anonymous those who are still serving members. Some of our comments draw on several individual comments to offer a collective viewpoint.

The Early Years

The earliest perspective by a Japanese employed at the Australian embassy in Tokyo exists in the form of a written memoir by the former head chauffeur, Jiro Takaya, who served for more than 30 years, from 1947 to 1978. Takaya began working for the Australian mission during the occupation period immediately after World War II, and was one of 40 locally engaged Japanese (including 10 drivers and nine room maids) whose wages were paid by the Japanese government. His initial reception was far from friendly; in the aftermath of the war, the Allied occupying troops sometimes displayed thinly veiled hostility towards Japanese people. But Takaya recalled that the Australian soldiers who were part of British Commonwealth Occupation Force (BCOF) were generally more relaxed than the British or Americans in their dealings with the local population. The food shortages during the occupation meant that black market trade between Japanese civilians and members of the BCOF, including Australian soldiers, was an important source of sustenance and therefore a necessary channel of regular communication.[10] Some of Jiro's most poignant memories include his resentment at the indignity of occupation for the Japanese people, especially the imperial dimension of the rule of US general Douglas MacArthur as supreme commander for the Allied powers. At the same time, he was also required to defend Australians who were caught up in violent anti-American protests that occurred at the time.

In addition to mostly generous reflections on the Australian heads of mission and some of the other diplomatic staff that he encountered as a driver, Takaya's long tenure enabled him to mark the growth of the Australian embassy and its evolving role in Japan. By the early 1970s, he recalled, there was a sudden increase of Australian children living at the embassy, reflecting the growth of Australians at the post. At its peak, there were 42 young Australians, ranging from very young children to teenagers at high school. It was Takaya's job to drive these children and teens to and from school every morning and evening, and was one of his more testing roles:

> I was just like a nursery schoolteacher, chiding quarrelling boys and soothing crying children. They were not quiet for more than two minutes. Then I made them sing songs while driving, I myself

---

10 Jiro Takaya, extracts from translated unpublished memoir, 12 April 1978, 1–6.

acting as the leader of the chorus. This method proved good for the lower graders, but higher graders were too much for me. They threw peelings and even spit [spat] at passers-by from windows of the running bus. From time to time, I stopped the bus and bid them to go home on foot. They asked me not to tell their parents on them, crying, but, as soon as they rode the bus again, they invented another mischievous thing. I bothered my brain on how to 'fight' with these 'little monsters' every day.[11]

In this description, as in other sections of his memoir, Takaya touched on the unsurprising cultural slippages that recurred during his decades as an embassy driver. His memories of Australian diplomats were partly organised in accordance with Japanese cultural expectations of personal style and behaviour in everyday interactions, significant elements in effective diplomatic communication. Takaya most admired those Australians based at the embassy who spoke with quiet voices, in contrast to those who were louder and seemed less sensitive to Japanese norms.[12] Takaya's categorisation was subtle but distinct, and perhaps most relevant to the time of his service during the early period of the embassy's work, in the transition from occupation to rebuilding and strengthening bilateral relations. From the late 1950s, both Australia and Japan were rapidly experiencing more overt forms of globalisation in their economies, communications and culture and this was to have an impact in the everyday forms of communication between Australians and LES staff.

Takaya's written reflection is an unusual document, and notable for its warm but frank insights. It does, however, highlight the need for future scholarly attention to the issues of Australia's diplomatic training, as well as to exploring the indirect influence of the individual style of ambassadorial and diplomatic appointments in the detailed diplomatic histories of Australia's foreign policy with Japan and, by extension, elsewhere in the Asia-Pacific. As the following section outlines, one key element in the capacity of Australian diplomatic staff to conduct effective business is tied to their language proficiency and certainly the translation and interpretation services provided by LES have been essential in this regard.

---

11   Ibid., 25.
12   Ibid., 1–26.

Language and Diplomacy

The history of Japanese-language learning in Australia, at both school and tertiary levels, has been a fundamental element of the development of bilateral relations between the two nations, and the deepening of person-to-person and institutional connections from the late twentieth century, as examined in other chapters in this volume.[13] Language proficiency is also important at the official level and in Australia's diplomatic representation in Japan. But how much does linguistic capability matter to the work of Australians serving in the Tokyo post?

At a general level, it is reasonable to assume that language knowledge is closely tied to the effectiveness of representing and pursuing Australian interests, and aids the acquisition of the level of expertise required for the diplomatic negotiation of policy and programs, and for the subtleties needed for clear communication in sensitive situations. This is the view of the former DFAT officer Trevor Wilson. In an unpublished manuscript on this very subject, Wilson argues that Japanese-speaking capacity among Australian diplomats has acted as a modest 'force multiplier', enabling the small but significant expansion of the nation's interests in Japan.[14] However, assessing what might have been gained or lost through Australia's very limited number of fully trained Japanese linguists appointed to the embassy in Tokyo prior to 1970s is a difficult task. While the advocates of greater linguistic skills as a component of training for foreign service can point to the likelihood of enhanced diplomatic finesse and nuance, it is hard to clearly determine the negative consequences for the bilateral relationship resulting from lower levels of Japanese-speaking Australians in senior diplomatic positions.

By the late 1960s the Department of External Affairs had in place policies for Japanese-language training prior to a posting in Tokyo, and this was to result in an expansion of linguistic capacity within a decade. At a symposium on Australia–Japan relations in Canberra held in 1974, the recently returned diplomat Colin Willis reported that eight of the current Australian staff in Tokyo could communicate effectively in Japanese; and

---

13   See Kate Darian-Smith, 'Australian–Japanese Cultural Connections', and David Carter, '"Scholars—Future Interpreters of Australia": Education, Cultural Diplomacy and Australian Studies in Japan', in this volume.

14   Trevor Wilson, 'The Impact of Australia's Japanese-Speaking Diplomats on Australia–Japan Relations', unpublished manuscript, 2017, 32.

three years later another study suggested that 31 officers had reached what was described as a 'good to high' rating in Japanese proficiency.[15] During the 1970s, Australia's Department of Foreign Affairs had an agreement to use the facilities of the US State Department's Foreign Service Institute Language School based in Yokohama. This allowed for up to four full-time Australians posted to Japan to undertake courses there, and it also became possible for their spouses to enrol in the short courses that were offered. However, it would be a mistake to equate the linguistic *progress* that was achieved through this training with a sharp increase in the levels of Japanese *proficiency* among Australians at the embassy. From the 1980s, the professionalisation of interpretation services in Tokyo, utilised by both the Japanese and Australian governments, was an important factor in reducing the potential for mistranslations and increasing confidence in the clear communications underpinning diplomatic exchanges.[16] This development, and its success, made Japanese proficiency for Australian representatives in Japan less urgent, and less of a priority in diplomatic training.

With these circumstances in mind, it is likely that locally engaged Japanese speakers were extremely helpful for Australian negotiations at sensitive junctures in the relationship. These included such moments as the amalgamation of the Australian Departments of Trade and Foreign Affairs in 1987, when Japanese governments revised their thinking on the role of their Self-Defense Forces, and when security, defence cooperation and coordination became important features of the relationship from the 1990s onwards. One locally engaged officer interviewed for this chapter commented that Japanese fluency does make a significant difference at the individual level, and singled out Ambassadors Ashton Calvert (1993–98) and Bruce Miller (2011–17) for their respective linguistic capabilities in Japanese. Indeed, Calvert is acknowledged more widely within Japanese political and diplomatic circles as being the first Australian ambassador appointed to Japan to possess high-level language skills.[17] The local staff member reflected further on the question of Japanese-language proficiency from the perspective of Japanese government negotiators:

---

15   Ibid., 6–7.
16   Ibid., 9–10.
17   Calvert's language skills were also commented upon by former Japanese ambassadors to Australia, Yoshio Okawara (1976–80), Masaji Takahashi (1998–2001) and Hideaki Ueda (2005–07) in discussion with the authors, 24 January 2017.

> If Australian ambassadors and diplomat staff can speak in Japanese then they [Japanese negotiators] speak very frankly, but if they think that the interpreter is going to interpret what they are going to say then what they say may be different.[18]

The golden era of maximum linguistic capacity among Australia-based members of the Australian embassy in Tokyo, according to one longstanding DFAT official, was during the 1990s and early 2000s. This was the product of the high priority attached to the Australia–Japan relationship during the 1980s and 1990s.[19] It coincided with the series of language policy and program initiatives launched in Australia from the mid-1980s to the mid-1990s which gave impetus to Japanese-language learning in Australian schools and universities, and an associated growth in Australians undertaking exchange programs in Japan.[20] The overall impact of such focused educational endeavours can be seen in the improved Japanese-language capacities, and cultural knowledge of Japan, possessed by many younger Australians recruited by DFAT from the 1980s onwards.

The uplift in Japanese-language proficiency among Australians in the late twentieth century coincided with the expansion of bilateral trade, and the subsequent growth of the expatriate Australian community in Japan, notably those working in the commercial sector for Australian and multinational companies. Much diplomatic work is devoted to expanding Australia's economic interests and influence, including in the mining and primary sector, but also in education and tourism. The success of the Australia Japan Business Co-operation Council, founded in 1964, and in more recent decades the multifarious activities of the Japan–Australia Diet members league, have been partly derived from the efforts of successive Japanese-speaking Australian diplomats who have been supported by LES. The league comprises Japanese politicians interested in Australia and has become a focal point for such activities as briefings, meetings and breakfasts with visiting Australian politicians.[21]

Furthermore, while it is impossible to evaluate precisely, the Japanese speakers—both Australian-based and locally employed—working in the realm of public diplomacy, including those in the public and cultural sections of the embassy and those connected to the Australia–Japan

---

18   LES Interviewee A, interviewed by Kate Darian-Smith and David Lowe, 23 January 2017.
19   DFAT Interviewee C, interviewed by David Lowe, 13 January 2017.
20   See Darian-Smith, 'Australian–Japanese Cultural Connections', this volume.
21   Wilson, 'The Impact of Australia's Japanese-Speaking Diplomats', 20.

Foundation (AJF), have enhanced the promotion of Australia and its relationship with Japan. As Trevor Wilson writes, 'It was also no accident that a series of excellent Japanese-speaking Australian staff were appointed to head the Australia–Japan Foundation office in the embassy after 1995'.[22] In 2011–16, Leonie Boxtel lived and worked at the Australian embassy with her young family while serving as director of the AJF, an appointment that utilised her high-level fluency in Japanese, gained through university study in Australia and Japan. Boxtel reflected that her Japanese-language skills gave her a distinct advantage in progressing the AJF's work in building Australia's brand, especially within the arts community and educational institutions and networks across Japan.[23]

Working at the Embassy

The Australian embassy building, designed by leading Australian architectural firm Denton Corker Marshall, is far more than a workplace. It is a modern compound that incorporates the public-facing offices and workspaces of the embassy with the ambassadorial residence and gardens, and apartments and other facilities for Australian staff.[24] The unification of work and home spaces encourages a sense of cooperation and esprit de corps. Social events and other collective activities, as well as programs to involve the spouses of DFAT representatives and embassy children, provide opportunities for informal networks around shared interests that transcend work-related boundaries. As one former Australian-based resident explained, 'Living in the compound was a great way to connect across the embassy'.[25] The proximity of work and home has also been a boon for the maintenance of a productive work-life balance, especially so for those Australian women working at the embassy who have caring duties for infants and small children. In addition to the embassy building's public spaces and reception areas, and the more formal meetings and entertainments held at the ambassador's residence and in the gardens, the well-appointed and relatively large residential apartments provide a welcoming space for embassy staff to offer hospitality to Japanese colleagues, thus blending work and home in diplomatic activities.

---

22 Ibid., 30.
23 Leonie Boxtel, interviewed by Kate Darian-Smith, 24 March 2017.
24 Alison Broinowski and Rachel Miller, 'Creation, Destruction and Re-creation: The Australian Embassy in Tokyo', and Philip Goad, 'Building Diplomacy: The Architecture of the Australian Embassy, Tokyo', in this volume.
25 Leonie Boxtel, interviewed by Kate Darian-Smith, 24 March 2017.

While LES service, facilitate and participate in both the formal and informal entertaining at the Australian embassy, and may be involved in social activities, they have a very different experience from Australian staff of the embassy compound. Local employees cannot live within the embassy apartments, and the majority commute a considerable distance from their homes every day, with travel time sometimes taking over one hour each way. Their spatial experience of the embassy overall is also restricted. LES are subject to security restrictions on their movements and barred from entering the upper floor where the ambassadorial offices are located. More broadly, external access to the building has also changed over the past 20 years. Following the terrorist attacks against the United States on 11 September 2001, security was increased at all of Australia's overseas postings. At the Australian embassy in Tokyo this meant the installation of a front fence, a screening station and clearance for all visitors, creating a small but nonetheless real and symbolic barrier between the embassy and the wider Japanese community.[26]

From the perspective of the LES staff interviewed for this study, the embassy operates as a workplace that is Australian in its regulations and character—though infused with some small and nuanced Japanese influences in the daily activity of how business and engagement are conducted. This is evident in several ways, many mundane but nonetheless significant. One example involves the observance of national public holidays. For more than 30 years, the embassy has taken a balanced approach, splitting the public holidays that are taken between those that are officially designated in Australia and Japan. However, such compromises are not always satisfactory, particularly as in this Japan has several more public holidays than Australia. Some local employees bemoaned missing out on a portion of the Japanese public holidays during Golden Week, and the toll that this took on family life. At the same time, our interviews revealed that LES appreciated many Australian attitudes and regulations towards such issues as gender equity within appointment structures and working conditions, and saw the embassy as a progressive working environment, in contrast to a typical Japanese government or commercial setting.

---

26 The increased security was to have a negative impact on the AJF Library, then the Australian Resource Centre, that was located within the Australian embassy until it was relocated in 2007; Yasue Arimitsu, interviewed by Kate Darian-Smith and David Lowe, 27 January 2017.

Local Japanese staff also spoke of their ability to both support and influence Australia's diplomacy in Japan and were proud of their contribution to what they saw as a collaborative effort with Australian diplomats. The interviews revealed a detailed understanding of the relative expertise and strengths of both local and Australian-based staff. To give an indicative example, one LES at the embassy commented that Australian staff possessed the background knowledge and understood the policy context in far greater detail. As a complement, local staff 'know the local market or we know Japan better than them so in that way we can collaborate and bring out results better', aiding Australian diplomats in making informed and advantageous decisions.[27] Other LES are proud of their 'insider' proactivity, and capacity to finesse the broad directive issued by DFAT, and as one commented:

> I think I have to be able to suggest what we can, what would be the best in Japan to commence some projects to the counsellor in my section, in our section. So, it's not just always accepting, accepting … I think we'd have to sometimes be proactive and say, 'No, this isn't, this wouldn't work here'. But it might be difficult to do that, but it's not against it, it's to help collaborate.[28]

There are, we were told, times where the insight of local staff is crucial, including in determining cost efficiencies relating to certain policy or project initiatives. If something is likely to fall flat, then it is better that Australian-based officers know sooner rather than later. LES are well placed to feed the views of Japanese opinion-shapers into embassy deliberations and to pick up quickly on the nuances of government-to-government and people-to-people communications. As one interviewee put it, 'in the end, of course the diplomats will be the decision makers' but LES can advise those in Canberra in the negotiations and process: 'because if you try to force what Australia thinks is best, which might not work at all in Japan, it's a waste of resource'.[29]

---

27   LES Interviewee X, LES Interviewee Y, LES Interviewee Z interviewed by David Carter, 22 June 2017.
28   Ibid.
29   Ibid.

Locally Engaged Women and Their Careers at the Embassy

Australia's missions abroad have, over time, provided Japanese employees with some distinctive opportunities to gain deep expertise in aspects of Australia's economy and culture, and to develop a career pathway that perhaps would not be possible within the Japanese bureaucracy. This alternative track has been particularly advantageous for some of the Japanese women employed at the Australian embassy, perhaps most especially in earlier decades. This point is illustrated by the career of Tomoko Nakamura, senior research officer in agriculture, who in an oral interview on the eve of her retirement in 2017 reflected on her 34 years of continual employment with the Australian government in Tokyo. Over this time, she had seen changes in the technology that shaped work practices, and she recalled the noise of the telex machine and typewriters in the 1980s and the excitement generated by the arrival of the embassy's first fax machine. Nakamura has also witnessed across her career significant shifts in attitudes towards gender and work, and how an increasing number of women, both Australian and Japanese, have been employed at the embassy and taken on senior roles.

In 1983, Nakamura commenced as an interpreter and translator for the minister, commercial, in what was then a separate trade office in the Sankaido Building in Akasaka, around two and a half kilometres from the chancery in Azabu-Juban.[30] This appointment was a landmark, situating Nakamura as the first locally engaged woman to hold a position within the Australian government that was not secretarial. With the relocation of Australia's trade and commerce activities to the new Australian embassy building after its completion in 1990, Nakamura assumed a new role as chief interpreter and translator under Ambassador Ashton Calvert. This was, she recalled, both stimulating and exhausting. The day often began with breakfast events, and translating commitments could run throughout the evening, with this work sandwiched by the one-and-a-half-hour commute each way to and from her home. Nakamura recalled that the scope of the work also involved extra hours of personal study 'because I had to cover everything. Agriculture, sports, education, defence, politics, economy, trade, everything'.

---

30   Tomoko Nakamura, interviewed by Kate Darian-Smith and David Lowe, 23 January 2017. Trade and Customs staff moved from the Mita site to more space in the Sankaido Building in 1968.

Tomoko's career at the Australian embassy can be interpreted in pioneering terms, and perhaps also a form of conditional liberation. As a woman employee, she broke the existing pattern in being appointed a more senior position than secretarial work. Translating and interpreting was viewed as both prestigious and highly skilled, and a position with the embassy offered some employment and financial stability as opposed to work with many different clients through an agency. The Australian embassy enjoyed a high standing for its translation support among other major diplomatic posts in Tokyo, such as the United States and France where translating and interpreting staff were also required.[31] In addition, Nakamura found that her role required some interesting travel throughout Japan, and she was also sponsored by the embassy to attend a professional development conference at the University of Queensland, thus giving her firsthand insight into the nation she was working for.

In the late 1990s, Nakamura transferred to the agriculture section of the Australian embassy as a research officer. She took pride in being a source of continuity with members of the Japanese Department of Agriculture, enabling smooth introductions for successive Australian diplomats arriving and working in Tokyo for fixed terms. From her perspective, negotiations between Australia and Japan on agriculture were generally hard fought, and it was the long game that was needed. Like many other LES, Tomoko bore the brunt of overly tight meeting scheduling, learning to adjust itineraries that omitted toilet breaks—or, in case of a visit by Resources Minister Peter Cook, to suddenly request such a break herself, in order to secure relief for her charge.[32]

While an exceptional case study rather than representative of many, Nakamura's experiences help chart the evolution of the crucial role played by LES in the work of the Australian embassy in Tokyo across time. In terms of numbers and in providing the skills and political and cultural capacity to undertake a broad range of both basic and more complex tasks, LES have always been important. As the Australian embassy has grown, so too have the numbers of LES staff, and as the embassy has relied even more on their skills, local employees have quickly stretched into new roles to fulfil new roles and expectations.

---

31   DFAT Interviewee H, interviewed by David Lowe, 11 January 2017.
32   Ibid.

Conclusion

In ways often invisible to the public eye, the Australian embassy has been indebted to the skills and hard work of local employees who labour as translators, administrators, liaison officers with government and industry, cultural and policy advisers, and, more mundanely, drivers, cleaners and caterers. For both incoming Australian diplomats and researchers, it is LES—especially those who are long-serving—who are important holders of the embassy's corporate memory and long-term relations within the Japanese bureaucracy. Their linguistic skills have been another constant asset through the variable levels of Japanese-language capacity among Australian diplomatic staff. Similarly, on matters of tone, register and timing and the cross-cultural dimensions of communication underpinning official meetings and exchanges the presence and guidance of LES staff have been a constant strength.

Reading between the lines of recollections such as those by Tomoko Nakamura and others, there have been significant employment benefits for LES members working at the Australian embassy, especially for women, but they have also often come with necessary compromises. LES members are constantly negotiating their relationship with the amorphous and vital bundle of values and policies making up 'Australia's national interest'. It is clear that many locally engaged Japanese staff have demonstrated high levels of commitment to Australian policy goals while, at the same time, adjusting to security provisions circumscribing their activities and their movements within the embassy building.

The interviews with LES members and with Australian diplomats revealed strong levels of mutual respect and appreciation between both groups, and in some instances these relationships moved beyond those of work colleagues to personal friendships. Interpreting and advocating for Australian interests and policy goals to the different segments of Japanese society and to policymaking groups requires unrelenting efforts, in which local staff often carry a big workload. As several LES interviewees were keen to emphasise, for diplomatic work to be pursued successfully in Japan on big issues such as trade and investment, there was a need to engage not merely with government ministers and departmental heads, but also with other members of the relevant departments and with key industry groups. In making progress with Japanese counterparts, or registering where progress is unlikely to be made, LES members have been fundamental to the day-to-day work of the embassy in furthering Australia–Japan relations.

Exchanges: Culture, Education, Politics

9

Australian–Japanese Cultural Connections

Kate Darian-Smith

In the 1950s, most Australians knew little of Japan and its people beyond recent wartime experiences and stock stereotypes, and this was mirrored by the very limited knowledge of most Japanese about the society and environments of modern Australia. As bilateral trade flourished as a result of economic growth in both nations, and the enmity that had existed during World War II quickly receded into the past, the relationship that developed between Australia and Japan over the next 70 years was distinctive and multilayered. Government-to-government relations frame what is now a myriad of institutional, community and personal connections between Australia and Japan—and indeed Australians and Japanese people—that span interests and generations.

This special and highly significant relationship between Australia and Japan is both established and evolving, and has been facilitated by the extraordinary revolution in communications and technologies across recent decades. The increased mobilities afforded by the development of mass tourism, and the expansion of higher education in both countries with an emphasis on international connections in both research and student experience, have contributed to the growth of personal links across the two nations. Accompanying these developments has been the deepened knowledge in both Australia and Japan about each nation's respective histories, populations and economic opportunities. Staff at the Australian embassy have continuously contributed to Australia–Japan relations by supporting Australians travelling, studying and conducting business in Japan, as well as Japanese people and corporations interested in Australia as a destination for tourism, education, trade and investment.

Although cultural and economic exchanges between the two countries can be traced to the nineteenth century, since the immediate post–World War II decades a new and quite remarkable Australian relationship with Japan has flourished.[1] This has been underpinned by an enthusiasm for Japanese popular culture, sometimes in unexpected ways. In the early 1960s, for instance, the Japanese television series *The Samurai* was hugely popular in Australia, with its leading star Ose Koichi selling out live shows in Sydney and Melbourne (and attracting larger crowds of young Australians than a tour by the Beatles).[2] By the 1980s, Japan was widely recognised for its technological expertise, and Japanese culture was embraced in Australia by the end of the century. Japanese food, particularly sushi, is now ubiquitous in Australia. Japan's regional cuisine has been widely promoted through the media, including celebrity chef Adam Liaw's *Destination Flavour: Japan* tour for television. Japanese animation, manga and electronic games continue to be consumed in Australia across generations.

Correspondingly, the last four decades have seen expanding knowledge within Japan about Australia, and its social and technological innovation. This built on limited foundations. To give one example, Sachiko Tamai recalled that when she was appointed to the position of senior cultural officer at the Australian embassy in Tokyo in 1986, many of her Japanese friends were puzzled, asking her what might constitute Australian culture beyond an interest in sports.[3] The development of government agencies and organisations in both countries that have focused on soft power relations and cultural exchanges have contributed, in subsequent decades, to a

---

1   Paul Jones and Vera Mackie, eds, *Relationships: Australia and Japan: 1880s to 1950*, University of Melbourne History Monograph 28 (Melbourne: University of Melbourne, 2001); Masayo Tada and Leigh Dale, eds, *On the Western Edge: A Colloquium on Comparisons of Australia and Japan* (Perth: Network Books, 2007); David Walker, *Anxious Nation: Australia and the Rise of Asia 1850–1939* (St Lucia: University of Queensland Press, 1999); David Walker, *Stranded Nation: White Australia in an Asian Region* (Crawley: University of Western Australia Publishing, 2019).
2   Kate Darian-Smith, 'Expanding Horizons: Australian Television and Globalisation in the 1950s–1970s', in Contemporary Australian Studies: Literature, History, Film and Media Studies in a Globalizing Age, ed. Yasue Arimitsu and Yugi Suzuki (Tokyo: Otowa-Shobo Tsurumi-Shoten Publishing, 2016), 111–12.
3   Sachiko Tamai, ed., *Reflections: Australian Artists Living in Tokyo* (Bloomington, Indiana: Balboa Press, 2019), 1.

discernible shift and increased reciprocal cultural understanding between Australian and Japan. During the 2000s, social media and promotions of lifestyle, travel, sports and the environment have been influential in both countries in deepening such respective knowledges well beyond simplistic images of people and places.

This chapter explores the educational, cultural and sporting connections between Australia and Japan from the mid-twentieth century to the present, and the significant role that the Australian embassy in Tokyo has played in initiating and supporting these programs and activities. It commences with an overview of the importance of language teaching and the education sector to the Australian–Japanese relationship, and then explores how people-to-people links between the two countries increased and strengthened from the 1980s through the expansion of mass tourism in both directions. It examines the place of the creative arts in forging bilateral understanding, with a focus on the success of the visual arts and residential exchanges. It concludes with an exploration of the increasing importance of sports as a dimension of the bilateral relationship and diplomatic effort.

Connecting through Education and Language

Language is a key channel in the development of cross-cultural connections, and there is a deep history of language instruction in Japanese in the Australian higher education and school sectors. Japanese was first taught at the university level in 1917 by the University of Sydney on behalf of the Commonwealth Department of Defence.[4] James Murdoch, an international expert on Japan, regularly travelled from Sydney to conduct classes for army cadets at the newly established Royal Military Academy at Duntroon in Canberra. In 1919 Murdoch was appointed as chair of Oriental studies at the University of Sydney, and began visiting Japan annually, providing a briefing to Australian authorities on his return about

---

4   Jennifer Baldwin, 'From Ancient to Modern: The Place and Importance for Languages Other Than English in Australia's National Interest' (PhD thesis, University of Melbourne, 2015), 17, 52; Jennifer Baldwin, 'World War I and the Development of Language Study at Australian Universities', in *The First World War, the Universities and the Professions in Australia 1914–1939*, ed. Kate Darian-Smith and James Waghorne (Melbourne: Melbourne University Press, 2019), 261–68.

Japanese public opinion and defence policy.[5] The teaching of Japanese language moved quickly to the secondary sector in New South Wales, initially with 50 boys enrolled at Sydney High School and North Sydney High School. This instruction was, as Murdoch explained, 'aimed entirely at the encouragement of commercial relations' with Japan and a small but active community of Japanese business interests concentrated in Sydney.[6]

The University of Melbourne introduced Japanese-language classes in 1919, and by 1935 instruction was offered at the progressive Mac.Robertson Girls' High School.[7] As Japanese-language teaching expanded in the interwar decades, the Japanese government offered some support, for example donating five sets of textbooks to Perth Technical School in 1934.[8] Interest in Japanese language remained strong; in 1937 the Queensland government introduced Japanese-language classes at the university and selected high schools.[9] The ABC also broadcast a popular program on Japanese history and language between 1935 and December 1941.[10] With the outbreak of the Pacific War, Japanese-language proficiency was of importance for Australian defence and security, with instruction offered to military personnel.

In the post–World War II years, as Australia's trade with Japan was rebuilt, this was accompanied by a revitalisation of Japanese-language teaching. From the 1960s, Japanese language was introduced at Australian universities, with the enrolments exceeding all other Asian and European language classes by 1990.[11] This growth at tertiary institutions was accompanied by new university subjects examining Japanese history and politics, in part spurred by Australia's involvement in regional security and trade in the Asia-Pacific and reflecting interest from younger Australians

---

5   Jennifer Joan Baldwin, *Languages Other Than English in Australian Higher Education: Policies, Provision and the National Interest* (Switzerland: Springer Nature, 2019), doi.org/10.1007/978-3-030-05795-4, 40, 107–8.
6   'The Japanese Language: Why NSW Is Teaching It', *Age*, 30 March 1918, 15; Jean Robertson, 'Japanese Language: The Commercial Aspect', *Argus*, 27 July 1918, 5; 'Japanese Language in Schools', *Daily Telegraph*, 4 September 1922, 8.
7   Senkichi Inagaki pioneered Japanese language at the University of Melbourne until he was interned in December 1941: Baldwin, *Languages Other Than English*, 40–41, 108–9; 'School Speech Nights: Mac.Robertson Girls' High School', *Age*, 11 December 1935, 8; 'Leaving Passes in Japanese Language', *Sun*, 4 February 1940, 1.
8   'Teaching Japanese: Gift to Technical School', *West Australian*, 31 July 1934, 17.
9   'Japanese Glad at Decision to Teach Language', *Telegraph*, 5 February 1937, 12; 'Teaching Students Japanese', *Labor Daily*, 5 February 1937, 12; 'The Japanese Language', *Daily Mercury*, 8 July 1939, 6.
10   Baldwin, *Languages Other Than English*, 109.
11   Ibid., 112–15.

about their place in Asia. In 1951, the intergovernmental Colombo Plan had been launched, and its support to developing Asian nations led to 20,000 sponsored students by 1985 undertaking education and training in Australia. The presence of international students from Asia was important in raising Australian awareness of Asian cultures and peoples.[12]

Amid Australia's booming economic relationship with Japan, government and public commentary during the 1960s and 1970s indicated anxieties about the limited proficiency in Japanese language and culture. Few business leaders or government officials were able to speak Japanese, and this led to cultural and commercial misunderstandings.[13] Over the next decade concerted efforts were made to improve mutual understanding. A cultural agreement was concluded between Australia and Japan in 1974; the Australia–Japan Foundation established in 1976; and the Working Holiday Program signed in 1980, enabling young Australians and Japanese to have a long-term stay in each other's country. In Japan, an Australian studies course was established at Tokyo University, and greater bilateral academic links encouraged.[14] In Australia, the most significant program in deepening appreciation of Japan was the rapid increase in the teaching of Japanese language at primary and secondary schools.[15] In 1981, a visiting American scholar noted a marked increase in Japanese-language teaching in Australia since he last visited in 1971. 'Australia is the only foreign country that makes a systematic effort to teach Japanese in high school and is to be praised for this', leading scholar Professor Donald Keene of Columbia University observed.[16] By this time, too, the first wave of Australian high school students were taking final year matriculation examinations in Japanese, and were eligible for advanced university instruction. At tertiary institutions, Japanese departments were also growing in number, and attracting increasing enrolments.

12   See Kate Darian-Smith and James Waghorne, 'Australian-Asian Sociability, Student Activism, and the University Challenge to White Australia in the 1950s', in *Australian Journal of Politics and History* 63, no. 2 (2016): 203–18, doi.org/10.1111/ajph.12245.

13   'Little Teaching about Asia in Schools', *Canberra Times*, 13 May 1972, 9; 'Language Difficulties: "Risks" in Dealing with Japanese', *Canberra Times*, 24 May 1972, 3.

14   'Australia–Japan Relations', *Australian Foreign Affairs Record* 51, no. 4 (April 1980): 98; 'Japan–Australia Relations (Basic Data)', Ministry of Foreign Affairs of Japan, www.mofa.go.jp/region/asia-paci/australia/data.html, accessed 7 May 2022.

15   'Australia–Japan Relations', *Australian Foreign Affairs Record* 51, no. 4 (April 1980): 98.

16   John Bryant, 'Teaching of Japanese Praised', *Canberra Times*, 11 December 1981, 9.

One feature of many university Japanese-language programs was the opportunity for students to visit Japan to study, or sometimes complete an internship, thus embedding young Australians in Japanese society.[17]

From the late twentieth century, the teaching of Japanese language within the Australian school system expanded considerably due to the economic importance of Japan, and opportunities for exchange and tourism between the two nations. A plethora of national and state language and curriculum policies framed this development. In 1982, the Fraser government commissioned a Senate inquiry to respond to community pressure for a national language policy. Reporting to the Hawke government in 1984, the inquiry recommended a comprehensive approach to national language planning that would address all of Australia's language and literacy needs. As Joseph Lo Bianco has noted, 'the ethos was one of collaboration by engaging all jurisdictions, as well as community level, non-government structures and agencies'.[18] The National Policy on Languages was endorsed with bipartisan support in 1987, identifying Japanese as a language of geopolitical significance.[19]

In 1992, the Keating government introduced a new Australian Language and Literacy Policy which shifted the funding balance towards English literacy and away from foreign languages.[20] The Asia Education Foundation was established the following year, with A$3.5 million in funding to promote studies of Asia in schools. In 1994, a report on Asian Languages and Australia's Economic Future resulted in the National Asian Languages and Studies in Australian Schools (NALSAS) program. This aimed to strengthen Australia's engagement with Asia by educating and enthusing a new generation of Australians about their region. A priority of 'Asian literacy' was language proficiency in Japanese, Bahasa Indonesia, Korean and Mandarin.[21] Despite the allocation of A$220 million to the program

---

17 Leonie Boxtel, interviewed by Kate Darian-Smith, 24 March 2017.
18 Joseph Lo Bianco, 'Asian Languages in Australian Schools: Policy Options', Melbourne Asia Policy Papers 7, May 2005.
19 R.J. Hawke, Speech delivered to the Asian Studies Bicentennial Conference, 11 February 1988, pmtranscripts.pmc.gov.au/sites/default/files/original/00007287.pdf, accessed 12 December 2019; Marilyn Harrington, 'Australia in the Asian Century: Asian Studies in Schools', Parliament of Australia, 2012, www.aph.gov.au/About_Parliament/Parliamentary_Departments/Parliamentary_Library/FlagPost/2012/November/Australia_in_the_Asian_Century_Asian_studies_in_schools, accessed 30 April 2021.
20 Lo Bianco, 'Asian Languages in Australian Schools'.
21 Juliet Pietsch and Haydn Aarons, 'Australian Engagement with Asia: Towards Closer Political, Economic and Cultural Ties', in *Australia: Identity, Fear and Governance in the 21st Century*, ed. Juliet Pietsch and Haydn Aarons (Canberra: ANU Press, 2012), doi.org/10.22459/AIFG.11.2012.03, 34.

and the privileging of Asian languages, the NALSAS learning outcomes fell below targets, and it ended in 2007.[22] A new impetus and funding was given to the study of Asian languages under the Rudd government, and the introduction of a national curriculum in schools has included languages as a key study area.

In the twenty-first century, and despite ongoing challenges, Japanese has remained the most studied foreign language in Australian schools and universities. The numbers peaked in the early 2000s, when about 426,000 students—representing about 10 per cent of all Australian school students—were studying Japanese language. At that time, Australia had the second-largest group of Japanese-language learners in the world, surpassed only by Korea.[23] Queensland and Victoria have the highest numbers of Japanese-language learners at school, partly accounted for by the deep teaching strengths that have been established. Over the last two decades, Australian universities have seen stability or even a small increase, especially at the beginner level, in enrolments in Japanese language and culture subjects. This can be explained by enrolments from international students at Australian campuses, but also by the enthusiasm among younger Australians for Japanese popular culture and a recognition of the importance of skills in cross-cultural communication in the global economy.

People-to-People Links: Exchange Programs and Tourism

One of the strengths of the Australian–Japanese relationship over the past 60 years has been the meaningful people-to-people relationships that have developed through programs of student exchange and the growth in tourism both ways. Indeed, in-country exchange programs for, respectively, Japanese and English language learners at all levels—and

---

22   Kevin Rudd, *Asian Languages and Australia's Economic Future* (Brisbane: Queensland Government Printer, Brisbane, 1994); Rebecca Cairns, 'Constructing Asia Literacy as a Policy Problem', *Australian Policy and History*, 13 November 2017, aph.org.au/2017/11/constructing-asia-literacy-as-a-policy-problem/, accessed 30 April 2021; Deborah Henderson, 'Politics and Policy-Making for Asia Literacy: The Rudd Report and a National Strategy in Australian Education', *Asian Studies Review* 32, no. 2 (2008): 171–95, doi.org/10.1080/10357820802064690.
23   Robyn Spence-Brown, 'Japanese Language Education in Australia Today: An Overview', 2, nsjle.org.au/nsjle/media/2014-NSJLE-04-ROBYN-SPENCE-BROWN.pdf, accessed 30 April 2021; Anne de Kretser and Robyn Spence-Brown, 'The Current State of Japanese Language Education in Australian Schools', The Tokyo Foundation for Policy Research, 15 December 2010, www.tkfd.or.jp/en/research/detail.php?id=174, accessed 30 April 2021.

including homestays with family groups—have increased dramatically in recent decades. Most of these exchanges are organised by Australian and Japanese secondary schools, universities, government bodies and by private organisations such as Rotary International.[24]

There is a long history of Australians travelling to Japan for language training. In the 1930s, at least two students from the University of Melbourne did so, funded as Mollison Scholars in Japanese.[25] After World War II, student exchange was increasingly recognised as contributing to cultural exchange and, for Western nations, was seen as an avenue for promoting democratic ideals and combatting communism in the political context of the Cold War. In 1952, the Japanese Education Ministry announced that, in return for outgoing exchange invitations from the United States and other nations, it would establish an incoming scholarship scheme 'to help young people of foreign countries to understand Japan'.[26]

In the 1960s, student exchange between Australia and Japan increased substantially, coinciding with deepening trade ties and also the growth in Australia of Japanese-language teaching.

Organisations such as Rotary International were instrumental to this development, sending Australian students to Japan and bringing Japanese students to Australia.[27] Rotary, originating in the United States in 1905 to promote professional interchange, had pre–World War II links with Japan and Australia. Embracing the ideals of the United Nations and world peace, from the 1950s Rotary was very active in promoting and funding student exchange between the two nations, particularly for senior secondary school students.

The Australian–Overseas Student Travel (AOST) Scheme funded Australian students to study Japan for the first time in 1963, and in 1965 funded Japanese students to Australia, arranging billets with Australian

---

24   Mayumi Parry, 'Lessons from Japanese Family Homestays', *New Voices in Japanese Studies* 1 (Dec 2006): 62–74, doi.org/10.21159/nv.01.07.

25   'Melbourne Student in Japan: Mr P.V. Russo's Successes', *Herald*, 25 May 1934, 19; 'W. T. Mollison Scholarship in Modern Languages', University of Melbourne, scholarships.unimelb.edu.au/awards/w-t-mollison-scholarship-in-modern-languages, accessed 30 April 2021; 'Friendship with Japan: Advice of Australian Student', *Recorder*, 24 November 1937, 1. For the Mollison scholarships, see www.unimelb.edu.au/__data/assets/pdf_file/0006/2824683/UTR-6.9-Amendment-W.-T.-Mollison-Scholarship-Certified-12-July-2018.pdf, accessed 7 May 2022.

26   'Japan Plans Foreign Student Scholarships', *Newcastle Sun*, 7 October 1952, 4.

27   'Student Arrives', *Biz*, 28 February 1962, 1; 'Rotary Student Tells of Modern Japan', *Nepean Times*, 7 June 1962, 7; 'Exchange Student', *Biz*, 31 July 1963, 41; 'Student Off to Japan', *Canberra Times*, 27 January 1980, 17.

households.[28] Other avenues available to Australian students who wanted to visit Japan included the National Union of Australian Students, which organised homestays for tertiary students in Japan; essay-writing competitions, which sent successful students to Japan; and the Australia–Japan Business Committee school-student exchange scheme. Among those young Australians was a future ambassador to Japan, Bruce Miller.[29]

Student exchange has typically involved linguistic and cultural immersion. Homestays, it was explained by the press to the Australian public in the 1980s, could 'promote mutual understanding between the ordinary citizens' of the two countries, which would then lead to improved trade relations.[30] This understanding included exposure to such Japanese customs as communal bathing, which could be very confronting, as Rosalind Dickson of Victor Harbor, South Australia, explained to her local newspaper when she returned from a 12-day tour of Japan as 'an ambassador of youth' for Australia.[31]

The year-long student exchanges sponsored by Rotary Clubs throughout Australia were particularly transformative for many young Australians, including those from rural communities. In 2020, when Melanie Brock received a Commendation from the Japanese foreign minister in recognition of her contribution to Japanese–Australian connections in business and culture, she recalled:

> I am ever so grateful to the blokes on the Albany [WA] Rotary youth exchange panel way back in the early 80s for sending me to Japan. It is now my home and my passion … People-to-people linkages underpin all areas of engagement, so we need to get more young people learning Japanese.[32]

Academic and journalist Libby Lester spent a year on a Rotary exchange from Devonport, Tasmania, and the experience 'was formative in a way little else has been since'. While she gained 'many of the things the scheme

---

28 'Homestays Urgently Required', *Tharunka*, 2 July 1965, 3.
29 'Vive La Diffence' [*sic*], *Tharunka* 16 September 1969, 4; 'Our Student Ambassadors' Tour: Japan', *Australian Women's Weekly*, 18 October 1978, 71; '2nd AFS Student to Japan', *Hamersley News*, 1 March 1983, 7; 'Canberra Student Wins Japan Exchange Award', *Canberra Times*, 14 August 1982, 13. See also Bruce Miller, 'The Tokyo Embassy, Past, Present and Future: Reflections', in this volume.
30 'Getting to Know Each Other', *Canberra Times*, 7 July 1982, 2.
31 David Green, 'Rosalind Enjoys Japanese Way of Life', *Victor Harbor Times*, 11 May 1988, 9.
32 Mark Mulligan, 'AFR Columnist Wins Award for Service to Japan–Australia Relationship', *Australian Financial Review*, 3 December 2020, www.afr.com/world/asia/afr-columnist-wins-award-for-service-to-japan-australia-relationship-20201203-p56k7y, accessed 3 February 2021.

intended—a language, an appreciation for another culture, a network of friends and families still in place today', her eyes were opened in unexpected ways to cultural and political developments. Lester reflected her year in Japan provided:

> my first real glimpse of soft power in action and is something I have carried through life—along with a penchant for beige trench coats and black stockings, the sensible and elegant uniform of the Japanese working woman.[33]

School tours in both directions have been built over time since the 1980s and have exposed generations of Australian and Japanese students to each other's country. Australia has been the most popular international destination for Japanese school groups, with around 60,000 students visiting annually prior to the COVID-related travel restrictions from 2020. Australian school visits to Japan have proved equally popular, and more recently have broadened their scope to include sciences and technology subjects. Around 650 formal partnerships between Australian and Japanese schools currently exist, some incorporating teacher exchange and online collaborative learning. After a decline in the early 2000s, student mobility between the two nations then strengthened, assisted by scholarships at secondary and tertiary levels. Since 2014, Australia's New Colombo Plan has sent more than 2,000 university undergraduate students to study and undertake internships in Japan.[34] Recent initiatives such as the Australian Olympic Connect 'Tomodachi 2021' have recharged connections between schools, with more than 600 classes in Australia and Japan involved in the lead up to the Tokyo Olympic Games in 2020 (ultimately held in 2021), and the Australian embassy actively encouraging Japanese participation.[35]

Cultural interactions between Japan and Australia extend to agreements of cooperation between municipal and state governments. All Australian states and more than 100 cities and towns have a sister relationship with Japan, accounting for over 20 per cent of all such relationships. However,

---

33 Libby Lester, personal communication to Kate Darian-Smith, 6 April 2021.
34 'Japan–Australia Education and Research', Australian Government Department of Education and Training, June 2017, internationaleducation.gov.au/International-network/japan/PolicyUpdates-Japan/Documents/2017-06%20A-J%20Education%20Research%20quick%20facts.pdf, accessed 5 March 2020; 'Japan–Australia Relations (Basic Data)', Ministry of Foreign Affairs of Japan, www.mofa.go.jp/region/asia-paci/australia/data.html, accessed 7 May 2022.
35 'Strengthening Links with Japan', Australian embassy in Tokyo, japan.embassy.gov.au/tkyo/pr2021_tk07.html, accessed 20 January 2021.

the growth in tourism between the two nations has been particularly important in opening up mutual appreciation of the culture and landscapes of the two nations. In 1964, 6,371 Australians travelled to Japan, the majority for holidays (5,074), with the remainder for business and study purposes.[36] Less than half that number of Japanese (2,598) travelled to Australia, primarily on business trips.[37] From the mid-1960s, the liberalisation of travel from Japan established that country's modern international tourism industry. Initially, the most popular destinations were the United States, Hawai'i and Hong Kong. By the 1980s, this had shifted. A 1986 Australian Tourism Commission International Visitor Survey found that about one-third of first-time Japanese travellers chose Australia as their preferred destination. Tourist arrivals from Japan to Australia grew rapidly, and by 1987 had increased by 48 per cent, accounting for 12 per cent of total international visitors.[38] This growth was supported by the relatively short travel distance, Australia's unique environments and the decline in the value of the Australian dollar.

The Australian government and the tourist industry also effectively promoted special events in Japan, including the Bicentennial and the Brisbane World Expo, both held in 1988. Indeed, by the late 1980s Australia was rated as Japan's most popular destination, and its tourism industry increasingly catered to Japanese visitors.[39] In 1992, a report by the Australia–Japan Research Centre noted that Australia was 'the number one honeymoon destination [for the Japanese], just ahead of Hawai'i'.[40] Japanese tourism to Australia peaked in 1997, with some 814,000 visits, but declined with the economic downturn in Asia, and the subsequent stagnation of the Japanese economy.[41] By 2016, when just 417,900 Japanese tourists travelled to Australia, tourist numbers from Japan had halved from what they were in 1997.[42]

---

36   'Australian Demographic Review, no. 217: Overseas Arrivals and Departures' (Canberra: Commonwealth Bureau of Census and Statistics, 1964), 18, 3401.0_12_1964-2, www.abs.gov.au/AUSSTATS/abs@.nsf/DetailsPage/3401.01964?OpenDocument, accessed 7 May 2022.
37   'Australian Demographic Review, no. 217', 14.
38   Ian Curnow et al., *Japanese Travel to Australia: Prospects and Issues*, Pacific Economic Paper No. 183 (Canberra: Australian National University, 1990).
39   Ian Curnow et al., *Japanese Travel to Australia*, 1, 8; Maree Tait, *Japanese Tourism to Australia* (Canberra: Australia–Japan Research Centre, 1992), 2, 4.
40   Maree Tait, *Japanese Tourism to Australia*.
41   Tourism Australia, *Annual Report 2005/2006*, *PP no. 43*, National Library of Australia (NLA): nla.gov.au/nla.obj-906354502, accessed 7 May 2022.
42   Carrington Clarke, 'Australia and Japan Reverse Tourism Relationship', ABC News, 16 January 2018, www.abc.net.au/news/2018-01-16/australia-and-japan-reverse-tourism-relationship/9332518, accessed 2 December 2019.

This same period has seen a reversal in tourism flows, with Australian visits to Japan sharply rising. In 1997 only 101,460 Australians travelled to Japan, as most Australians found the country too expensive because of the exchange rate. During the 2000s, with the weakening of the yen, Australians have been increasingly attracted by more affordable food and accommodation in Japan, as well as the opportunity to ski during the Southern Hemisphere summer, and Japan's hosting of major events. During 2016, more than 445,230 Australians visited Japan, and by 2018 this number had risen to half a million—indicating Japan's importance as a tourist destination for Australians prior to border closures and travel restrictions due to the global pandemic.[43]

Australian–Japanese Arts and Cultural Connections

From the early 1970s, the Australian government expanded its programs of cultural or public diplomacy with Japan. The recognition of the value of what Joseph Nye has termed 'soft power' has incorporated diplomatically sanctioned programs that aim to share ideas and showcase Australia's creative and technological expertise, and build institutional, community and people-to-people links.[44] The promotion of Australia's cultural and creative industries overseas has been key to its cultural diplomacy and development of a wider Asia literacy, and has been particularly prominent in its ties with Japan. Central to popular perceptions of Japan within Australia are Japan's cultural traditions alongside its artistic as well as technical innovation, with the arts 'serving as key drivers of the intimacy of ties at both the elite and grassroots level'.[45]

The Australia–Japan Foundation (AJF) was launched in 1976 and is Australia's oldest cultural council, supporting programs underpinning bilateral and regional relationships in the Asia-Pacific. Initially a statutory

---

43   'Japan Attracts a Record Number of Australian Tourists in 2018', Japan National Tourism Organization, www.japan.travel/en/au/media-releases/japan-attracts-a-record-number-of-australian-tourists-in-2018/, accessed 7 May 2022.

44   Christiane Keys-Statham, 'Australia's International Cultural Diplomacy', *Australian Policy and History* 13 November 2017, aph.org.au/2017/11/australias-international-cultural-diplomacy/, accessed 6 December 2020.

45   Shiro Armstrong, *Reimagining the Japan Relationship: An Agenda for Australia's Benchmark Partnership in Asia* (Canberra: Australia–Japan Research Centre, The Australian National University, 2021), 52.

body, the AJF received a sizeable budget in recognition of the importance of Australia–Japan relations and funded a Tokyo-based director who worked and later lived at the Australian embassy. A review of the AJF under the Howard government re-situated it within Department of Foreign Affairs and Trade (DFAT), and its headquarters are now in Canberra, with an office at the Australian embassy in Tokyo. Eminent Australians appointed to the AJF board provide expertise and input to Australia's foreign policy and economic and diplomacy priorities. Through its grants program, the AJF aims to increase mutual awareness and understanding of Australia's and Japan's shared cultural and economic interests, and to foster programs of collaboration and exchange spanning the arts, media, education, business, science, technology and sport, with these initiatives often supported by the embassy.[46]

Other government agencies, including the Australia Council for the Arts, and organisations such as Asialink, have been important in fostering mutual appreciation of Australian and Japanese culture and the arts. On the Japanese side, the Japan Foundation was established in 1972 to promote international exchange, with a focus on showcasing Japanese culture and Japanese-language teaching overseas. The Japan Foundation opened its first Australian office in 1977, and today has offices, a library and a gallery in Sydney. It has played a role, through its grants program, in supporting Japanese studies in Australia and contributing to bilateral ties across many fields of creative endeavour.

Indeed, from the 1970s there has been an extraordinary growth in the creative exchanges between Australia and Japan. Australian theatrical performers, musicians, puppeteers, dancers, writers and artists who work across many artforms have visited Japan to perform and to collaborate with Japanese artists and cultural institutions in the creation of new works, exhibitions and performances. These activities have highlighted Australia's creative economy, and individual and collective artistic innovation, and have often been funded by the Australian and Japanese governments through their respective cultural agencies, as well as through philanthropic and corporate sponsors. Such showcasing has spanned traditional and contemporary practice. For instance, in the field of dance, both the Australian Ballet and the Indigenous contemporary Bangarra Dance Theatre have toured Japan with great success over the past few years.

---

46 'Australia–Japan Foundation', Australian Department of Foreign Affairs and Trade, www.dfat. gov.au/ajf, accessed 18 November 2020. See also Chapter 8 in this volume.

In return, Asia-focused exhibitions and festivals, such as the Asia-Pacific Triennial of Contemporary Art and the newer Asia-Pacific Triennial of Performing Arts have brought many Japanese creative artists to Australia.

The visual arts, in particular, have proved an important channel of cultural exchange, and offer a case study for exploring Australia's cultural diplomacy in Japan and how this has evolved over the past 50 years. This brief overview begins with the Biennale of Sydney, launched in 1973 to widen Australian access to contemporary art in the Asia-Pacific. It proved to be an important site for Japanese artists, notably those working with performances and cutting-edge technologies, to exhibit in Australia and was to be the precursor of many later artistic exchanges. By 1981, influential ties were established when groups of artists based in Melbourne arranged an exchange of group exhibitions with Japanese artists. The works challenged conventional notions of art, and were displayed to widespread acclaim at seven gallery sites across Melbourne under the banner of *YOIN: Ideas from Japan Made in Australia*.[47] This large-scale project had been organised with assistance from Stelarc, an Australian performance artist then living in Tokyo, and student volunteers from Melbourne's art colleges assisted in the exhibition installation.[48]

Two years later, in a complementary exchange, the landmark *Continuum '83* exhibition of Australian contemporary art was held in Tokyo. This showcased the work of 27 Australian artists and video artists in multiple commercial galleries across Tokyo during Australia Week, and was funded by the Australia Council, the AJF and the Japan Foundation. On-the-ground support came from Alison Broinowski, cultural counsellor at the Australian embassy, with Ambassador Neil Currie hosting a reception in the embassy gardens for the Australian and Japanese artists, gallery directors, curators and the media.[49]

---

47   Alison Holland, 'Innovation, Art Practice and Japan–Australia Cultural Exchange during the 1970s and 1980s', *Asia Pacific Journal of Arts & Cultural Management* 9, no. 1 (December 2012): 24–31; see Alison Broinowski, *The Yellow Lady: Australian Impressions of Asia* (Melbourne: Oxford University Press, 1992), 170.

48   Stelarc, 'My Tokyo Connection', in Tamai, *Reflections*, 26–30.

49   Tamai, *Reflections*, 15; Ken Scarlett, 'Australia, Japan and Continuum '83', in *Continuum '83: The 1st Exhibition of Australian Contemporary Art in Japan, 22 August–3 September 1983* (Tokyo: Japan–Australia Cultural & Art Exchange Committee, 1983), 3; Emiko Namikawa, 'Art Exchanges between Australia and Japan', in Tamai, *Reflections*, 10–21.

By the mid-1980s, Australian visual artists were engaged in a more intense relationship with Asia, and particularly Japan, than their counterparts in Europe or North America. Japanese visual art was seen as at the epitome of ultra-style, and as a 'a locus of ultra-modern creativity'.[50]

The *Continuum '85: Aspects of Japanese Art Today* brought contemporary Japanese art to the Australian Centre for Contemporary Art and other galleries in Melbourne in 1985, showing installation, graphics, video art, film and performance art.[51] Exchanges between Australian and Japanese galleries were developed, with a partnership between the Queensland Art Gallery and Saitama Museum of Modern Art providing the model for the ongoing and highly successful Asia-Pacific Triennial of Contemporary Art.[52] Since the 1990s, Australian galleries and museums have also developed their collections of traditional and contemporary Japanese art, and bilateral residencies and exchanges for individual artists and students have deepened the relationship.

High-profile exhibitions of Australian art commenced in Japan during the 1980s. In 1987, *Contemporary Australian Art*, hosted by the Museum of Modern Art in Saitama, celebrated sister relations between Saitama Prefecture and Queensland, and the Australian Bicentennial Authority's *Edge to Edge* contemporary art exhibition toured in Japan during 1988. The Australian embassy staff both initiated and supported these events, working in partnership with other government agencies and providing sponsors. For instance, the major retrospective *Two Hundred Years of Australian Painting* held in 1992 at the National Museum of Western Art in Tokyo and the National Museum of Modern Art in Kyoto was proposed by staff at the Australian embassy and realised with funding and promotion from the AJF and Japanese media company Nihon Keizai Shimbun (now Nikkei).[53]

In 1989, Asialink was established as a joint initiative of the Australian government's Commission for the Future and the philanthropic Myer Foundation in response to growing investment in Australia's interactions within the Asia-Pacific. Asialink's role was to build Australia's influence within the region through leadership training across programs spanning

---

50 Broinowski, *The Yellow Lady*, 187, 174.
51 Namikawa, 'Art Exchanges between Australia and Japan', 18–25.
52 Caroline Turner, 'My Memories of Art Projects in Japan', in Tamai, *Reflections*, 22–25.
53 Tamai, *Reflections*, 6.

business, education and the arts.[54] Asialink Arts was formed in 1991, headed by the art administrator and curator Alison Carroll, who had lived in Japan in the early 1970s. Its arts projects were often supported by the Australia Council and DFAT, and by 1993 included an Arts Exhibition Touring Program that included Japan.[55] By the early 2000s, an emphasis on developing professional links between Australian and Japanese curators and arts institutions led to an active program of exhibitions between the two nations.[56] Through the AJF, Australian artists were not only exhibiting work but also connecting with curators and galleries, including across regional Japan.[57] Asialink's *Sun Gazing* initiative, for instance, organised a series of exhibitions of Australian contemporary art and craft to Japan in 2002–04, with the expectation that a number of Japanese exhibitions would come to Australia. These attracted an audience of nearly 300,000 people, with Patricia Piccinini's hyper-realist sculptures breaking attendance records at the Hara Museum of Contemporary Art in Tokyo.[58] In 2006, the official 'Year of Exchange', the first Australia–Japan Visual Arts Forum was held in Tokyo, and hosted by the Australian embassy.[59]

By the late 1980s, small commercial galleries in Tokyo were exhibiting traditional Australian Indigenous art.[60] By the early 1990s, public galleries in Japan began presenting Aboriginal art to wider audiences; as Japanese tourism increased to Australia, there was increasing interest in learning about the nation and its peoples. In 1992, *Crossroads – Toward a New Reality: Aboriginal Art from Australia* was shown at national art museums in Kyoto and Tokyo.[61] Japanese reviewers made connections across cultures, praising the works as possessing a vitality that was perceived

---

54   'Shaping the Future: An Uncommon History of Asialink 1989–2017', University of Melbourne, asialink.unimelb.edu.au/stories/shaping-the-future-an-uncommon-history-of-asialink-1989-2017, accessed 16 May 2022.
55   Alison Carroll and Carrillo Gantner, 'Finding a Place on the Asian Stage', *The Conversation*, 11 June 2012, theconversation.com/finding-a-place-on-the-asian-stage-7189/, accessed 7 May 2022.
56   Alison Carroll, *Asialink Arts: Through the Looking Glass, the Asialink Arts Program, 1990–2010* (Melbourne: Asialink, University of Melbourne, 2012), 12–13.
57   Leonie Boxtel, interviewed by Kate Darian-Smith, 24 March 2017.
58   Alison Carroll, 'People and Partnership: An Australian Model for International Art Exchanges— the Asialink Arts Program, 1990–2010', in *Contemporary Asian Art and Exhibitions Connectivities and World-making*, ed. Michelle Antionette and Caroline Turner (Canberra: ANU Press, 2014), doi.org/ 10.22459/CAAE.11.2014.11.
59   Alison Carroll, ed., *Sun Gazing: The Australia–Japan Art Exhibitions Touring Program 2002–04*, (Melbourne: Asialink Centre, University of Melbourne, 2004), 3; Asialink, *Annual Report 2006* (Melbourne: University of Melbourne, 2007).
60   Kayo Tamura, 'Australian Aboriginal Art in Japan' (MA thesis, University of Melbourne, 1994), 6.
61   Ibid., 1–4.

to be now 'lost from contemporary Japanese life'.[62] Asialink also funded an exhibition of contemporary Aboriginal art from private collections staged in Matsunoyama, Tokyo and Hokkaido during 2003, which was accompanied by a major publication on Aboriginal art produced in Japanese.[63]

In 2008, the popularity of Indigenous Australian art in Japan was exemplified by the resounding success of the *Utopia: The Genius of Emily Kame Kngwarreye* touring exhibition, mounted at the National Museum of Art in Osaka and the National Art Center in Tokyo, and then shown at the National Museum of Australia, in Canberra.[64] It was the largest exhibition of an Australian artist ever held internationally, with around 200 works by the Western Desert artist Emily Kame Kngwarreye (c. 1910–1996). Japanese audiences of over 100,000 attended across the two venues, a visitation record for any Australian art exhibition.[65]

The tour of the *Utopia* exhibition to Japan has been described as the 'kind of extended, cross-cultural, governmental-corporate collaboration that was virtually without precedent in exhibitions of Australian art'.[66] It was developed over many years, with initial support from Asialink, and ongoing negotiations between the participating institutions, curators and the Australian embassy.[67] *Utopia*'s principal curator was Indigenous Australian Margo Neale, who was based at the National Museum of Australia. Her co-curator—the Japanese poet and curator Akira Tatehata—had initiated the exhibition after attending Neale's exhibition of Kngwarreye's work in Australia in 1998. Tatehata approached Murray McLean, Australia's ambassador in Tokyo, with a proposal for the exhibition; in turn, McLean approached the Australian federal

62 Ibid., 8.
63 Timothy Morrell, 'Spirit Country: Contemporary Australian Aboriginal Art from the Gantner Myer Collection', *Artlink*, June 2002, www.artlink.com.au/articles/2379/spirit-country-contemporary-australian-aboriginal-/, accessed 7 May 2022.
64 Margo Neale, ed., *Utopia: The Genius of Emily Kame Kngwarreye* (Canberra: National Museum of Australia Press, 2008); Gay McDonald and Laura Fisher, 'Emily Kame Kngwarreye in Japan', *Artlink*, 1 June 2015, www.artlink.com.au/articles/4318/emily-kame-kngwarreye-in-japan/, accessed 7 May 2022.
65 'Cultural Diplomacy', Australian embassy in Tokyo, japan.embassy.gov.au/tkyo/art_culture_aust.html, accessed 7 May 2022; Alison Carroll, ed., *Sun Walking: Australian Visual Arts Partnership, Program, 2005–9* (Melbourne: Asialink Centre, University of Melbourne, 2009), 30.
66 McDonald and Fisher, 'Emily Kame Kngwarreye'; Department of Foreign Affairs and Trade, *Annual Report 2008–2009* (Canberra: Australian Government Department of Foreign Affairs and Trade, 2009), 191.
67 Carroll, *Sun Walking*, 5.

government for support. The Australian embassy in Tokyo then assisted with the project's realisation and promotion through staff contributions, principally from Hitomi Toku (cultural officer), Ross Westcott (counsellor, public diplomacy) and Bruce Miller (minister, political).[68]

Interviewed by the *Japan Times* in February 2008, the 'suave, chain-smoking' Tatehata predicted that the *Utopia* exhibition will 'make Japanese face the question, "What does multiculturalism really mean?" … Making an effort to understand a foreign culture like Kngwarreye's is very important'.[69] For the Japanese, the exhibition raised the problem of where to place Australian Indigenous cultural production within the canon of Western art history, and both reviews and audience responses highlighted this issue while also responding positively to the work.[70]

The Australia Council for the Arts has also supported the exposure of Australian visual and performing arts in Japan for several decades. In 1991, under the Keating government, the Australia Council allocated at least half of its international budget to the Asia-Pacific region, although this was to decline sharply by the mid-1990s. Developing arts connections with North Asia was a key focus area for the Australia Council's international grants throughout the 2000s, and Australia's artistic connections with Japan are deeper and more developed than elsewhere in the region.

One of the most significant programs was instigated in 1987 by the Australia Council's Visual Arts and Craft Board when it set up its Tokyo Studio, with sculptor Noelene Lucas as the inaugural artist-in-residence. The studio was initially located in a small, rented prefabricated house on the rooftop of a building in Monzen-Nakacho, in Tokyo's 'old downtown', which was furnished by the Australian embassy. In 1995, the studio was relocated to an apartment block in Takadanobaba. While the Australia Council managed the program, the artists who came for a three-to-four-month stay were supported personally and professionally through the

68   McDonald and Fisher, 'Emily Kame Kngwarreye'; Tamai, *Reflections*.
69   Edan Corkhill, 'Dreamtime on Canvas', *Japan Times*, 21 February 2008, www.japantimes.co.jp/culture/2008/02/21/arts/dreamtime-on-canvas/, accessed 7 May 2022.
70   McDonald and Fisher, 'Emily Kame Kngwarreye'; see also Nakamura Kazue, 'A Dialogue to Find Ourselves and Others: The Reception of Emily Kngwarreye in Japan', *Australian and New Zealand Journal of Arts* 9, no. 1–2 (2008): 22–27, doi.org/10.1080/14434318.2008.11432789; Corkhill, 'Dreamtime on Canvas'; and John McDonald, 'Emily Kame Kngwarreye in Osaka', *John McDonald* (blog),1 February 2008, www.johnmcdonald.net.au/2008/emily-kame-kngwarreye-in-osaka/, accessed 7 May 2022; Andrew Pike, director, *Emily in Japan: The Making of an Exhibition* (Ronin Films, 2008), www.roninfilms.com.au/video/0/120/2142.html, accessed 7 May 2022.

cultural work of embassy staff. Sachiko Tamai recalled that Tokyo was 'not very internationalized in the late '80s. Life in Tokyo was so fresh and different for most Australian artists who took up the residency'.[71] She worked as the senior cultural officer for the Australian embassy in Tokyo from 1986, offering assistance to resident artists, and when she retired in 2000 this was continued by other embassy staff for some years.[72]

For the artists-in-residence at the Australia Council's Tokyo Studio until its closure in 2016, the experience was to influence their creative practice and often led to collaborations with Japanese artists and return visits to that country.[73] To give one of many examples, Megan Keating spent time at the studio in 2003, and recalled that she found Tokyo 'literally littered with exaggerated representations of nature … Everywhere you turn nature has been preened, prepared, perfected and the re-presented'.[74] This infused her subsequent work.

People-to-people and institutional connections between Australia and Japan were also fostered through Asialink's Arts Residency Program, which from the 1990s until 2018 funded Australian artists, performers and writers to visit Japan to create new work and collaborate with Japanese communities and artistic partners. A related Australia–Japan Arts Network sent senior arts managers in Australia to Japan to work in key cultural institutions.[75] In all these activities involving the arts, and countless more, the Australian embassy played a key role as initiator, supporter and promoter of Australian cultural production and creativity.

While the extent of artistic and creative interchanges can only be sketched out in this chapter, where the focus has been on the visual arts and arts residencies, there is no doubt that the cultural sector as a whole has clearly been a substantial factor in strengthening the bilateral relationship between Australia and Japan for almost five decades. However, diminishing federal and state funding for the arts in Australia over the past decade, the cessation of international residency programs and, most recently, the impacts of COVID-19 on the arts sector all present challenges. As a recent

---

71   Sachiko Tamai, 'VACB Tokyo Studio', in Tamai, *Reflections*, 32–34.
72   Ibid., vii.
73   Ibid., vii, 4, 35.
74   Megan Keating, 'A Floating World', in *Floating World*, ed. Jonathan Holmes and Paul Zika, exhibition catalogue (Tokyo: Plimsoll Gallery, University of Tasmania, 2007), 35.
75   Asialink, *35,000 Days in Asia: The Asialink Arts Residence Program* (Melbourne: Asialink Centre, University of Melbourne, 2004), 3. The Australia–Japan Arts Network ran from 1998 to 2002.

report has advocated, these are among the factors that underlie the need for Australia to consider fresh models for cultural engagement across the arts in Japan in the future.[76]

Sports and Diplomacy

Today, Australia and Japan are known as sporting nations, with national teams participating in international and regional sporting competitions across a range of codes and audiences consuming sports events and games not only through in-person attendance but via multiple media formats. Japan has deep traditions in distinctive sports such as sumo and martial arts, while team sports such as cricket, football and tennis have shaped Australia's settler identity since the early colonial era. However, from the mid-twentieth century, both nations have also invested heavily in the hosting of prestige global sports events, such as the Olympic Games, as a means of furthering national objectives at home and abroad, including fostering national identity and asserting influence across the Asia-Pacific region and on the world stage. In the post–Cold War era of globalisation, sports diplomacy has emerged as a potent form of soft power, not merely in ad hoc ties between clubs and networks, but increasingly through government.[77] Scholars Steven Jackson and Stephen Haigh note 'an ever-closer convergence of sport and foreign policy', as states turn to sport as a foreign policy instrument to respond to social, political, cultural and economic pressures.[78]

Sport as a bridge between Australia and Japan can be traced back to the early twentieth century. In 1924, three warships and 2,500 men of the Imperial Japanese Naval Squadron visited Australia on a friendly training mission under the leadership of Admiral Makoto Saitō (who was to serve as prime minister of Japan, 1932–34). Addressing an Australian audience at the Millions Club at Farmer's department store in Sydney, Saitō spoke

---

76   Armstrong, *Reimagining the Japan Relationship*, 50–55.

77   David Black and Byron Peacock, 'Sport and Diplomacy', in *The Oxford Handbook of Modern Diplomacy*, ed. Andrew F. Cooper, Jorge Heine and Ramesh Thakur (Oxford: Oxford University Press, 2013), doi.org/10.1093/oxfordhb/9780199588862.013.0040, 708–14; Kambiz Abdi, et al., 'Identifying Sports Diplomacy Resources as Soft Power Tools', *Place Branding and Public Diplomacy* 15 (2019): 147–55, doi.org/10.1057/s41254-019-00115-9; Yoav Dubinsky, 'From Soft Power to Sports Diplomacy: A Theoretical and Conceptual Discussion', *Place Branding and Public Diplomacy* 15 (2019): 156–64, doi.org/10.1057/s41254-019-00116-8.

78   Steven J. Jackson and Stephen Haigh, 'Between and beyond Politics: Sport and Foreign Policy in a Globalizing World', *Sport in Society* 11, no. 4 (2008): 352, doi.org/10.1080/17430430802019169.

of the Japanese tennis team, which from 1921 competed in the Davis Cup tournament, and the growing popularity of football among Japanese children. 'By friendly rivalry in sport', he stated 'we will cement this friendship between us.'[79] In 1927 Japan's Waseda University rugby team toured Australia, and when an Australian intervarsity rugby team later visited Japan a crowd of 20,000 watched the game.[80] These early sporting exchanges ceased as conflict approached in the Pacific.

After World War II, Australian and Japanese sporting rivalry intensified. Seeking to re-establish its regional and global standing, modern Japan has recognised the significance of sport for building national pride and international diplomacy. As Wolfram Manzenreiter has explained, 'along with its former colonies Korea and China, Japan has appropriated football [soccer] to express and negotiate ideas of identity, power, status and global norms in international relations'.[81] Australia has also been active in football diplomacy across sporting codes, although this has evolved gradually. In 1956, an Australian soccer team played for the first time at the Olympics in Melbourne, defeating Japan 2–0. However, it was only in the 2000s, when Australia joined the Asian Football Confederation, and especially after 2006, that this rivalry has strengthened. Australian and Japanese soccer teams have competed in almost every World Cup qualifying final, generating more attention from supporters and the media in both countries each year.

79   'Friendly Relations', *Sun*, 29 January 1924, 12.
80   'Football', *Evening News*, 29 June 1927, 7; 'Australia Beats Japan', *Brisbane Courier*, 17 August 1927, 6; 'Keep Together', *Sun*, 23 August 1927, 5; 'Football: Australia Wins in Japan', *Advocate*, 8 February 1934, 7; 'Rugby Football', *Argus*, 12 February 1934, 16.
81   Sandra Collins, '"Samurai" Politics: Japanese Cultural Identity in Global Sport—The Olympic Games as a Representational Strategy', *The International Journal of the History of Sport* 24, no. 3 (2007): 357–74, doi.org/10.1080/09523360601101345; Wolfram Manzenreiter, 'Football Diplomacy, Post-colonialism and Japan's Quest for Normal State Status', *Sport in Society* 11, no. 4 (2008): 417, doi.org/10.1080/17430430802019359. See also Sandra Collins, 'East and West: Confrontational Diplomacy', *The International Journal of the History of Sport* 24, no. 8 (August 2007): 1003–41, doi. org/10.1080/09523360701376573; Wolfram Manzenreiter, 'Global Movements, Sports Spectacles and the Transformation of Representational Power Asia', *Pacific World* 1 (2010); Joel Rookwood and Kola Adeosun, 'Nation Branding and Public Diplomacy: Examining Japan's 2019 Rugby World Cup and 2020(21) Olympic Games in the Midst of a Global Economic Downturn and the COVID-19 Pandemic', *Journal of Global Sport Management* (2021), doi.org/10.1080/24704067.2021.1871860; and David Rowe, 'Football, Diplomacy and Australia in the Asian Century', in *Sport and Diplomacy*, ed. J. Simon Rofe (Manchester: Manchester University Press, 2018), doi.org/10.7765/97815261310 65.00018.

Australia–Japan competition in many other professional sports has likewise accelerated in recent decades. A prime example is rugby union, which had seen extraordinary growth after Japan hosted the Rugby World Cup in 2019. The Japanese Brave Blossoms and the Australian Wallabies are now well matched, player exchanges are occurring between rugby clubs in both nations, cross-national media coverage of the sport has grown and discussions are underway about Japan joining the prestigious Southern Hemisphere's top-tier Rugby Championship alongside Australia and other teams. Australia's championing of Japan in international rugby is also supported, at a lower level, by the alignment of Australian Super Rugby clubs with Japanese teams; the partnership between the Melbourne Rebels and Osaka's Hanazono Kintetsu Liners has demonstrated the potential of bilateral commercial opportunities developing through sporting and club ties.[82]

At the non-professional and community levels of sports participation in Australia and Japan, the support of government and the AJF has been notable if somewhat sporadic. In an early example, in 1978 Australian golfers were supported to play the Japanese in winning the Australia–Japan Foundation trophy. The inaugural tournament was held in Victoria in February 1978, with 32 leading golfers from Australia and Japan involved, and subsequent tournaments were held in Tokyo and Canberra.[83] Australia and Japan have also worked together in the development of surf lifesaving. The AJF provided support and guidance for the establishment of the Japan Lifesaving Association in 1982, and this work has had a significant impact in subsequent decades in Japan. A survey of AJF grants for the exchange of sports expertise between Australia and Japan is instructive and shows the breadth of this on-the-ground diplomacy. Training sessions for communities and teams; two-way touring of athletes and sports leaders; and professional development aimed at improving sports skills, umpiring and sports administration have been funded by a range of grants. Sports and activities that have been funded since 2000 include rugby union, rugby league, Australian rules football, surf lifesaving, table tennis, hammer-throwing, croquet (or 'gateball'), gymnastics, judo, baseball and volleyball. Many grants fund the connection of small clubs and community groups between the two nations, as well as state or national associations. Some are directed

---

82 Armstrong, *Reimagining the Japan Relationship*, 58–59.
83 'Two-Way Trade in People', *Sydney Morning Herald*, 8 May 1978, 8; 'Aust. Golfers Slump', *Sydney Morning Herald*, 7 July 1979, 52; 'Golf to Australia', *Sydney Morning Herald*, 10 March 1980, 56.

at widening participation, including of women, children and those with a disability.[84] Staff at the Australian embassy in Tokyo have been closely involved in the promotion, advocacy, liaison implementation and documentation of these diplomatic sporting initiatives for over four decades, and alongside the arts these activities have strengthened person-to-person and community relationships.

While sport has been important for Australia's informal international influence, Australia has also been a pioneer in the formalisation of sports diplomacy within foreign policy.[85] Australia's first government strategy was launched in 2015, recognising the capacity for sport to advance national interests and bolster the economy through associated tourism and international partnerships. Its focus on the Asia-Pacific included the negotiation of sports agreements with several Asian nations. A Memorandum of Understanding on Sport Cooperation was signed with Japan in January 2017 during Prime Minister Shinzō Abe's visit to Australia, acknowledging the potential for sporting organisations in the two countries to strengthen existing ties and expand programs of athlete and coaching exchange and business development. Since then, Australia has introduced a national sports plan which is complemented by a renewed international strategy known as *Sports Diplomacy 2030*.[86] The document recognises sport as a 'universal language that can break down cultural barriers', projecting Australia's 'values and identity' internationally, and cultivating partnerships across the world.[87]

The Australian embassy has been driving this on the ground in Japan through the AUS+RALLY, an initiative association with Rugby Australia, the Australian Olympic Committee and Paralympics Australia. The embassy has encouraged Japanese local government authorities and organisations to sign up as 'Friends of Australia', with the idea that they host visiting Australian sporting teams. While impacted by the

---

84   See Australia–Japan Foundation, *Annual Report* (Canberra: Australian Government Publishing Service): see annual reports from 2000 through to 2020.

85   Stuart Murray, 'Sports Diplomacy in the Australian Context: A Case Study of the Department of Foreign Affairs and Trade', *Sports Law eJournal* 1, no. 1 (2013): 1–15, doi.org/10.53300/001c.6399; Stuart Murray and Geoffrey Allen Pigman, 'Mapping the Relationship Between International Sport and Diplomacy', *Sport in Society* 17, no. 9 (2014): 1098–118, doi.org/10.1080/17430437.2013.856 616. See also Rowe, 'Football, Diplomacy and Australia in the Asian Century'.

86   Department of Health, *Sports Diplomacy 2030* (Canberra: Australian Government Department of Health, 2019), www.dfat.gov.au/sites/default/files/sports-diplomacy-2030.pdf, accessed 4 January 2021; see Armstrong, *Reimagining the Japan Relationship,* 56–59.

87   Department of Health, *Sports Diplomacy 2030,* 7.

COVID-19 pandemic, this program demonstrates how sports diplomacy connects Australia and Japan at multiple levels, from local communities through to peak sports bodies and international competitions.[88]

Conclusion

The promotion of Australia's cultural and creative industries overseas has been key to its cultural diplomacy in Japan, as have sporting exchanges and participation. Over many decades, these endeavours have built up a depth and breadth of cross-cultural connections in the arts that underpin Australia and Japan's relationship. As this chapter shows, these connections have been developed within a broader context that encompasses Japanese-language teaching in Australia, and knowledge of the English language and Australian society in Japan. This has, particularly since the 1990s, resulted in the reciprocal exchanges of people that have been facilitated and promoted through programs of student exchange, tourism and working holidays, and educational programs that range from the school sector to universities. While the extent of artistic and creative interchanges can only be sketched out here with a focus on the visual arts and arts residencies, the cultural sector as a whole has clearly been a substantial factor in strengthening the bilateral relationship between Australia and Japan in a people-centred way. So too have sporting exchanges, and the 2032 Olympics in Brisbane will provide a range of opportunities for Australian–Japanese relations.

In concluding this chapter, I turn to Australia House, a structure that was originally built for the fourth Echigo-Tsumari Art Triennale as part of a program of artistic exchange. In 2011, Australia House collapsed in a powerful aftershock from the Tohoku earthquake.[89] However, with the support of the Tokamachi City government, the AJF, the Australian embassy and local residents, it was rebuilt and can be visited in Urada, Tokamachi City, Niigata Prefecture. Following an international competition, the winning design by Sydney architect Andrew Burns incorporates environmental sustainability and natural disaster prevention to reflect a merger of Australian and Japanese expertise and provide a space

---

88 'Sports Diplomacy', Australian embassy in Tokyo, japan.embassy.gov.au/tkyo/sportsdiplomacy. html, accessed 10 January 2021.

89 See also Murray McLean, 'The Australian Embassy in Tokyo and the Tohoku Earthquake and Tsunami of March 2011', in this volume.

for exhibitions and artists-in-residence.[90] The story of Australia House is particularly pertinent to the bilateral relationship, as it is one of resilience and deep community ties that attest to the depth of Australian–Japanese collaborations. Looking to the future, here are also fresh opportunities for Australia–Japan connections, whether in the arts or through sport, to strengthen. This will depend, in part, on appropriate support from government agencies and the ongoing efforts of those at the Australian embassy to facilitate this rich and special relationship at institutional and community levels.

90 'Australia House', Australian embassy in Tokyo, japan.embassy.gov.au/tkyo/australiahouse.html, accessed 17 December 2021.

10

'Scholars—Future Interpreters of Australia': Education, Cultural Diplomacy and Australian Studies in Japan

David Carter

The rapid expansion of Australia–Japan economic relations in the late sixties and throughout the seventies in many ways caught Australia unprepared. We had produced few specialists on Japan, in economic or other fields, and we had taken no trouble to teach Japan something of the realities of life in Australia. It is difficult for Japanese who have spent their whole life in a monocultural society existing in a compact, densely populated, well watered land to imagine the different conditions pertaining in a comparatively dry country of vast distances and small population. Particularly since the establishment of the Foundation, steps have been taken to equip Australians and Japanese to deal more realistically with each other. Had these steps been taken earlier, some, perhaps many, of the mistakes of the past might have been avoided.[1]

1   Australia–Japan Foundation (AJF), *Australia–Japan Foundation Annual Report 1982–83*, Parliamentary Paper (PP) No. 45/1984 (Canberra: Australian Government Publishing Service, 1983), 3. The quotation in the chapter heading is taken from AJF, *Australia–Japan Foundation Annual Report 1984–85*, PP no. 58/1986 (Canberra: Australian Government Publishing Service, 1985), 7. For assistance with compiling this essay, I would like to acknowledge Professor Yoichi Kibata, formerly of Tokyo University, and Ms Hitomi Toku and Ms Ikuko Kohara, Public Diplomacy section of the Australian embassy and the Australia–Japan Foundation, Tokyo.

It might seem to be merely stating the obvious to assert that education is an important dimension of cultural diplomacy for Australia as for many other nations. In practice, however, in the division of labour through institutional structures within the larger Australian embassies—including in Tokyo—and in the distribution of portfolios across government ministries, the two areas will often be separated and function in quite different domains. The focus of overseas activity in the education portfolio is on institutional and research linkages, student exchanges, and, above all, the recruitment of international students to Australia. Cultural affairs, by contrast, are often focused on one-off headline events such as the visits of major arts companies or exhibitions, cultural festivals, international sporting events or large-scale programs of promotions and events such as that mounted in 2018 under the banner *Australia Now* throughout Japan.

But cultural diplomacy typically also involves a range of smaller scale, often ongoing engagements, which are lower key perhaps but also longer lasting in their impacts. These involve activities such as maintaining relationships with Australia–Japan friendship associations and sister city groups, managing residency programs for artists, writers and scholars, promoting Australian expertise in areas as diverse as English language teacher training, aged care or surf lifesaving, and, not least, supporting the study of Australia in schools and universities.

The last of these—the support of Australian studies broadly defined—has been a long-term focus of Australian cultural diplomacy in Japan, largely through the programs of the Australia–Japan Foundation (AJF) but also through initiatives from the Japanese side. Here education and cultural diplomacy work hand in hand. The aim on the Australian side is the 'classic' objective of cultural diplomacy: to build an informed, up-to-date and positive understanding of Australian culture and society in Japan. Its particular significance for Australia is what I have referred to elsewhere as the nation's 'reputational deficit'.[2] Australia has a positive image internationally but of a peculiarly limited kind. To some extent international travel, global communications and indeed the work of

---

2   David Carter, 'Living with Instrumentalism: The Academic Commitment to Cultural Diplomacy', in *Cultural Diplomacy: Beyond the National Interest?* ed. Ien Ang, Yudhishthir Raj Isar and Phillip Mar (Abingdon: Routledge, 2016), 114–29. This article was also published in a special issue of *International Journal of Cultural Policy* 21, no. 4 (2015): 478–93, doi.org/10.1080/1028663 2.2015.1042470.

Australian agencies have produced change. Perceptions of Australia are no longer restricted to tourist images of marsupials and landscape or knowledge of Australia as a reliable source of coal and other primary products.

To these clichéd images we might add an increasing awareness of Australia as an education destination for students around the world and as a continent that is environmentally 'rewarding'. Among students, Australia's multiculturalism and Indigenous cultures are also points of interest. Still, in comparative terms, the positive images which have accrued to Australia lack the kind of historical and social dimensions that can easily be converted into other forms of prestige or capital—cultural prestige, the weight of tradition or the glamour of modernity, or forms of leadership or exemplarity. This is a middle power problem, magnified by Australia's regional situation: 'Australia's relationship with Asian countries is comparatively thin and instrumental, characterised by a major sense of cultural distance … a structural disconnect.'[3]

Allied to the reputational deficit is a kind of 'distinctiveness deficit'. Apart from its Indigenous cultures, it is difficult for Australia to promote an Australian culture in the way that French, Chinese, Japanese, Italian or even American governments can (whatever mythologies are exploited in the process). It is no accident that Indigenous cultures have such a large presence in Australia's cultural diplomacy programs. There is no language distinctiveness either of the kind that can justify state-subsidised language training institutions such as the Alliance Française or Confucius Institutes. The reputational stakes, then, are very different for Australia than for these other larger and more prominent nations, arguably giving education about Australia a much greater significance within the broad range of public diplomacy activities in Japan and elsewhere.

The present chapter examines the history of Australian studies in Japan within this challenging context, above all in the university sector but also with mention of the critical work done in the Japanese school system around developing new knowledge of Australia. The broad history of Australian studies in Japan is then focused in the second part of the chapter on the story of the position in Australian studies, now a visiting professorship, at Tokyo University. The chapter is written on the basis of a firm belief in the significance of increased academic work on Australia in Japan, not just within academic circles alone but as part of a much

---

3   Ien Ang, 'Smart Engagement with Asia', *Humanities Australia*, no. 8 (2017): 30–31.

wider network of bilateral relations and of influence within the wider Japanese professional occupations. Australian studies in Japan is a critical part of Australia's public and cultural diplomacy program, although this emphasis has always needed to be made and reiterated in Australia itself. The Australian embassy in Tokyo has played a key role in supporting the professorship at Tokyo University and many other key activities, such as the Australian Library at Otemon Gakuin University and support for the Australian Studies Association of Japan. But understood as part of a cultural diplomacy program, Australian studies demands close attention to its aims, methods and outcomes, not least in terms of what have been called networked and multidirectional models of bilateral relations.

The recent academic literature in this field has distinguished between older and newer modes of cultural or public diplomacy. Although this distinction is as much a matter of alternative strategies as a paradigm shift, 'older' approaches are characterised as being hierarchical, 'centred on intergovernmental relations and top-down communication', and primarily concerned with image projection or 'messaging', as in nation-branding campaigns. The 'new' public diplomacy, by contrast, is based on a network or networked model, dialogue rather than messaging, and 'horizontal communication as well as multidirectional flows and exchange of information'[4]—or, in the terms of the 2015 *Smart Engagement with Asia* report: 'Rather than the one-way outward projection and promotion of Australia's national interest, smart engagement focuses on the patient cultivation of genuine partnerships through mutually beneficial cooperation and collaboration.'[5] Cultural diplomacy is often understood as one element within the broader field of public diplomacy, as in the Australian government's 2014 Public Diplomacy strategy, although the terms are sometimes used interchangeably. Either way, it is useful to highlight the distinctive features of cultural diplomacy.[6]

If the theory struggles to get beyond abstract generalisations, the networked model does offer a good account of the kinds of cultural diplomacy that happen 'beneath' the level of the higher profile major cultural events but which, indeed, will often be crucial to their success. It offers the best

---

4   Terry Flew and Falk Hartig, 'Confucius Institutes and the Network: Communication Approach to Public Diplomacy', *IAFOR Journal of Asian Studies* 1, no. 1 (2014): 5, doi.org/10.22492/ijas. 1.1.02; Brian Hocking, 'Rethinking the "New" Public Diplomacy', in *The New Public Diplomacy: Soft Power in International Relations*, ed. Jan Melissen (Basingstoke: Palgrave, 2007), 35.
5   Ang, 'Smart Engagement with Asia', 23.
6   Carter, 'Living with Instrumentalism', 117.

model for understanding programs supporting Australian studies overseas. It also highlights the day-to-day work of Australian embassy staff, so much of which involves building and maintaining professional and grassroots relationships and 'filtering' general policy objectives through often very particular local contexts. As an early AJF report put it, such work is 'knowledge intensive and labour intensive'.[7]

Australian Studies in Japan

The policy of developing Australian studies in Japan has been a persistent if uneven feature of AJF programs from the outset, and its waxing and waning provide an informative history of the shifting understanding of its priority in the broader field of cultural diplomacy. Although the foundation's earliest strategic decision was to establish the first long-term intensive Japanese-language course in Australia, its 1977–78 annual report also announced that its budget would be allocated in 'approximately equal portions between activities designed to increase Australian understanding of Japan and Japanese understanding of Australia'.[8]

In relation to the latter, planning had begun for schemes to promote Australian studies in Japan in both teaching and research, for the situation was that:

apart from one or two specialist groups concentrating on economic studies, there are few courses of study on any aspect of Australia undertaken or taught at Japanese universities and none taught in the Japanese language by Japanese teachers.[9]

And in the realm of research:

Notwithstanding a growing awareness of Australia throughout all sections of the Japanese community it remains the fact that research on Australia outside the economic field remains low on the scale of Japanese priorities.[10]

---

7   AJF, *Australia–Japan Foundation Annual Report 1980–81*, PP no. 122/1982 (Canberra: Australian Government Publishing Service, 1982), 3.
8   AJF, *Australia–Japan Foundation Annual Report 1977–78*, PP no. 271/1979 (Canberra: Australian Government Publishing Service, 1979), 2.
9   Ibid., 7.
10   Ibid., 11.

A program of research grants and a publications program were announced to augment the existing travel grants, as was the intention to open a library of Australian books and related materials in Tokyo, a very high priority. In July 1979 the foundation moved into its own office in Tokyo and the AJF Library came into being.

Across the 1980s, the Australian studies in Japan program very often had top billing in the AJF annual reports, and a dedicated, well-funded program designed to lay the foundations for and then help build Australian studies activities was established.[11] The growth of the Australian studies program over the period can be charted in a series of key steps. These steps, and subsequent developments, might also be mapped against four phases identified by the AJF itself as characterising its programs from 1976 to 1999:

> engaging Australian interest in Japan (1976–1984); developing bilateral networks (1985–1990); building Australians' language and Japanese cultural skills (1991–1995); since 1995, advancing Australia's interests in the relationship ... through partnership, mutual concerns and interests.[12]

First, Australian studies courses taught in Japanese by a Japanese academic began at Keio University in April 1983, following the AJF's support for lecturer (later professor) Masami Sekine, of the Faculty of Law and Politics, to study in Australia for three years. These were the first such courses offered in Japan, although visiting Australian lecturers were offering courses in English at Tokyo University, as discussed below. Second, the first Australian Studies Symposium—an AJF initiative—was held in June 1985, with 280 participants, becoming an annual event.[13] Third, a new Australian Studies Centre was established at Nanzan University, Nagoya, in 1986, and was to host the second Australian Studies Symposium. Fourth, the Australian Studies Association of Japan (ASAJ) was launched in 1989, an initiative that had been flagged by the foundation in 1984

---

11   See especially AJF, *Australia–Japan Foundation Annual Report 1983–84*, PP no. 238/1985 (Canberra: Australian Government Publishing Service, 1985); AJF, *AJF Annual Report 1984–85*; AJF, *Australia–Japan Foundation Annual Report 1985–86*, PP no. 57/1987 (Canberra: Australian Government Publishing Service, 1986).
12   AJF, *Australia–Japan Foundation Annual Report 1998–99*, PP no. 222/1999 (Canberra: Australian Government Publishing Service, 1999), 5.
13   AJF, *AJF Annual Report 1984–85*, 4–6.

and was a key part of the strategy behind organising the Australian studies symposia.[14] A directory of Australian studies scholars in Japan was published for the first symposium, and listed 360 scholars.

These major steps were underwritten by a series of general grants (travel grants and research grants) and then dedicated Australian studies funding schemes. These included an annual Australian Lecture series, begun in 1982, with Professor Geoffrey Blainey as the inaugural lecturer; an annual AJF–*Asahi Shimbun* symposium from 1988; ongoing investment in the AJF Library; and a very active publications program. In 1981–82 the AJF Senior Fellowship and Postgraduate Scholarships were launched, 'to carry out studies in the humanities and social sciences'. One of the first two recipients of the postgraduate award was Yasue Arimitsu, who studied at The Australian National University (ANU). She was later to be a professor at Doshisha University, Kyoto, the president of the ASAJ, a guiding presence behind the ongoing Gendai Kikakushitsu series of translations of Australian literature, and the author of *Australian Identity: Struggle and Transformation in Australian Literature* (2003).

The AJF's 1985–86 annual report—on the foundation's 10th anniversary—reviewed its Australian studies activities in some detail. At that point in time, five scholars were being funded under the fellowships scheme and 18 through postgraduate scholarships, and around 50 grants had been made to Japanese research projects on Australia or Australia–Japan relations.[15] As the report put it:

> The provision of grants-in-aid under this program to Japanese scholars was largely instrumental in establishing an infrastructure of Japanese scholarship on Australia which provided the basis for development of Australian studies in Japan.[16]

Due to these successes, a new Australian studies grants scheme was announced.

The range and scale of activities, and the investment, was significant. In 1986–87, for instance, Australian studies grants funded seven projects undertaken by Japanese researchers, for a total of A$43,000, in addition to A$93,000 for AJF fellowships (for academics) and A$116,000

---

14   AJF, *AJF Annual Report 1983–84*, 3.
15   The AJF 1983–84 annual report makes an explicit reference to the US Fulbright Scheme as a model. Ibid., 1.
16   AJF, *AJF Annual Report 1984–85*, 2.

for postgraduate scholarships. Nine Australian academic books had been translated into Japanese and published, and eight more were in preparation. Titles included Dean Jaensch, *An Introduction to Australian Politics*; James Gleeson, *Australian Painters*; Norma Grieve and Patricia Grimshaw, *Australian Feminist Perspectives*; Ross M. Martin, *Trade Unions in Australia*; Geoffrey Dutton, *The Literature of Australia*; Miriam Dixon, *The Real Matilda*; Kenneth Maddock, *The Australian Aborigines*; Don Aitken, *Australian Political Institutions*; Jean Martin, *The Migrant Presence*; Craig MacGregor, *The Australian People*.[17] By this stage the foundation's library had 3,000 members, 8,000 books, and 6,000 visitors per year.[18] It would be hailed as the foundation's 'flagship activity'.[19] Together with the AJF's Tokyo office, the library relocated to the new Australian embassy building in mid-1990, in a prominent, accessible location. In 1998 it was renamed the Australian Resource Centre, reflecting its wider role and investments in digital technologies.

The AJF's programs for Australian studies in Japan were established on the basis that the Japanese universities involved 'should ultimately take full responsibility for their respective activities'. The foundation's role was 'to encourage, to advise and to provide initial funds for the development of library resources and for academic staff training'. There was little point in investing in the area if the institutions did not intend 'to eventually take responsibility for the programs'.[20] This was an important strategy for embedding programs within Japanese institutions rather than managing programs through ongoing gifts from the Australian side.

Similar commitments continued through to the early 1990s, although the Fellowship and Scholarship schemes were discontinued. In 1989–90, the AJF underwent a major review and a new set of priorities were set in place. The primary emphasis was now on Japanese-language education in Australian schools and universities. In the foundation's annual reports, Australian studies largely disappeared as an explicit program.

---

17 Previous works published included Manning Clark, *A Short History of Australia*; Geoffrey Sherrington, *Australia's Immigrants*; Geoffrey Blainey, *The Tyranny of Distance*; Blanche D'Alpuget, *Bob Hawke: A Biography*; Y. Gushikata, ed., *Twentieth Century Australian Poetry*.
18 AJF, *Australia–Japan Foundation Annual Report 1989–90*, PP no. 405/1990 (Canberra: Australian Government Publishing Service, 1990), 15.
19 Ibid., 10.
20 AJF, *AJF Annual Report 1985–86*, 5.

But then in 1992–93, another reorientation occurred, with the new emphasis falling (again) on the importance of 'changing attitudes about Australia among the Japanese public'.[21] The focus, however, turned to Australian studies in Japanese schools rather than the tertiary sector— with little or no mention of the latter over several years, perhaps because it was felt that at least the foundations for university Australian studies were already in place. Work on *Discovering Australia*, a video and information kit for junior high school students and their teachers was commenced, with the kit being introduced into 11,500 junior high schools in Japan in 1995—an extraordinary achievement. Tertiary Australian studies retained a small presence through the ASAJ Australian Studies Symposium, with the AJF providing general grants for researchers, and publication subsidies for *Southern Hemisphere*, the journal of the Australia and New Zealand Literary Society of Japan (ANZLSJ).

In 1998–99, the *Discovering Australia* Teacher's Kit was revised, following its review by a Japanese Advisory Committee, launched in May 2000 and later digitised.[22] The Australian Resource Centre, now a full reference and lending library, had become one of the most comprehensive collections of Australian books and related resources to be found outside Australia. It also hosted seminars, and received over 11,000 visitors in 1998–99. Finally, the AJF managed *Australia Web*, first launched in March 1996, a site presenting a wide range of materials, information and links regarding contemporary Australia. Australian studies represented 87 per cent of the AJF's education budget and together with the Australian Resource Centre 41 per cent of overall expenditure on activities.[23] As the AJF chair put it in 1997:

> Three of the Foundation's major projects—*The Australia Web*, *Discovering Australia* and the Australian Library—are tools for promoting understanding and attitudinal change. Images are very important in our dealings with each other and have repercussions through the full range of interaction between countries: cultural, social, defence, trade and business. All levels of contact are affected by the way we view each other.[24]

21   AJF, *Australia–Japan Foundation Annual Report 1992–93*, PP no. 375/1993 (Canberra: Australian Government Publishing Service, 1993), 1.

22   The names of the Japanese Advisory Committee are listed in: AJF, *Australia–Japan Foundation Annual Report 1996–97*, PP no. 299/97 (Canberra: Australian Government Publishing Service, 1997), 2.

23   AJF, *AJF Annual Report 1998–99*, 7–12 and 24–26.

24   John L. Menadue, 'Chairman's Message', in *AJF Annual Report 1996–97*, 1.

By the time of the 1999–2000 annual report, 'Australian Studies' had once again become a major headline item.

At the tertiary level, the most important development at this time was the introduction of the Sir Neil Currie awards for graduate students and academics researching and publishing on Australian topics. First offered in 2000–01, they eventually offered Early Career Researcher, Postgraduate, Curriculum Development and Publication schemes, with five or six awards most years from approximately 30 applications. In the same year a major survey of Australian studies in Japan was commissioned, and the foundation contributed to the translation and publication costs for three Australian crime novels.[25] Other developments included an Australian studies resource for senior high school and university students—*Austr@ lia_Go>Land, People, Culture*—launched in May 2000 (but without much follow-up); the appearance of *Aus E-Study*, an online Australian studies bulletin; a *Teach Australia* workshop held in November 2002, for academics and senior high school teachers; and exchange programs for publishers, debating teams and art exhibitions. In 2002, the foundation also launched the *Experience Australia* kit, this time for teachers and students in primary schools, which introduced 'integrated studies' across a range of disciplines on aspects of Australian life and culture.[26] By 2010, more than 1.9 million Japanese school students had used the kits.[27] In late 2005, the *Discover Eco Australia* kit was added to *Discovering Australia*, to 'promote Australia's progressive approaches to conservation and management of natural and cultural heritage'.[28]

This kind of broad investment in Australian studies across all levels of education peaked in the late 2000s when priorities, funding procedures and budget allocations changed. The Australian Resource Centre in the embassy was closed in May 2007 for a mix of security and budgetary reasons alongside the greater accessibility of resources online. The collection was transferred to Otemon Gakuin University in Osaka,

25   The three novels were published by Bungeishunjū in December 2002. The titles included Shane Maloney, *The Brush Off*; Marele Day, *The Last Tango of Dolores Delgado*; Peter Doyle, *Get Rich Quick*.
26   AJF, *Australia–Japan Foundation Annual Report 2002–03* (Canberra: Australian Government Department of Foreign Affairs and Trade, 3 November 2003), 7, www.dfat.gov.au/sites/default/files/ajf-annual-report-2002-03.pdf, accessed 28 August 2020.
27   AJF, *Australia–Japan Foundation Annual Report 2009–10* (Canberra: Australian Government Department of Foreign Affairs and Trade, 18 November 2010), 18, www.dfat.gov.au/sites/default/files/ajf-annual-report-2009-10.pdf, accessed 28 August 2020.
28   AJF, *Australia–Japan Foundation Annual Report, 2005–06* (Canberra: Australian Government Department of Foreign Affairs and Trade, 3 October 2006), 14, www.dfat.gov.au/sites/default/files/ajf-annual-report-2005-06.pdf, accessed 28 August 2020.

which had its own Center for Australian Studies (indeed, the first such centre in Japan, established in 1967, with a strong focus on economics and trade) and published the journal *Osutoralia kenkyu kiyo* (1975–2015).[29] The library was housed in a new purpose-built facility with significant institutional support. The collection was thus maintained as a collection, but accessibility and visibility were inevitably reduced given the university's location, and the collection's location within a university rather than the embassy.

Although the Otemon Center for Australian Studies has remained very active, the relocation of the Resource Centre from its prominent location in the Australian embassy in Tokyo was seen a major blow to public 'Australian studies' activities in Japan. The AJF also donated 370 books to the Center for Pacific and American Studies at Tokyo University as the basis for an Australian studies collection at the university, the home of the Visiting Professor in Australian Studies, as discussed later. The *Aus E-Study* bulletin disappeared after a year or two, and the Neil Currie awards were discontinued in 2014–15,[30] in part because the demand appeared to be shrinking, but also because priority was given to the Australian government's broader Endeavour fellowship scheme—which, however, did not have a dedicated Australian studies program.

Nonetheless, in other ways, the commitment to Australian studies at the tertiary level in Japan has been maintained, and indeed, over time, expanded. The AJF's annual report for 2006–07 foregrounded the 'Australian Studies program', again named as such. This program included increased support for the ASAJ through an open lecture series; a review of Australian studies in Japan, conducted by Kate Darian-Smith, then at the University of Melbourne; and funding for the ASAJ's annual conference.[31] The 2008–09 report prioritises 'capacity building for the Australian Studies Association of Japan'.[32] From 2007, the AJF organised its programs and projects into five priority areas: Economics and Trade; Security, Regional and International Relations; Education and Science (including Australian

---

29   *The Otemon Journal of Australian Studies* (1975 to December 2015); since 2016 the centre has published *The Journal of Australian and Asian Studies*.
30   The Early Career Researcher, Postgraduate and Curriculum Development schemes were discontinued but the Publication scheme continued.
31   Kate Darian-Smith, 'Research, Teaching and Cultural Diplomacy: The Current Profile of Australian Studies in Japan', *Otemon Journal of Australian Studies* 36 (2010): 131–39.
32   AJF, *Australia–Japan Foundation Annual Report 2008–09* (Canberra: Australian Government Department of Foreign Affairs and Trade, 31 October 2009), 17–18, www.dfat.gov.au/sites/default/files/ajf-annual-report-2008-09.pdf, accessed 28 August 2020.

studies); Society and Culture; and Communication, Information and Advocacy. Within this greater dispersal of areas, Education and Science remained the largest single category through to 2011–12, when it fell just behind the closely related Society and Culture.[33]

Establishing the Visiting Associate Professor in Australian Studies

The key element of the educational profile that clearly has grown in significance is the position of Visiting Professor in Australian Studies at Tokyo University. The position indeed has a long history, in two distinct phases. It was not an initiative from the Australian side—and indeed, rather strangely, there is no mention of the position in the AJF annual reports until 2005. It would now be seen as one of the foundation's major engagements. Professor Akio Watanabe, who had completed his PhD at ANU in 1967 and was later a foundational figure in establishing the ASAJ, took the initiative to establish a visiting position for an Australian scholar at Tokyo University's Komaba campus, where area studies and interdisciplinary humanities are located.

The first appointment was that of Trevor Matthews, from the Department of Government at the University of Sydney, in April 1978. An Australian selection committee made recommendations to Tokyo University, which made the final selection. The position was generally for two years at associate professor level, initially in the International Relations Section of the Department of Social Sciences for the first nine appointments (1978–93), overseen by Professor Watanabe, and then in the English Section of the Department of Foreign Languages for three further appointments through to September 1999, overseen by Professor Yoichi Kibata. Hosting by the English section meant the appointees were required to teach English as well as Australian studies. They often also taught at Tsuda University and/or Keio University. The full list of appointments can be viewed in Table 10.1.

---

33 No annual reports are available after 2011–12. However, the foundation's current strategic plan can be accessed online: AJF, 'Australia–Japan Foundation Strategic Plan: 2017–2022', Australian Government Department of Foreign Affairs and Trade, n.d., www.dfat.gov.au/people-to-people/foundations-councils-institutes/australia-japan-foundation/governance/Pages/ajf-strategic-plan-2017-2022, accessed 28 August 2020. It defines the foundation's commitment to public diplomacy and includes Education and Australian Studies as one of five priority areas. The visiting professorship at Tokyo University is highlighted.

Table 10.1: Visiting Associate Professors in Australian Studies to Tokyo University (1978–99).[34]

Period	Name	Home institution (at time of appointment)	Principal research field(s)
1978–80	Trevor Matthews	University of Sydney	Political science
1980–81	Roy Forward	University of Queensland	Political science
1981–82	Robyn Lim	University of New South Wales/Australian Office of National Assessments	International relations
1982–84	Allan Patience	Flinders University	International relations
1984–86	Rodney Tiffen	University of Sydney	Politics, media studies
1986–88	William Purcell	University of New South Wales	Business studies
1988–90	Humphrey McQueen	Independent scholar	Australian history, culture
1991 (April–Sept)	Colin McKenzie	Osaka University	Economics
1991–93	Dennis Rumley	University of Western Australia	International relations, geopolitics
1993–96	Peter King	University of Sydney	International relations, politics
1996–98	Robin Gerster	Monash University	Australian literature, cultural history
1998–99	David Day	Independent scholar	Australian history, politics, diplomatic history

Source: Yoichi Kibata, personal communication with author, 2019.

As a Tokyo University position—rather than an appointment managed by the Australian embassy or other agency—the 'job description' was academic rather than having an explicit cultural diplomacy brief. Nonetheless, the larger and longer impacts of the position were significant. Students at Komaba were recruited to Australian studies, including Teruhiko Fukushima, later professor at the National Defense Academy of Japan and president of the ASAJ, taught by Trevor Matthews. Many of the appointees produced significant publications on Australia–Japan relations and regional politics and a number maintained significant engagements with Japan.

---

34 I thank Professor Yoichi Kibata, formerly of Tokyo University and a major supporter of the chair position, for providing details of the appointments for this period and for general assistance in researching this essay.

The international relations field is especially strong. For example, Robyn Lim went on to become professor of international relations at Nanzan University and author of *The Geopolitics of East Asia* (2003). Allan Patience and Rodney Tiffen became leading scholars in the fields of Australian politics and media, foreign policy and regional relations. Their books include the former's *Australian Foreign Policy in Australia: Middle Power or Awkward Partner?* (2018) and the co-edited collection *On the Western Edge: Comparisons of Japan and Australia* (2007), and the latter's *Scandals: Media, Politics & Corruption in Contemporary Australia* (1999) and *Diplomatic Deceits: Government, Media and East Timor* (2001). Peter King's field was also politics and international relations, and he was co-editor with Yoichi Kibata of *Peace Building in the Asia Pacific Region: Perspectives from Japan and Australia* (1996) and author of *West Papua and Indonesia since Suharto: Independence, Autonomy or Chaos?* (2004).

Humphrey McQueen was probably the highest-profile figure at the time of his appointment with a suite of influential books already published, including *A New Britannia* (1970) and *Social Sketches of Australia, 1888–1975* (1978). Further books, *Japan to the Rescue: Australian Security around the Indonesian Archipelago during the American Century* (1991) and the memoir *Tokyo World: An Australian Diary* (1991), followed his incumbency. Robin Gerster—the first appointment from a literature department—also published a memoir of his Tokyo tenure, the provocative *Legless in Ginza: Orienting Japan* (1999), followed later by *Travels in Atomic Sunshine: Australia and the Occupancy of Japan* (2008) and, more recently, the co-authored *Pacific Exposures: Photographs in the Australia–Japan Relationship* (2018). David Day's many books include *Reluctant Nation: Australia and the Allied Defeat of Japan, 1942–45* (1992), *Claiming a Continent: A History of Australia* (1996), and biographies of Australian prime ministers Fisher, Curtin, Chifley and Keating.

While the appointees often had close relations with and support from the AJF, the Resource Centre and other staff based in the embassy—Gerster testifies to the support he received from the 'tireless' Sachiko Tamai of the Cultural Relations office[35]—official support from the Australian side, including financial investment, was minimal. However, when the position was at risk of disappearing, Australian personnel did become more actively involved and the AJF's relation to the position changed significantly.

---

35   Robin Gerster, *Legless in Ginza: Orienting Japan* (Melbourne: Melbourne University Press, 1999), 46.

Later Years: The Visiting Professor in Australian Studies

Towards the end of the 1990s, Tokyo University's central administration was seeking to reduce the number of teaching staff and in this context the future of the Australian studies position became uncertain. The Australian ambassador at the time, Peter Grey, met with the president of the university in order to make the case for maintaining the position, and, one might guess, with the promise of greater contributions from the Australian side. Despite the danger of the position disappearing, the timing in fact was fortuitous. The university's then Center for Research Materials in American Studies was in the process of being reconstituted and the Ministry of Education insisted that this reconstitution should include significant, visible change in its profile. The decision was made that a new centre would be formed, extending its scope to the Pacific and Australasia. The Center for Pacific and American Studies (CPAS) was launched in 2000, incorporating the newly named position of Visiting Professor in Australian Studies, in effect an upgraded definition of the post, placing it alongside similar visiting positions at the Menzies Centre at the University of London and at Harvard University. It also provided the model for the BHP Billiton Chair in Australian Studies established at Peking University in 2011.

The position would now be for one academic year, and its location within CPAS rather than within a particular department encouraged greater interdisciplinarity in the range of potential candidates. We might say it became more of an 'Australia Studies' appointment in the sense that that term is used to cover interdisciplinary humanities and social sciences–based approaches. Professor Kibata and, later, Professor Toshiko Ellis (Graduate School of Arts and Sciences) played major roles in supporting the position. The first appointment under the new arrangements was Dr Stephen Alomes, from the Australian studies team at Deakin University.[36] The 20th visiting professor at Komaba, Professor David Lowe, is also, as it happens, from Deakin University. Members of the AJF board in Australia formed the selection committees in the early years, until in 2004 the AJF funded the Australia-based International Australian Studies Association to manage this process, with an Australian-based selection committee led by senior

---

36   See Stephen Alomes, 'The 21st Century Model: Teaching Australian Studies at the University of Tokyo', *Crossings* 6, no. 1 (2001): 33–35.

Australian studies academic Professor Kate Darian-Smith, plus a CPAS representative (often the centre's director), making recommendations to Tokyo University for the ultimate decision. At the time of writing, the COVID pandemic had disrupted the movement of new Australian appointments to Tokyo University: Professor Nicole Moore (University of New South Wales Canberra, specialising in Australian literature and media) is due to visit in September 2022, Professor Barbara Pini (Griffith University, rural studies, gender studies, sociology) in September 2023.

Table 10.2: Visiting Professors in Australian Studies to Tokyo University (2000–2020).

Period	Name	Home institution (at time of appointment)	Principal research field(s)
2000–01	Stephen Alomes	Deakin University	Australian history, Australian studies
2001–02	Joanne Scott	University of the Sunshine Coast	Australian history, Australian studies
2002–03	Chilla Bulbeck	University of Adelaide	Sociology, women's studies, Australian studies
2003–04	Allan Kellehear	La Trobe University	Sociology, public health
2004–05	Christine Nicholls	Flinders University	Art history, Aboriginal art
2005–06	Les Terry	Victoria University	Sociology, policy studies
2006–07	David Day	Independent scholar	Australian history, politics, diplomatic history
2007–08	David Carter	University of Queensland	Australian literature, cultural history, Australian studies
2008–09	Michael Ackland	Monash University	Australian literature
2009–10	Gay Hawkins	University of New South Wales	Cultural and media studies
2010–11	Baden Offord	Southern Cross University	Human rights, cultural studies
2011–12	Anne Collett	University of Wollongong	Australian and postcolonial literature
2012–13	Justin Dabner	James Cook University	Comparative taxation law
2013–14	Catriona Elder	University of Sydney	Australian studies, cultural studies
2014-15	Anna Johnston	University of Tasmania	Australian literature, postcolonialism, history
2015–16	Maria Nugent	The Australian National University	Australian history, Aboriginal history

Period	Name	Home institution (at time of appointment)	Principal research field(s)
2016–17	David Carter	University of Queensland	Australian literature, cultural history, Australian studies
2017–18	Helen Gilbert	Royal Holloway, University of London	Theatre studies, postcolonialism
2018–19	Melanie Oppenheimer	Flinders University	Australian history
2019–20	David Lowe	Deakin University	Australian history, diplomatic history

Source: Author's summary.

The visiting professor has a full teaching load, comprising one course each semester at each level—junior undergraduate, senior undergraduate and graduate—an arrangement that pretty much guarantees interdisciplinarity across the offerings whatever the incumbent's disciplinary background. Where topics are relevant, the position assists postgraduate students (most from British or American studies) working on their dissertations. Most incumbents have also taught at Keio University, and given academic lectures and public presentations in venues in different Japanese cities. In addition to contributing to CPAS's seminar series and publications (the *CPAS Newsletter* and the journal *Pacific and American Studies*), and in many cases organising a conference or symposium during their tenure, the visiting professor also delivers a special keynote at the ASAJ annual conference, later published in the association's *Journal of Australian Studies*. On return to Australia, the visiting professor has also contributed a reflection on their experience in Japan to the *Journal of Australian Studies*, the Australian-based publication of the International Australian Studies Association.

The broader Australian studies remit for the position is perhaps less likely to produce new books on the Australia–Japan relationship, at least in the domain of international relations, but the most significant point for present purposes is the deepening of understanding on the Australian side of the potential of the visiting professorship as an asset in cultural diplomacy. In the 2000–01 AJF annual report there is a passing reference to Visiting Professor Joanne Scott presenting a lecture, but from 2005, the appointment and the chair's activities become a regular, prominent element alongside fuller accounts of the work of the ASAJ. A much closer relationship has developed between the new centre and the AJF, and while the position remains first and foremost a Tokyo University academic appointment, there is greater financial investment from the AJF (and from ambassadors). The foundation provides a research and travel grant for the professor and seeks to engage the holder in a wide range of foundation/embassy activities.

However, while the cultural diplomacy dimension of the appointment is now more fully appreciated, there remains significant scope for expanding the public role of the position and, more directly, its role in building Australian studies across Japanese institutions. Australian studies in Japan is now well established through the ASAJ and the ANZLSJ, their conferences and journals, courses in several universities and the visiting professorship at Tokyo University.[37] But bringing a new generation of scholars into the field remains a challenge. Despite the firm foundations that have been laid and the active Australian studies community now established, in a much more crowded and competitive environment it is still the case that research on Australian topics, except perhaps in the fields of trade and international relations, remains a relatively low priority in Japanese universities. The departure of the Australian Resources Library from Tokyo would likely have had a negative effect on generating new interest in Australian studies. Here is a major role for the Visiting Professor in Australian Studies, working with Japanese colleagues across the university system to encourage new research from emerging scholars and graduates.

Australian studies might well sound like a narrow or inward-looking academic discipline, but the position at Tokyo University in the context of the active ASAJ and a range of other academic and general public activities gives this broad, interdisciplinary field a significant role to play not just in the teaching and research of Australian topics but also, through classroom contact, in influencing a large body of future professionals in the Japanese system. Australian studies at its strongest is open to a very wide range of scholarly fields and student and public interest; many individuals working in areas of public policy, cultural management, cultural institutions or environmental policies, as well as trade and economics, can be engaged by Australian expertise. For the future of Australian studies in Japan, in addition to maintaining a strong record of appointments to the

---

37   See Darian-Smith, 'Research, Teaching and Cultural Diplomacy'; Yasue Arimitsu, 'The Contemporary State of Academic Appraisal of Australian Literature in Japanese Universities', *Antipodes* 25, no. 1 (2011): 7–13.

professorship and strong support for participating Japanese organisations, increased and better targeted support for Japanese academic staff and, very strongly, for master's and doctoral research students should be crucial in future planning. Grants are still available for Australian studies projects under the AJF's grant programs—now administered from Canberra—but there are no schemes specifically dedicated to Australian studies, research fellowships or postgraduate study. While the current grant guidelines include 'support for the teaching of Australian studies in Japan and the maintenance and expansion of Japanese academic interest and expertise on Australia' among its priority areas, they also advise that 'proposals for study tours and academic research projects, particularly those that lack a strong communications component, are generally not competitive'.[38] The history of government engagement through the Australia–Japan Foundation—and comparisons with activity in China, for example— does suggest that a dedicated program of grants and/or fellowships for academic and postgraduate research projects in Australian studies is a key element in generating and maintaining engagement in the field among younger scholars and over the longer term.

---

38 Department of Foreign Affairs and Trade, 'International Relations Grants Program: Australia–Japan Foundation 2020 Guidelines', Australian Government Department of Foreign Affairs and Trade, 20 December 2019, www.dfat.gov.au/sites/default/files/ajf-irgp-grant-guidelines-2020.pdf, accessed 28 August 2020.

11

Japan as Number One: Relations with Australia in the 1980s and 1990s

Richard Broinowski

I feel qualified to comment on the development of postwar relations between Japan and Australia because of my own involvement in it: as a young diplomat in Tokyo in the early 1960s, as Japan desk officer in Canberra following that posting, as executive director of the Japan Secretariat in Canberra from 1979 to 1982 and as general manager of Radio Australia in the early 1990s.[1]

This chapter focuses on the 1980s and 1990s, in particular. By 1980, the mutual benefits of Australia's relations with Japan were increasingly clear. Here were two wealthy and politically stable democracies with highly compatible trade interests. Australia had raw materials feeding a burgeoning industrial sector in Japan, and primary products helping to satisfy the needs of a Japanese community with rising standards of living. Japan was producing high-quality Japanese manufactured products for an expanding Australian domestic market.

---

1   I have been generously assisted with ideas and reminiscences for this chapter by Geoff Miller and Rawdon Dalrymple, two former Australian ambassadors to Japan, and Kim Jones, minister and deputy chief of mission of the embassy during the 1980s. Allan Gyngell, a senior adviser to Prime Minister Keating and current president of the Australia Institute of International Affairs, referred me to the following readings: Allan Gyngell, *Fear of Abandonment: Australia in the World since 1942* (Carlton: La Trobe University Press, 2017); Paul Keating, *Engagement: Australia Faces the Asia-Pacific* (Sydney: Macmillan, 2000).

The nascent postwar commercial relationship with Japan was reinforced by two bilateral agreements. As outlined in previous chapters, the first was a far-sighted commodity-based Agreement on Commerce, signed by Australian trade minister John McEwen and Japanese foreign minister Nobusuke Kishi in Hakone in July 1957. The second was a much broader Basic Treaty of Friendship and Cooperation signed by the two nations' prime ministers, Malcolm Fraser and Takeo Miki, in Tokyo in June 1976. The former applied most-favoured-nation treatment to bilateral trade in agricultural and manufactured commodities, meaning that under the rules of the WTO (World Trade Organization) neither country could discriminate against the other by granting more favourable conditions to third countries. The Treaty of Friendship expanded bilateral cooperation to cover political, economic, labour, human rights, legal, scientific, technical, social, cultural, professional, sporting and environmental issues.

Buttressing the relationship with such treaties was well and good, but it did not altogether allay some Australian anxieties. For one thing, the signing of the 1957 agreement with Kishi reminded some observers of his record as a war criminal, and the atrocious treatment some Australian POWs had experienced at the hands of their Japanese captors. For another, the Japanese economy was almost too perfect. Japan had the world's highest rate of personal savings, almost strike-free labour relations, and rates of unemployment five points below those of other advanced industrial democracies. It was the world's leading creditor nation with net capital exports in 1984 of just under US$50 billion. It was also the world's preferred supplier of motor vehicles and consumer electronics.[2] Two books by influential American academics amplified Australian concerns about the overwhelming economic power of Japan—Ezra Vogel's *Japan as Number One*,[3] and Herman Kahn's *The Emerging Japanese Superstate*.[4] A common theme in these works was the prediction that Japan would very shortly achieve enormous economic, technological and financial stature, and become very powerful in international affairs, more able and

---

2   Chalmers Johnson, 'The Japanese Economy: A Different Kind of Capitalism', in *Japanese Models of Conflict Resolution*, ed. S.N. Eisenstadt and Eyal Ben-Ari (London: K. Paul International, 1990), 39.
3   Ezra Vogel, *Japan as Number One* (Cambridge, MA: Harvard University Press, 1979), doi.org/10.4159/harvard.9780674366299.
4   Herman Kahn, *The Emerging Japanese Superstate: Challenge and Response* (Englewood Cliffs, NJ: Prentice Hall, 1970).

inclined to dictate terms of trade to its main trading partners, including Australia. Ronald Conway's *The Land of the Long Weekend*[5] invidiously compared Australia with Japan.

Australia's Lack of Commercial Coordination

Australian officials and traders were faced with a novel situation—for the first time they had to deal with a major trading partner outside the Anglosphere. Not only that, but a country commercially disciplined by an arcane process of coordination through the *keiretsu* system, whereby manufacturers, supply chain partners and distributors worked closely together in industrial silos, each led by a bank. Their efforts were strongly supported and coordinated by a highly educated central bureaucracy represented by the powerful Ministry of International Trade and Industry (MITI). In their dealings with Australian suppliers, Japanese companies studied the market and tended to pick and choose between firms, creating competition and driving down prices in the process.

Accustomed to dealing primarily with the United Kingdom and the United States, Australian traders were ill-prepared for what was commonly regarded as the Japanese 'miracle', its phenomenal recovery since devastation in the Pacific War and the outstanding cohesion of its industries. They saw themselves as having a far less effective management structure than Japan. The federal government had exclusive jurisdiction over some, but not all, external affairs powers. The extent to which Australian states could participate in foreign relations was untested but showed signs of being substantial. In the federal bureaucracy were overlapping areas of policy formulation between different departments, and some areas of intense rivalry and jurisdictional jealousy in conducting relations with Japan. Australian companies had never considered a coordinated strategy and lacked knowledge about Japanese tactics, having only short-term perspectives about prices and insufficient information about Japan's short- and long-term buying strategies. Furthermore, few Australian bureaucrats or businesspeople had even the faintest knowledge of Japanese law, language or culture.

5   Ronald Conway, *The Land of the Long Weekend* (South Melbourne: Sun Books, 1978).

A special effort to get Australia's act together began in 1968. It was precipitated by a singular case concerning the employment of Japanese workers in a Western Australian oil and mineral project. Lack of coordination between relevant Commonwealth government departments in dealing with the issues had resulted in adverse publicity in Japan. Consequently, the Department of External Affairs proposed that an interdepartmental committee comprising itself and the Departments of Trade and Resources, Labour and National Service, Science and Technology, Primary Industry, Customs and Excise, and Interior (responsible for ANIB, the Australian News and Information Bureau) should meet monthly to try to coordinate policy at the federal level. However, these meetings were unsuccessful in solving the problem. The committee lacked an independent secretariat, was plagued by in-fighting, and lost its authority as junior officials were delegated to attend the meetings over more senior figures. Accordingly, federal policies remained uncoordinated and duplication of effort continued, and there was no long-term planning and no attempt to engage the private sector.

In 1978, the Fraser government recognised this as a chronic problem. As a result, Melbourne businessman and philanthropist Sidney Baillieu Myer was invited to chair a standing committee of senior bureaucrats, business leaders and a trade union official. All had plenty of clout. Aside from Myer, the committee included figures such as the prominent economist Sir John Crawford; Gordon Jackson of CSR (what was earlier known as the Commonwealth Sugar Refinery); Peter Nolan, secretary of the Australian Council of Trade Unions; Doug McKay, secretary of the Department of Overseas Trade; and two External Affairs deputy secretaries, John Rowland and Alf Parsons. The committee invited an extraordinarily large cross-section of the Australian community to make submissions, including expatriates in Japan. It also held in camera interviews in Canberra, Melbourne and Sydney.

Myer's report recommended Australia coordinate its policy towards Japan at three levels—within the Canberra bureaucracy, between the bureaucracy and the private sector, and between the federal and state governments. Thus, three committees were created—a Standing Committee on Japan (SCJ), comprising the permanent heads of seven Commonwealth government departments most involved in trade with Japan; a Consultative Committee on Relations with Japan (CCRJ), comprising the SCJ plus representatives of business, union peak councils, primary industry and the academic community; and a Commonwealth–States Committee.

The chairs of these committees included Peter Henderson, secretary of the Department of Foreign Affairs, Sir Gordon Jackson, CEO of CSR, and Sir Arvi Parbo, chairman of Western Mining. Among the members of the inaugural CCRJ in 1979 were Simon Crean, federal secretary of the Storemen and Packers' Union; David Asimus of the Wool Corporation; Bruce Watson, CEO of Mount Isa Mines; and Professor Wang Gungwu of The Australian National University.

The whole coordinating machinery was given coherence by having a secretariat in Canberra, which was to arrange committee meetings, prepare agendas and write research papers on subjects for discussion. I was appointed its executive director. I was joined by Dr Alan Rix, an academic specialising in Japan; Geoffrey George, a former intelligence officer; and a small support staff.

The SCJ and CCRJ met monthly in Canberra, while the Commonwealth–States Committee met only infrequently. Much to the irritation of at least one of the permanent heads on the SCJ and CCRJ,[6] members were not allowed to delegate their attendance to deputies. As Myer observed in his report:

> The experience of Commonwealth inter-department committees had shown that once a secretary delegated to a deputy secretary, the latter would in turn delegate at the next meeting to a first assistant secretary, and so on down the line until whoever represented a particular department would have no authority to decide anything. And this would lead to the kind of report devoid of clear recommendations that Prime Minister Gough Whitlam caustically rejected in 1973 when he was advised to take an 'on the one hand … on the other hand', 'welcome though not seek', 'neither emphasise nor ignore' response to a problem.[7]

The small secretariat had considerable clout in determining the agendas and choosing subjects for research. Topics were diverse, including such things as the impact of Australian industrial relations problems and their possible impact on Japanese confidence in the reliability of Australian suppliers; Japanese banks' reactions to the Campbell Report on Australia's financial system; the problem of the size of Japanese bluefin tuna

6   John Stone, secretary of the Treasury.
7   Ad Hoc Working Committee on Australia–Japan Relations, *Australia–Japan Relations: Report of the Ad Hoc Working Committee on Australia–Japan Relations, May 1978* (Canberra: Australian Government Publishing Service, 1978).

fishing catches in Australian waters; the future of Japanese tourism in Australia; how Australia was portrayed in Japanese school textbooks; the implications of Japanese–European Union relations for Australia; the psychology behind Japan's whaling industry; the future of uranium and woodchip exports to Japan; United States and European Community pressures on Japan to correct trade imbalances; regional strategic and military developments; the reactions of Pacific Island countries to Japan's proposal to dump radioactive wastes in the Pacific; and whether Japanese application of new industrial materials such as carbon fibres, ceramics and amorphous metals would impact on Australia's traditional iron ore and coking coal exports.

Between 1979 and 1982, the secretariat produced 28 research papers. It was also instrumental in negotiating a Migratory Birds Agreement with Japan. It is difficult to calculate the degree to which these activities sharpened Australia's trading approaches towards Japan, but they must have had some effect on corporate awareness, and better-informed trade delegations to Japan. Some research papers became standard texts in Australian government departments and company board rooms.

Japanese–Australian Relations in the 1980s and 1990s

Japan's business practices were not Australia's only concern. Since the 1970s, Japan had been developing an international reputation as an unstoppable economic power, buying up property and trophy assets, notably in the United States, but also in Australia, much like China's behaviour today. But the Plaza Agreement of 1985, an agreement between the United States, France, Britain, Germany and Japan that persuaded Japan to revalue the yen against the US dollar, put a stop to such speculations. American exports became cheaper, Japanese goods more expensive. This caused Japan to reduce its imports or negotiate lower prices for them, including Australia's minerals, which coincided with an economic downturn in Australia's own economy. In an informal exchange I had with him over the preparation of this chapter, Geoff Miller observed that during his time as ambassador to Japan in the 1980s, Tokyo resource prices were a source of great bilateral tension during meetings of the Australia–Japan Ministerial Committee and Australia Japan Business Co-operation Committee. Each side accused the other of collusive selling and buying, and Australian ministers, including John Dawkins, Paul Keating's treasurer from 1991 to 1993, paid a number of visits to Japan that did not end happily.

Another source of tension concerned the opening up of the Japanese beef market. In direct competition with the United States, Australia was concerned that Washington might try to persuade the Japanese trade authorities to substitute American beef for imports from Australia. Great efforts were made by the embassy and the Australian Meat and Livestock Corporation to prevent this from happening, and it did not. In fact, Japan became Australia's biggest market for frozen and fresh beef. We were still a long way from negotiating the kind of certainties of demand sought by the Australian suppliers to Japanese companies, but it was a start.

During the eighties, some other developments served to broaden the narrow base of Australian raw material exports to Japan. First, electronics, including early model computers, televisions, car radios and hi-fidelity stereophonic equipment, quite rapidly emerged as an industry rivalling steel. For the first time, Australian silicon (a tetravalent metalloid), and rare earths from beach sands were in demand in Japan as semiconductors for these new industries. Second, the Japanese public, encouraged by a successful Australian 'clean and green' advertising campaign, developed an attraction for Australian horticulture products which began to stock supermarket shelves. These included not just fruit, vegetables and dairy products, but one or two indigenous products such as *jumpu stēki*, kangaroo meat. Third was a sudden fascination for Australian wildlife. This may have been prompted by the arrival in a Japanese zoo of a pair of koalas, or a striking and wildly popular television advertisement showing a frill-necked lizard, an *erimakitokage*, running across the screen on its hind legs. Long queues of the Japanese public shuffled past the koala cage at the zoo, and the Australian Treasury was bemused at the sudden demand in Japan for its newly minted two-cent coins portraying a frill-necked lizard.

Another product of Japan's economic miracle was an expansion in people-to-people contacts. Sister city relations were established between over 60 towns and cities in Japan and their Australian counterparts. Surf clubs began to appear at Japanese beaches, even though the surf might be negligible. Japanese tourism to Australia climbed, although this benefited Japanese entrepreneurs more than it did Australians. Australian companies in the trade were not often given a chance to make a profit as most tourists paid in advance to Japanese companies, and their discretionary expenditure in Australia was channelled into buses, shops and restaurants owned by Japanese agents or entrepreneurs. The practice of Japanese sticking together in tight pelotons behind a leader waving a flag while they collectively viewed the strange ways of Australian *gaijin* (literally, outside persons or foreigners) was orderly, although the locals found it somewhat irritating.

A curious consequence of the Japanese tourist trade was an attempt by some Japanese entrepreneurs to establish retirement homes for elderly Japanese along the Australian coast, particularly in Queensland and northern New South Wales. Geoff Miller recalled to me that one such scheme was called 'Silver Colombia'. Needless to say, such schemes for walled villages were not well received by Australians, and died an early death. However, as mentioned in Chapter 3, a similar Japanese proposal was met with initial enthusiasm.

During a visit he made to Australia in 1987 to attend a meeting of the Australia–Japan Ministerial Committee, the Japanese minister for international trade and industry, Hajime Tamura, proposed that Australia allow a new kind of city to be built in Australia with Japanese involvement. Awkwardly called a 'Multifunction Polis' by the MITI, the city was planned to have a population of between 20,000 and 200,000, many of them coming from abroad (meaning, some said, from Japan). Based on 'techno-polises' already in existence in Japan, it would include state-of-the-art urban technology and sophisticated leisure facilities, and would be commercially viable. Attracted to the prospect of job creation and infusions of capital, the governments of Queensland, New South Wales, Victoria and South Australia all studied Tamura's concept and made proposals to host it.

Various Australian think tanks also studied the idea. Seminars were held in 1989, open to those who could pay a substantial fee. Although Tamura had proposed the city as an international venture, Japan would obviously be the dominant partner along with Australia. The Australian public only got to know of such plans later, and mainly through press releases. Some suspected Japanese motives and elitism. Rumours arose, amplified by the press, that the whole concept was a ploy by Japan to establish a science city in a nice place for Japanese inhabitants by the Australian sea. Some suggested it would be a 'Trojan Horse', others a 'Pandora's Box'.[8] The idea eventually died when the decision was made to offer a swampy and chemical-ridden wasteland near Port Adelaide for the city. Some Australian entrepreneurs, from Adelaide, in particular, had visions of commercial opportunities that a multifunction polis would create and regretted the outcome.

Another missed opportunity occurred when David Hill, managing director of the ABC, decided in the early 1990s to cancel Radio Australia's short-wave Japanese-language broadcasts, believing short-wave to be an outdated 1930s technology. As the newly appointed general manager of Radio Australia in 1990, I argued against Hill's proposal, and obtained his agreement to go to Japan to see how many listeners we had. The answer was that tens of thousands of listeners belonged to short-wave clubs throughout Japan, and that Radio Australia was one of their favourite stations. Sony had even developed a radio set that had pre-programmed cards that slotted into the receivers and obviated the fiddly business of tuning. The cards included Radio Australia frequencies. I returned to Melbourne with my findings, but Hill was obdurate. I had to close our longstanding Japanese service and sack its broadcasters. Radio Australia became a shadow of its former self, closing some of its short-wave transmitters, using geo-stationary satellites to beam radio and television signals into an increasingly crowded Asian space, and shifting uneasily between commercial and ABC management of the service. One of the most ill-judged decisions was taken in 2000 by Australian foreign minister Alexander Downer when he approved the sale of Radio Australia's transmitters at Cox's Peninsula, near Darwin, to a private evangelical Christian broadcaster which used them to send short-wave messages over Indonesia, the world's largest Muslim country.

Growth of Australian Political Expectations

As seen from the perspective of a succession of Australian prime ministers, the relationship with Japan continued to be a priority among their international policies.[9] On a visit to Japan in February 1984, Bob Hawke

---

8   See Ross E. Mouer and Yoshio Sugimoto, eds, *The MFP Debate: A Background Reader* (Bundoora: La Trobe University Press, 1990).

9   Australia's prime ministers during this period were as follows: Malcolm Fraser (1975–83), Bob Hawke (1983–91), Paul Keating (1991–96) and John Howard (1996–2007).

was delighted to establish his kind of matey 'Bob' and 'Yasu' relationship with Prime Minister Yasuhiro Nakasone. This did not prevent Japan from reducing the amount of iron ore, coking and steaming coal, and beef it imported from Australia as a result of an economic downturn and pressure from the United States to increase its own shares of these markets. However, Hawke was able to offset this by getting Japan to increase its investments in Australia in motor vehicle production, tourism, cattle feedlots and Queensland real estate.

In his first year as prime minister, Paul Keating reminded Australians that Japan took one-third of Australia's exports and was our third-largest source of foreign investment. Yet due to a variety of developments in Japan during his tenure, Keating's faith in the continuation of a robust Japanese economy appeared to waver. Long-term deflation reduced Japan's economic growth to just 0.8 per cent annually, Japan's working-age population peaked and began to decline, and more and more of its productive capacity moved offshore to other Asian countries. Furthermore, there was a major earthquake in Kobe, a terrorist gas attack in Tokyo's subways by the fanatical group Aum Shinrikyo, and an uncharacteristically rapid turnover of prime ministers. From 1994 to 1996, the conservative Liberal Democratic Party which had virtually ruled Japan since the end of the Pacific War, briefly gave way to a leftist government led by Tomiichi Murayama of the Japan Socialist Party.

A symbol of the importance a country places in its relations with another is the prominence of its embassy. As Bob Hawke's treasurer in the late 1980s, Keating degraded Australia's physical presence in Tokyo by selling off the ancient embassy gardens which had enormous historical significance. Chapters 6 and 7 have touched on this still-controversial move. The reason was financial expediency. In order to correct the Commonwealth budget deficit, Keating decided, with Hawke's blessing, to divest some of Australia's overseas assets. As Japan was experiencing a huge property bubble at the time, with land in Tokyo worth millions of yen a square metre, Australia's embassy and its ancient garden in Mita tempted both sellers and buyers. The land was subdivided. Most of the garden was sold, and a new embassy combining a chancery and staff apartments designed by Melbourne architects Denton Corker Marshall was constructed. The move into the new premises was a complicated and time-consuming business, and there has been plenty of debate as to whether the new embassy has been a success or not. As Rawdon Dalrymple, Australian ambassador from 1989 to 1993, observed:

The dominant issue for me in Tokyo was not a matter of bilateral relations—it was the completion and then occupying the new embassy building and all the complex of associated issues. [There were] many problems with reconciling staff to accepting smaller living quarters than they had been used to.[10]

In the 1980s and 1990s, most Australian prime ministers, including Fraser and Howard, had consistently seen Japan as Australia's most important trade partner, not just in the region but the world. Prime ministers, foreign and trade ministers, and state premiers made frequent visits to Japan, which were not often reciprocated by the Japanese. Looking beyond narrow trade considerations, Hawke, Keating and Howard began to see Japan as a potentially valuable ally in regional diplomacy. During a visit to Seoul in 1989, Hawke launched his Asia-Pacific Economic Cooperation (APEC) concept, lightly disparaged at the time by Foreign Minister Gareth Evans as four adjectives in search of a noun. But the concept sank its roots in fertile Asian soil. The Japanese in particular were strong supporters of the concept, and insisted on the participation of the United States, which was not what Hawke had originally planned. On his watch, Keating expanded his concept of Japan's potential role in building regional institutions, stating that 'the health of the international system as a whole requires the world's second-largest economy to play a more substantial role in the world'.[11]

Beyond Trade — Regional Cooperation

During the eighties and nineties, Japan and Australia cooperated in other aspects of regional diplomacy, including involvement in the Association of Southeast Asian Nations (ASEAN 'plus') councils. Consultations with the 10 ASEAN members[12] plus Australia, Japan and New Zealand (ASEAN plus three), were formulated in December 1997 and institutionalised at the Third ASEAN Summit in Manila in 1999.[13] Australia and Japan also signed the ASEAN Treaty of Amity and Cooperation. They were also the two main drivers in establishing the ASEAN Regional Forum in 1994, which comprises the 10 ASEAN members, plus 10 other countries with

---

10 Rawdon Dalrymple, email to the author, 1 May 2019.
11 Keating, *Engagement*, 70.
12 The ASEAN members are Brunei, Cambodia, Indonesia, Laos, Malaysia, Myanmar (known as Burma until 1989), the Philippines, Singapore, Thailand and Vietnam.
13 Russia, China and the United States were subsequently invited to join a regular forum with the 10 ASEAN countries, plus the original three (ASEAN plus three plus three).

an interest in security in Asia—Australia, Canada, China, the European Union, India, Japan, New Zealand, Russia, South Korea and the United States. There are also countries with observer status, including North Korea and Papua New Guinea.

However, Japanese and Australian regional interests did not always coincide, particularly in defence and strategic matters. In the early Cold War period, Australia feared that releasing Japan too soon from the cocoon of its pacifist Constitution might presage the country's remilitarisation. Moreover, Australia did not have any interest in backing Japan's contest with China and Korea over the sovereignty of islands in the Japan Sea and East China Sea, or in supporting Japan's bid to have Russia return four islands in the Kurils seized at the end of the Pacific War.

But as the Cold War moved on, Australian officials accepted that Article Nine of the Japanese Constitution, which forbade Japan from settling international disputes by military means, and from raising military forces, was being more honoured in the breach rather than the observance. By the 1980s, Japan had acquired very competent ground, air and naval forces, euphemistically called the Self-Defense Forces (SDF). There was a growing feeling in Canberra, as well as Washington, that they should be capable of being deployed abroad, at least in peacekeeping and disaster relief operations. The phrase 'not pulling their weight' was an opinion frequently expressed within such circles. In response, the Japanese adapted their force capabilities during the eighties and nineties to allow aircraft and naval vessels to range beyond Japan's territorial waters. In 1992–93, ground self-defence forces were, for the first time, permitted to take part in overseas operations, specifically in peacekeeping operations under the United Nations Transitional Authority in Cambodia. Self-Defense Force personnel were also involved as peacekeeping observers in East Timor in 2001, and from 2004 to 2006, ground forces were authorised to send a battalion to support reconstruction after the invasion of Iraq, which were guarded by Australian Army units.

In 1995 Keating signed a Joint Declaration on the Australia–Japan Partnership, and described a 'relationship of unprecedented quality', a foundation on which both countries pledged to build 'an enduring and steadfast partnership'. At the same time, Japan affirmed that Australia was 'an indispensable partner in regional affairs'.[14]

---

14   Gyngell, *Fear of Abandonment*, 225.

In March 1996, the Australian Liberal–National Party coalition won a general election and John Howard became prime minister. Like his predecessor, he placed great importance on the bilateral relationship with Japan, but introduced a different perspective. He asserted that Australians 'do not have to change who we are' (meaning mainly Europeans with a European culture) and that Australia did not have to put Asia at the centre of its foreign policy. He refuted Labor's 'East Asian Hemisphere' policy, and foreshadowed that his new government would put Australian views more forcefully in Asian forums in future. This ruffled a few Japanese feathers, but in a visit to Tokyo in June 1996, Howard's new foreign minister, Alexander Downer, calmed the atmosphere when he declared that Australia highly valued the contribution Japan had made to regional stability through supporting the strategic engagement of the United States in the Western Pacific.

The Japanese appeared to adjust to the difference of emphasis, although other events early in Howard's tenure raised eyebrows in the Foreign Ministry about the reactionary nature of the new Australian government. They included Howard's initial failure to distance himself from Pauline Hanson, a newly elected parliamentarian who delivered an anti-Asian maiden speech in federal parliament in 1996; Howard's success in sabotaging the 1999 referendum on whether Australia should become a republic; and his reluctance to distance himself from his caricature as the United States' 'deputy sheriff' in Asia. The issues attracted adverse publicity in Japan, particularly the Hanson phenomenon. Artist Kariya Tetsu ran an illustrated story in the popular comic book *Oishinbō* ('The Gourmet') in which he questioned whether One Nation meant that Australia was for white people only.[15] How enduring, Japanese officials may have wondered, were anti-Asian feelings in Australia, and for how long would Australia cling to Britain's apron strings?

Conclusions

By 2021, although eclipsed by its trade with China, Australia's trade with Japan remains Australia's second-largest in value, ahead of that with the Republic of Korea and the United States. Coordinating machinery is no longer needed to manage it.

---

15 Alison Broinowski, *About Face: Asian Accounts of Australia* (Melbourne: Scribe Publications, 2003), 162.

In contrast to their narrow trade-based postwar beginnings, Australia's relations with Japan have broadened far beyond commercial considerations. Neither government now sees the need for frequent formal gatherings of ministers to bolster the relationship, although there are many individual ministerial visits each way. Social and cultural links have also matured and broadened through a myriad of sister city relations, and student and cultural exchanges. Before the COVID-19 pandemic struck at the beginning of 2020, Japan was the fifth-largest source of short-term visitors to Australia. These are expected to resume after the pandemic has been contained. The Australia–Japan Foundation finances cooperation in science and technology, sports, the arts, education and people-to-people exchanges.

Conservative Australian officials have for many years advocated that Australia should encourage Japan to loosen the restraints imposed by Article Nine of its Constitution and develop military forces commensurate with its economic status. But Japan doesn't need much encouragement. Its SDF surpasses in size and sophistication all but the military forces of the US, Russia and China. Under a succession of conservative leaders, especially Japan's longest-serving prime minister, Shinzō Abe (2006 and 2007, and from 2012 to 2020), the SDF has expanded its operations well beyond its own borders to participate among other campaigns in the US-led occupation of Iraq and the Australian-led UN transitional military authority in Cambodia. Closer to home, Australian and Japanese defence cooperation has expanded through formal arrangements, beginning with a Joint Declaration on Security Cooperation in 2007, a Comprehensive Partnership in 2008 and a Special Strategic Partnership in 2014.

It now involves annual discussions between Australian and Japanese foreign and defence ministers (the '2+2') and regular air and sea exercises, both bilaterally or in conjunction with the United States and other countries in the region. The driver for such cooperation, although never made explicit, is the perceived threat from China. Instead, it is said to be about shared values of democracy, the rules-based international order, freedom and human rights.

I conclude my chapter with some thoughts on the current parlous state of relations between Australia and China. They are parlous in the sense that we have two factions in Australia pulling in different and counterproductive directions. On the one hand are the traders—the iron ore and coal producers and farmers who sustain our largest and most profitable exports to China. On the other are a collection of officials and think-tank characters in Canberra who pillory China as the greatest threat to the region and think up war games to counter the threat. The Chinese naturally take exception, and impose trade and other barriers against Australian imports.

What is urgently needed is coordinating machinery similar to that which we developed in our responses to the Japanese government and traders in the 1980s. A standing committee on China could involve the permanent heads of key policy departments in Canberra, including Defence and the intelligence agencies, and a consultative committee on relations with China could include those senior officials plus a selection of miners and producers deeply involved in the China trade. Like the machinery we had with Japan, this would need the support of politicians and a secretariat to guide its deliberations and undertake research. A counterpart body in China, if one could be set up, would be a great mutual asset.

12

The Tokyo Embassy, Past, Present and Future: Reflections

Bruce Miller AO

As a (retired) practitioner of international relations and a former Australian ambassador to Japan, I aim to use this concluding chapter to describe the role of the Australian embassy in Tokyo as it has evolved over the last 30 years, and its contribution to achieving Australian goals in Japan.[1] I start, however, with a personal perspective.

Personal Journey

I have had a long association with the embassy. I first visited it in April 1978, when I was in my last year of high school on a Japan Foundation–sponsored study visit to Japan. The occasion was to attend the annual cherry blossom event hosted by the then ambassador, John Menadue, which even then attracted the cream of Japan's business and political worlds. I could not have imagined that I would attend that same function 14 times, hosting it six times as ambassador. That visit sparked my fascination with Japan and was the impetus for my study of Japanese language, literature and history at the University of Sydney, including

---

1   I owe Bill Wise, who served several times at the embassy in Tokyo, a debt of gratitude for his assistance with preparing this chapter.

a year studying in Japan. Before long, after I had completed a law degree, I found myself working at the then Department of Foreign Affairs (DFAT) in Canberra.

I have lived and worked in the current embassy building over three different postings for 14 years out of the last 26 (my first posting began in November 1992). My years in Japan as a student and a diplomat— in junior and later more senior jobs and finally as ambassador—have given me a box seat from which to observe, as well as contribute to the strength and diversity of the relationship between the two nations. The late Dr Ashton Calvert, who was Australian ambassador from 1993 until 1998, and for whom I worked during my first Tokyo posting, always emphasised that many people over several decades have put a great deal of work into the relationship. No one person can claim credit for all that has been achieved, although few would dispute that Ashton contributed more than anyone else over his four postings in Tokyo.

In that spirit, I aim to offer a balanced account of the embassy and its role over my 40 years of personal and 26 years of professional association with it. This will not be a full picture of postwar relations. Rather, I will focus on the periods when I was involved and leave to historians the more dispassionate and comprehensive account.

The Embassy and Its Neighbourhood

The embassy in Mita, in Minato ward, near the government and business heart of Tokyo, is where Australia is represented and pursues its interests in Japan. It is located on an old *daimyō* (feudal lord) estate, the city residence during the Edo period first of the Shimazu family of southern Kyushu (Satsuma and Hyuga, now Kagoshima and Miyazaki), and later the Hachisuka family of Awa (present-day Tokushima).

Australia rented the property after World War II for the use of its representatives to the supreme commander for the Allied powers. We had apparently also rented it for Australia's short-lived legation before the war. When Japan regained its sovereignty with the entry into force of the Treaty of San Francisco in 1952,[2] Australia was in the market for an embassy. After hard-fought negotiations with the Hachisuka family, we bought the

---

2   Okinawa remained under US administration until 1971.

property through an intermediary.[3] The family had fallen on hard times because of their extravagance over many years, and then, as a final blow, the wealth taxes levied after the war on owners of property.[4]

At the time of the Meiji Restoration in 1868, the Azabu and Mita districts were dotted with many such old estates. These estates, together with numerous shrines and temples, occupied the ridges, while the villages were on the flat around the Furukawa River. Those that have survived intact have done so because foreign governments acquired them as embassies.[5] They have otherwise been sold and subdivided.

The combination, however, of earthquakes, particularly the Great Kanto earthquake of 1923, and the loss of much of Tokyo to firebombing during World War II, left little of the physical built environment of the Edo and Meiji periods. But you can still use an Edo-period map to navigate the district, because, despite many modern buildings, the boundaries are still apparent between the *daimyō* estates (now mainly embassies), the temple and shrine grounds, the Azabu-Juban area (a commercial centre since the middle of the Edo period) and residential areas.

Immediately opposite the embassy there are no fewer than three Buddhist temples, while the 1,100-year-old *Moto-shinmeigū*, the local shrine for the district, is just down the road. Even now, as you descend the back steps to Mita 1-chome, you get a strong sense of entering a village, with many small houses and shops, and until recently, a working public bath. Over the last 10 years, much of the low-lying area has been redeveloped, particularly that portion facing onto main roads, where local zoning regulations permit high-rise buildings. Behind the high-rise, as you approach the ridge on which the embassy is built, you can still find the higgledy-piggledy residential areas characteristic of the early postwar period.

---

3   The embassy in Tokyo has an unclassified file that includes documents that relate to the history of the embassy, including its purchase in 1952, partial sale in 1989 and negotiations over the subsequent use of the sold land.

4   Decades later, during an embassy function in the garden in the late 1970s, an elderly woman joined the queue of arriving guests. She said that she was Marquis Hachisuka's daughter, had been born in the house and hoped to look around, which was quickly arranged. I owe this anecdote to Dr Richard Rigby, emeritus professor at The Australian National University, who served in Tokyo in the late 1970s.

5   The embassies of France, Germany, Italy and the Netherlands, in addition to that of Australia.

The old Hachisuka residence collapsed during the 1923 earthquake and the owners replaced it with a replica of an English country house, which Australia used at first as the ambassador's residence and chancery offices, and then just as the residence once a separate chancery was built in the 1960s. The garden, however, is much older. It has a moon-viewing hillock, which probably goes back to the foundation of the garden 250 years ago. The garden is famed for its cherry blossom trees, which have been replanted over the centuries. It has the full range—the well-known *Somei yoshino* (Yoshino cherry), the *yaezakura* (double-layer cherry blossom) and some *shidare-zakura* (weeping cherry). Many of these were planted as a gift from the late Kenneth Myer AC, whose family has had a long and distinguished association with Japan. Wattle trees were planted in the middle of the 1960s. While a good idea to have an Australian element in the garden, it was a mistake to mix them with the cherry blossoms, as they interfered with the Japanese aesthetic of appreciating the evanescent and delicate colours of the blossom. Some years later, a native garden was planted, sensibly separated from the traditional Japanese garden, and the wattles in the main garden died a natural death after seven or eight years and were not replaced.

In 1972, two now impressive cherry blossom trees were planted by political foes: the left-wing governor of Tokyo, Minobe Ryōkichi, and the minister of international trade and industry (later the prime minister), Nakasone Yasuhiro, hailing from the conservative Liberal Democratic Party. During my term as ambassador, we acquired a weeping cherry thanks to Sumitomo Forestry. It is a clone of the famous tree at Daigoji in Kyoto, under which Toyotomi Hideyoshi held a celebrated flower viewing in 1598. Over the past 15 years, the embassy has pursued a conservation program for the cherry trees to stave off ageing, and a plan to replace those which were likely to die off over the next decade.

One of two eucalypts planted at the same time as the wattles remained on the land Australia sold in 1988. It flourished in humid Tokyo to a point that is uncanny for any Australian used to the gnarled and twisted forms of the gum tree that we have in a much dryer climate. The garden, mysteriously, also has several cycad palm trees. These palms are found naturally in Japan only in the southern tip of Kyushu and Okinawa. I like to think that they may have been planted at the behest of the first owners of the garden, the Shimazu family, whose lands were in southern Kyushu, but I have no proof. The garden also has number of impressive

Edo-period stone lanterns, including a small one located outside the ambassador's residence that looks quite exotic, and may have originated on the Korean Peninsula.

I cannot leave a discussion of the embassy without talking about the sale of half the property, including the lower garden, the demolition of the Hachisuka residence, and the rebuilding project that took place from 1988 to 1992. It was the right decision to release the accumulated value of the property through sale for the benefit of the Australian taxpayer and to do so at the height of the Japanese property boom. The new building, designed by Denton Corker Marshall, is itself a fine piece of architecture that represents modern Australia well. As someone who actually lived in it for 14 years, I can say that parts of it are a triumph of form over function. The black marble facades to the new residence prevent most natural light from entering the ambassador's living quarters. Many of the offices also lack natural light, having only porthole-sized windows. Returning Australian diplomats likened working in the new building, with its lower ceilings and narrower corridors, to serving on a submarine.

It was more important to keep the 250-year-old garden than the less historic residence. I believe, however, it would have been possible to keep the old residence while erecting a new chancery and apartment building. You have only to look at the waste of space as you enter the modern embassy through a large windswept courtyard, where nobody wants to linger and which evokes a prison exercise yard, to realise that there was room on the site to preserve the old residence. Sadly too, much of the internal decoration of the old residence was also lost, and the finest artworks, including some early Edo-period screens were sent on consignment to a suburban museum which did not put them on display for nearly 30 years.[6] The retention of some wood and stained-glass screens in the public areas of the new residence and of the magnificent old porte-cochère as an attractive (if pointless) feature in the garden, are poignant reminders of what was sacrificed.

The plans for the sold land did not go ahead because of a combination of the collapse in Tokyo's real estate bubble, the slowing of Japan's economy and zoning complications for the proposed commercial development. A temporary apartment building was erected on the site, which otherwise

---

6   My successor as ambassador, the Hon. Richard Court AC, has recovered these screens from the museum for display at the residence.

lay fallow for nearly 25 years until 2011, when one of my first acts as ambassador was to receive a delegation from the owners. On sale, Australia had prudently retained the contractual right to be consulted over proposals for development. I asked that the new luxury residential complex be set back further than planned and separated from us by a new security fence, and for the retention of the tall trees between our garden and the new development.

Role of the Embassy

The embassy is the fulcrum for Australia's presence in Japan—physically and metaphorically. It has many roles that range from the practical to the symbolic. The embassy tells a story to Japan about Australia: that we are a serious country, with a weighty presence in a nation that matters a great deal to us. It helps preserve Australia's access to the most senior levels in Japan, as everyone wants to visit, most more than once (no ambassador should pretend his or her charm alone persuades VIPs to turn up). The embassy is among the top five in Tokyo in size of staff and profile (only those of the United States, China, South Korea and Russia are larger). Before mass tourism and the internet, the embassy provided the only window onto Australia for many Japanese.[7] The embassy is also the place that Australians visit to receive consular assistance, register the births of children and vote in Australian elections.

The embassy monitors developments in Japan that affect Australia and advocates our trade, political and security interests. Much of this activity takes place outside the embassy, as staff interact with the Japanese political, business, cultural and bureaucratic worlds. But the embassy and its grounds are themselves a vital tool for advocating Australia. Over the decades, generations of Japanese politicians, businesspeople, government officials and cultural and sporting figures have visited the embassy and associate it with Australia. In my time as ambassador, I hosted over 1,500 sit-down lunches and dinners, and many buffets and breakfasts as well, following the high-tempo pattern set by my predecessors. We did not do this for the fun of it, but rather because we wanted each and every one of those events to secure something specific for Australia.

---

7   In addition to the embassy, Australia had a separate trade office in Akasaka and an office for the Australia–Japan Foundation in Aoyama, both of which closed when the new embassy opened in 1990. We also have a consulate-general in Osaka and used to have consulates in Nagoya, Sapporo, Fukuoka and Sendai.

The annual cherry blossom viewing party in April attracts industry leaders, politicians, senior officials and cultural figures, trade union leaders and representatives of grassroots organisations, with an interesting sprinkling of former Imperial Family members and prominent sporting figures. Successive ambassadors made a point of inviting as wide a range of people as possible. Australian companies also capitalised on the event to promote their commercial interests in Japan. The embassy hosted many dinners for politicians, for example, to lobby for the free trade agreement or to gain their support for defence agreements that led to better cooperation. With senior executives of Japanese companies, we argued the case for more investment, and rebutted misapprehensions about political and regulatory developments in Australia that affected their businesses, while also reporting concerns raised back to Canberra. I would use the embassy as a backdrop for my appearances on Japanese television, promoting the best about Australia, and to showcase our finest food and wine to restaurants, hotels, educators and the gourmet press.

Finally, in Tokyo the embassy is the place where Australian diplomats and their families live in apartment buildings adjoining the chancery. Australians are not used to living with work colleagues, but I was always pleasantly surprised at the live-and-let-live attitude taken by staff. The design helped: that there were several entrances and only two apartments on each floor of each block helped preserve privacy.

Evolution of the Australian Presence in Japan

For 40 years Japan was Australia's largest trading partner, until China overtook it. However, Japan remains Australia's largest Asian investor in terms of total stock. Japan, as a fellow democracy, committed to the rule of law and the global rules-based order, has for many years been a vital partner for Australia. This has been clear in such areas as the Asia-Pacific Economic Cooperation (APEC) group, seeking peace in Cambodia, building regional security institutions, coordinating international economic policy coordination through the G-20, and, more recently, building defence links. Additionally, the people-to-people links, tourism and education, in particular, are strong.

Australia's embassy has helped achieve outcomes and sustain ties over the long haul, with representation from many parts of the Australian government. It has performed these functions with teams composed of both Australians posted from home as diplomats, and locally hired Japanese and Australians. I pay tribute to the embassy's local staff, who give essential support and, critically, continuity—in some cases over several decades—to Australian-based diplomatic staff who rotate through embassy positions every three or four years. This includes people like Tomoko Nakamura, who worked at the embassy for close to 40 years, first interpreting, then supporting the agriculture section's work in opening up market access and quarantine barriers; Hitomi Toku who drives our cultural relations program, and who in her own right is a well-known figure in the Tokyo cultural scene; and Yoshiko Kuwazawa, who for 50 years kept the embassy building and property ticking over and settled in generations of diplomats and their families.

Australia has been successful in Japan because it has had diplomats at the embassy who could speak the language and who knew the country well. To advance Australian interests, the embassy needs staff who not only can communicate in Japanese but also know how decisions are made and how we can influence them. Speaking Japanese is not just a matter of language but also one of understanding how to press the levers of power. Just imagine how a foreign embassy in Canberra would fare if its staff could not speak English and all its dealings with Australians had to be through interpreters.

While there have been constant elements to Australia's presence in Tokyo since its inception, many changes—notably shifts in the balance of power and advances in technology leading to new areas of cooperation—tell a story of an evolving partnership. Defence is one example. Japan's war history and Peace Constitution meant it played a negligible regional security role for decades, so our defence relationship was not well developed and the resources devoted to it at the embassy were consequently minimal—a fraction of Australia's defence presences in Washington, London and Jakarta. Now, however, the change in the power balance in the region has driven the normalisation of Japan's defence posture and led to greatly enhanced cooperation on security. Japan sees Australia as a partner second only to the United States (with which both have security alliances). The recent burgeoning in Defence staff numbers at the embassy reflects this, with a tripling in the size of the Defence team.

For the last decade it has no longer been possible for the embassy to see itself as the sole, or at times, even principal channel of communication between the two countries. Technology, through email and videoconferencing, allows long-distance dialogue among subject matter experts, in technical areas such as arms control, quarantine, APEC, international financial cooperation and free trade agreement (FTA) negotiations. Frequent meetings and constant inter-sessional contact between negotiators of our bilateral FTA and of the Trans-Pacific Partnership (TPP), and its successor the TPP-11, saw the lion's share of the negotiations taking place directly among trade ministers and chief negotiators and their teams, rather than through the embassy to Japan's government. Nonetheless, the embassy worked closely with the negotiators, and retained the critical roles of troubleshooter and provider of the most authoritative advice on Japan and how to handle Australia's interests there. For example, we identified politicians linked to vested interests who were blocking progress, whom we then targeted for lobbying, travelled to regional Japan to defuse farming lobby concerns about greater Australian agricultural access, or advised on the complex, often impenetrable details of Japan's import regulatory frameworks. The embassy, the ambassador in particular, would be the first port of call at the Japanese political level, and troubleshooter in the final stages. For example, one of Prime Minister Abe's most senior advisers came to me privately in the last few days of the FTA negotiations to map out the last few steps.[8]

I describe the modern ambassador's role as strategic: envisioning the future relationship and establishing the connections on the ground to move that vision forward. But it is also akin to that of foreman on a building site, looking out for problems, troubleshooting, escalating, facilitating communication, watching the cranes, ensuring deliveries, telling ministers unpalatable truths, putting the last brick in place, and usually standing up and giving a speech at the launch. In the end, however, the measure of any ambassador's effectiveness remains the extent to which an Australian prime minister and senior ministers wants to know his or her views before taking action. That successive prime ministers and ministers wanted to know the views of ambassadors in Tokyo showed we were successful.

---

8   I write more on my personal experiences and on the importance of good diplomatic tradecraft in advancing Australian interests in Japan in an Australian Institute of International Affairs monograph (forthcoming).

Decades of Achievement

I will cover the milestones reached in the bilateral relationship over the years, focusing on those with which I have had the closest association.

It took political leadership at the highest level to reconcile Australia and Japan after World War II, beginning with the commitment shown by Prime Ministers Sir Robert Menzies and Nobusuke Kishi in 1956–57. Embodying those first steps in reconciliation was the bilateral Australia–Japan Commerce Agreement in 1957, which normalised the economic relationship by extending most-favoured-nation treatment to Japan. Although Australia had made its peace with Japan, war history remained a sensitive matter for decades. It was only in 1992 that an Australian defence minister visited Japan for the first time.

One of the highlights of being ambassador was hosting annual reconciliation visits for former prisoners of war, funded by the Japanese government. It was a privilege to meet the elderly veterans, and to experience their varied reactions to Japan, which few had visited since the war, and to accompany them to the Commonwealth War Cemetery in Yokohama.

At the time of my first visit to Japan in 1978 as a high school student, sponsored by the Japan Foundation, there were few Australians studying or living there. The Japanese government's Japan Exchange and Teaching program, now very popular among Australians, was not yet established, and the New Colombo Plan was a long way off.

Of course, the two nations' economic ties were already strong and becoming more sophisticated. In April 1978, Australia's then prime minister, Malcolm Fraser, visited Japan and met his then counterpart Takeo Fukuda. Unusually, the two prime ministers focused their meeting on international economic affairs, rather than bilateral trade matters, which had been the mainstay of discussion between Japanese and Australian leaders. We were starting to think about our relationship in a regional and global context. But that kind of thinking was still quite novel. And Australia–Japan strategic and defence relations were still in their infancy. The countries had only just signed the Basic Treaty of Friendship and Co-operation two years earlier (famously rescued from stalling by then first secretary at the embassy Ashton Calvert), and it was in 1978 that a parliamentary committee recommended that Australia start sharing its strategic thinking about the region with Japan.

I returned to Japan as a diplomat from 1992 to 1996, working under Ambassador Calvert to find that much had changed in the Australia–Japan relationship. High-level dialogue on strategic and defence issues, known as Pol-Mil talks, with senior representation from DFAT and Defence (both civilian and military) began in 1996. This was a major breakthrough that foreshadowed the modern special strategic partnership between the two countries.

Japan also welcomed that Australia was focusing more than ever on its relationships in the Asia-Pacific—including that with Japan. In May 1995, then prime ministers Tomiichi Murayama and Paul Keating signed the Joint Declaration on the Australia–Japan Partnership, in which Japan 'welcomed Australia's decision to create its future in the region' and underscored that Australia was 'an indispensable partner in regional affairs'.[9]

Though the Japanese economy had gone into recession in 1990, and Japan grew very little that decade, Australian merchandise exports to Japan grew by 60 per cent in the 1990s. Australia's trade in services was also adding diversity and depth to already complementary trade ties. Moreover, both countries had been striving to secure and entrench the economic gains being felt in the wider region. The establishment of APEC in 1989 was a result of close bilateral cooperation. When I arrived at the embassy in 1992, governments were preparing the ground for prime ministers to attend APEC's first leaders' summit in 1993.

My second posting to Tokyo, as minister-counsellor, was in 2004–08, this time working for two distinguished ambassadors in succession, John McCarthy and Murray McLean. By that time, Australia and Japan were in a position to announce several landmark bilateral events. Prime Ministers Abe and Howard signed a Joint Declaration on Security Cooperation in March 2007. This has proven to be a solid foundation for Australia and Japan's now wide-ranging cooperation on issues such as defence,

9   'Joint Declaration on the Australia–Japan Partnership', May 1995, Department of Foreign Affairs and Trade, www.dfat.gov.au/geo/japan/Pages/key-documents, accessed 10 November 2020.

law enforcement, border security, counterterrorism, disarmament and counter-proliferation of weapons of mass destruction, maritime and aviation security, and peacekeeping.

Also in 2007, the two prime ministers made the momentous decision to start FTA negotiations. Howard had paved the way for that in 2005 by gaining the commitment to an FTA feasibility study from then prime minister Koizumi. By June 2007, the respective prime ministers were holding the first Australia–Japan Joint Foreign and Defence Ministerial Consultations in Tokyo, which underlined that our interests were no longer just regional but also global. Recognising Japan's advocacy for global nuclear non-proliferation and disarmament, Australia joined forces to launch the International Commission on Nuclear Non-Proliferation and Disarmament in 2008.

I should also mention the tragic events of March 2011 that saw Japan assailed by earthquake, tsunami and a nuclear disaster. This took place in the final months of the term of my predecessor as ambassador, Murray McLean, who led Australia's national response with great energy and professionalism and who reflects on that crisis in Chapter 2 in this volume. Australia delivered its significant humanitarian assistance through a whole-of-government effort, much of it through deployed defence assets, including three of our four C-17 transport aircraft.

I became ambassador in August 2011. It was a privilege to serve in that role when many of the ground-breaking initiatives I have earlier described had become a natural and normal part of the relationship—simply the way Japan and Australia do business. The economic relationship continues to anchor our modern ties, but in a break from the past, our strategic and defence cooperation now assumes equal billing. That change has been driven by much bigger forces: by major shifts in the global and regional balance of power, by ever stronger economic complementarity and by mutual trust and shared values. The bolstered security and defence ties between the countries are also possible because of Japan's willingness and greater ability to make a security contribution.

Working under the now well-established '2+2' foreign and defence ministers' framework, strategic cooperation is much more meaningful and includes sophisticated exercises, regional capacity building, defence science and technology cooperation in the fields of hydrodynamics, autonomous systems and materials research. This complements longstanding peacekeeping cooperation, ever stronger service-to-service collaboration, and defence materiel cooperation (notably Japan's acquisition of Australian-made Bushmaster vehicles). Much sophisticated cooperation also occurs under trilateral United States–Japan–Australia auspices. Joint Australia–Japan efforts on humanitarian assistance and disaster relief, too, continue to highlight the regional importance of the partnership.

On the economic side, the two countries have expanded the relationship from the always strong resources and energy base, and have shifted the trade relationship from one of persistent conflict over agricultural market access, to one of compromise in the FTA and collaboration in regional trade negotiations, such as the TPP and more widely in other trade negotiations such as the Regional Comprehensive Economic Partnership. I was delighted to be ambassador when Australia and Japan finally signed and ratified the FTA in 2014 after seven long years of negotiation. It has had substantial commercial outcomes, as well as a head-turning effect in getting business to have another look at opportunities in the other country, particularly in investment.

Japan remains Australia's largest Asian source of investment by stock, and annual flows remain consistently high. The A$34 billion Ichthys project near Darwin, headed by Japan's INPEX, started production in late 2018, and is the first Japanese-operated liquefied natural gas project anywhere in the world. For many years, Japan's demand for Australia's raw materials and energy exports, and Australia's demand for Japan's manufactured products dominated economic ties. They remain important factors, but the two have a new complementarity. Japan's population is falling, and so major players in the domestic consumer goods sector and the services sectors have sought new markets abroad, through investment. Notable examples from which Australia has benefited include Kirin Beer, Asahi, Dai-ichi Life Insurance, Nippon Life Insurance, Nippon Paint and Kajima Corporation.

Another strength of the relationship is our people-to-people links, although COVID-19 has put a stop to tourism for now. Up until the onset of COVID-19, Australians and Japanese had been visiting each other's countries more; in the year to March 2020,[10] 443,000 Japanese visited

---

10 'International Market Performance Statistics', Tourism Australia, 2020, www.tourism. australia.com/en/markets-and-stats/tourism-statistics/international-market-performance.html, accessed 10 November 2020.

Australia—well up on five years ago—and over 620,000 Australians visited Japan in 2019.[11] Air links have been much healthier too, as airlines have revived unused air routes, and more airlines have begun competing in the market.

In education, Japanese remains the most studied foreign language in Australia (although too few Australian students study any foreign languages). Nearly 6,000 Australian students go to Japan to study every year, and some 60,000 Japanese come to Australia to study or undertake student exchanges. Importantly, 2,300 New Colombo Plan scholars have studied in Japan, either short-term or long-term. These links are supported by Australia–Japan societies in both Australia and Japan, Australia–Japan sister city relationships and state–prefecture relationships.

Strong science and research links also exist, with over 400 partnerships between Australian and Japanese universities and science institutes. Collaboration has yielded advances in fields as diverse as nuclear and physical sciences, Antarctic research, space science technology and applications, and marine science and ocean observations.

Into the Future

Geopolitical and geo-economic developments will see Australia and Japan cooperating ever more closely. The shift in global economic weight—the rise of China and India—is dispersing strategic influence and military power further. That makes Japan focus more on its security, including energy and food security, and pushes Australia–Japan defence and security cooperation further.

Both countries strongly support rules-based frameworks for trade, investment, non-proliferation and dispute settlement, and each wants flexible, representative global institutions and a rules-based international framework to support these markets. China and the United States in their different ways are challenging existing rules-based frameworks, prompting Australia and Japan to work together more closely in response.

---

11 'Japan-Bound Statistics', JTB Tourism Research and Consulting Company, 2020, www.tourism.jp/en/tourism-database/stats/inbound/, accessed 10 November 2020.

The United States withdrew from the TPP but instead of the whole framework collapsing, which appeared likely, Australia and Japan took the lead to keep it on foot as the TPP-11, without the United States.

Japan remains a major economy, and a key enabler of regional economic development through investment, aid and technology. Its enormous stock of cumulative overseas investment, which reached over US$1.8 trillion by 2019, ensures it continues to wield great influence.[12] Even as US trade policy under former US president Trump challenged global supply chains, these will continue to be influenced by decisions made in boardrooms in Japan, among others. Australia will be a part of those supply chains and concerns about economic security and reducing dependence on China will only strengthen those connections.

Australia and Japan's history of stable and predictable bilateral corporate and government dealings will see them turning ever more to one another in an age of growing uncertainty. As patterns of global supply and demand change even more rapidly owing to technological change and growth, producers will seek greater stability and predictability. As strong and important as Japanese investment in Australia already is, it will almost certainly grow stronger. Japan pumped out a record annual flow of US$160 billion in overseas investment in 2017, second only to the United States globally.[13] This figure is four times that of 15 years ago. The Australia–Japan FTA also created the conditions for easier Japanese investment in Australia.

The Australia–Japan bilateral relationship will remain important to both countries, because of our strong economic complementarity and shared interests in bolstering regional stability and the rules-based international system, and the relationship will continue to be sustained by strong people-to-people links. The embassy will remain central to the advancing of Australian interests in Japan. Its role and functions will keep evolving, but I am confident it will keep making its unique contribution, so long as it continues to be staffed by people who know Japan and understand how to manage its systems towards Australia's benefit, and to achieve bilateral advantage for both countries.

---

12 'FDI Stocks', OECD Data, 2020, data.oecd.org/fdi/fdi-stocks.htm#indicator-chart, accessed 11 November 2020. Also available as: OECD, *OECD International Direct Investment Statistics 2019* (Paris: OECD Publishing, 2020), doi.org/10.1787/g2g9fb42-en.

13 'FDI Flows', OECD Data, 2020, data.oecd.org/fdi/fdi-flows.htm#indicator-chart, accessed 10 November 2020. Also available as OECD, *OECD International Direct Investment Statistics 2019*.

If Australia was paying low rent in an ageing skyscraper in an unfashionable part of town, which is where so many Australian embassies around the world are accommodated, the Japanese would draw their own conclusions about Australia and our weight in the world. They would have been unlikely to treat us seriously, and we would have had far less chance of negotiating the big-ticket agreements of the last 20 years that have benefited Australia so much.

Of course, the embassy building is but part of the story of the Australia–Japan relationship: it is the people who staff it, and their knowledge of Japan, and capacity to pull the levers of power and influence to advance Australian interests in Japan that will drive our success as a country there.

Select Bibliography

Oral Histories

Dalrymple, Rawdon, interviewed by David Lowe, 23 May 2017, National Library of Australia (NLA): ORAL TRC 6870/2.

Dunn, Hugh, interviewed by Michael Wilson, 27 August 1993, NLA: ORAL TRC 2981/1.

McCarthy, John, interviewed by David Lowe, 8 May 2017, NLA: ORAL TRC 6870/1.

McLean, Murray, interviewed by David Lowe and Kate Darian-Smith, 3 August 2017, NLA: ORAL TRC 6870/3.

Miller, Bruce, interviewed by David Lowe and Kate Darian-Smith, 14 August 2017, NLA: ORAL TRC 6870/4.

Miller, Geoff, interviewed by David Lowe, 28 August 2017, NLA: ORAL TRC 6870/5.

Plimsoll, James, interviewed by Clyde Cameron, 26 March 1984, NLA: ORAL TRC 1967.

Watt, Alan, interviewed by Bruce Miller, 11 December 1974, NLA: ORAL TRC 306.

Other Sources

Ang, Ien. 'Smart Engagement with Asia'. *Humanities Australia*, no. 8 (2017): 23–33.

Armstrong, Shiro. *Reimagining the Japan Relationship: An Agenda for Australia's Benchmark Partnership in Asia*. Canberra: Australia–Japan Research Centre, The Australian National University, 2021.

Asialink. *35,000 Days in Asia: The Asialink Arts Residency Program*. Melbourne: Asialink Centre, University of Melbourne, 2004.

Austin, R.W.L. *The Narrow Road to a Far Country: Intimations of Things Japanese*. Australians in Asia Series No. 7. Nathan: Centre for the Study of Australia–Asia Relations, 1991.

Australia–Japan Foundation – Department of Foreign Affairs and Trade. *The Reconstruction Initiative: Australia–Japan Foundation's Response to the 2011 Japan Earthquake and Tsunami*. Report. Canberra: Australian Government and AJF, 2015. www.dfat.gov.au/sites/default/files/the-reconstruction-initiative. pdf, accessed 15 August 2020.

Baldwin, Jennifer. 'World War I and the Development of Language Study at Australian Universities'. In *The First World War, the Universities and the Professions in Australia 1914–1939*, edited by Kate Darian-Smith and James Waghorne, 261–68. Melbourne: Melbourne University Press, 2019.

Baldwin, Jennifer Joan. *Languages Other than English in Australian Higher Education: Policies, Provision and the National Interest*. Switzerland: Springer Nature, 2019. doi.org/10.1007/978-3-030-05795-4.

Beaumont, Joan, Christopher Waters, David Lowe and Garry Woodard. *Ministers, Mandarins and Diplomats: Australian Foreign Policy Making 1941–1969*. Melbourne: Melbourne University Press, 2003.

Black, David and Byron Peacock. 'Sport and Diplomacy'. In *The Oxford Handbook of Modern Diplomacy*, edited by Andrew F. Cooper, Jorge Heine and Ramesh Thakur, 708–14. Oxford: Oxford University Press, 2013.

Broinowski, Alison. *The Yellow Lady; Australian Impressions of Asia*. Melbourne: Oxford University Press, 1992.

Cairns, Rebecca. 'Constructing Asia Literacy as a Policy Problem'. *Australian Policy and History*, 13 November 2017. aph.org.au/2017/11/constructing-asia-literacy-as-a-policy-problem/, accessed 30 April 2021.

Carroll, Alison. *Asialink Arts: Through the Looking Glass, the Asialink Arts Program, 1990–2010*. Melbourne: Asialink, University of Melbourne, 2012.

Carroll, Alison. 'People and Partnership: An Australian Model for International Art Exchanges—the Asialink Arts Program, 1990–2010'. In *Contemporary Asian Art and Exhibitions Connectivities and World-making*, edited by Michelle Antionette and Caroline Turner, 199–217. Canberra: ANU Press, 2014. doi.org/10.22459/CAAE.11.2014.11.

Carter, David. 'Living with Instrumentalism: The Academic Commitment to Cultural Diplomacy'. In *Cultural Diplomacy: Beyond the National Interest?* edited by Ien Ang, Yudhishthir Raj Isar and Phillip Mar, 114–29. Abingdon: Routledge, 2016.

Cotton, James. *The Australian School of International Relations.* London: Palgrave Macmillan, 2013. doi.org/10.1057/9781137308061.

Crawford, J.G., ed. *Australian Trade Policy 1942–1966.* Canberra: Australian National University Press, 1968.

Crawford, J.G. and Saburō Ōkita. *Raw Materials and Pacific Economic Integration.* Canberra: Australian National University Press, 1978.

Dalby, Liza. *All-Japan: The Catalogue of Everything Japanese.* New York: Quill, 1984.

Darian-Smith, Kate. 'Expanding Horizons: Australian Television and Globalisation in the 1950s–1970s'. In *Contemporary Australian Studies: Literature, History, Film and Media Studies in a Globalizing Age*, edited by Yasue Arimitsu and Yugi Suzuki, 95–119. Tokyo: Otowa-Shobo Tsurumi-Shoten Publishing, 2016.

Darian-Smith, Kate. 'Pearl Harbor and Australia's War in the Pacific'. In *Beyond Pearl Harbor: A Pacific History*, edited by Beth Bailey and David Farber, 173–93. Lawrence, Kansas: University Press of Kansas, 2019. doi.org/10.2307/j.ctvqmp3br.13.

Darian-Smith, Kate and James Waghorne. 'Australian-Asian Sociability, Student Activism, and the University Challenge to White Australia in the 1950s'. *Australian Journal of Politics and History* 63, no. 2 (2016): 203–18. doi.org/10.1111/ajph.12245.

de Kretser, Anne and Robyn Spence-Brown. 'The Current State of Japanese Language Education in Australian Schools'. The Tokyo Foundation for Policy Research, 15 December 2010. www.tkfd.or.jp/en/research/detail.php?id=174, accessed 30 April 2021.

Debenham, Howard. *Waiting 'Round the Bend: A Life in Australia's Foreign Service.* Canberra: Barrallier Books, 2017.

Dee, Moreen. *Friendship and Co-operation: The 1976 Basic Treaty between Australia and Japan.* Canberra: Department of Foreign Affairs and Trade, 2006.

Dittmer, J. *Diplomatic Material: Affect, Assemblage and Foreign Policy.* Durham, North Carolina: Duke University Press, 2017. doi.org/10.1515/9780822372745.

Doran, Stuart and David Lee, eds. *Documents on Australian Foreign Policy: Australia and Recognition of the People's Republic of China 1949–1972*. Canberra: Department of Foreign Affairs and Trade, 2002.

Dorman, Shawn. 'Profiles: Who Works in an Embassy'. In *Inside a U.S. Embassy: Diplomacy at Work, All-New Third Edition of the Essential Guide to the Foreign Service*, edited by Shawn Dorman, 9–68. Lincoln: University of Nebraska Press, 2011. doi.org/10.2307/j.ctt1djmhxq.8.

Drysdale, Peter. 'Did the NARA Treaty Make a Difference?' *Australian Journal of International Affairs* 60, no. 4 (2006): 490–505. doi.org/10.1080/1035771 0601006994.

Drysdale, Peter. 'The Relationship with Japan: Despite the Vicissitudes'. In *Policy and Practice: Essays in Honour of Sir John Crawford*, edited by L.T. Evans and J.D.B. Miller, 66–71. Canberra: Australian National University Press, 1987.

Dunn, Hugh. *The Shaping of a Sinologue of Sorts*. Australians in Asia Series No. 1. Nathan: Centre for the Study of Australia-Asia Relations, 1988.

Flew, Terry and Falk Hartig. 'Confucius Institutes and the Network: Communication Approach to Public Diplomacy'. *IAFOR Journal of Asian Studies* 1, no. 1 (2014): 1–18. doi.org/10.22492/ijas.1.1.02.

Galligan, Brian. *Utah and Queensland Coal: A Study in the Micro-Political Economy of Modern Capitalism and the State*. Brisbane: University of Queensland Press, 1989.

Garnaut, Ross. *Australia and the Northeast Asian Ascendancy: Report to the Prime Minister and Minister for Foreign Affairs and Trade*. Canberra: Australian Government Publishing Service, 1989.

Gerster, Robin. *Travels in Atomic Sunshine: Australia and the Occupation of Japan*. Melbourne, Scribe, 2019.

Hamilton, Walter. *Serendipity City: Australia, Japan and the Multifunction Polis*. Sydney: ABC Books, 1991.

He, Baogang. 'Australian Ideas of Regionalism'. In *Navigating the New International Disorder: Australia in World Affairs, 2011–2015*, edited by Mark Beeson and Shahar Hamieri, 105–23. South Melbourne: Oxford University Press, in association with the Australian Institute of International Affairs, 2016.

Henderson, Deborah. 'Politics and Policy-Making for Asia Literacy: The Rudd Report and a National Strategy in Australian Education'. *Asian Studies Review* 32, no. 2 (2008): 171–95. doi.org/10.1080/10357820802064690.

Henderson, W. *West New Guinea: The Dispute and Its Settlement*. South Orange, NJ: Seton Hall University Press, 1973.

Hocking, Brian. 'Rethinking the "New" Public Diplomacy'. In *The New Public Diplomacy: Soft Power in International Relations*, edited by Jan Melissen, 28–43. Basingstoke: Palgrave, 2007. doi.org/10.1057/9780230554931_2.

Holland, Alison. 'Innovation, Art Practice and Japan–Australia Cultural Exchange during the 1970s and 1980s'. *Asia Pacific Journal of Arts & Cultural Management* 9, no. 1 (2012): 24–31.

Hood, Christopher P. *Shinkansen–From Bullet Train to Symbol of Modern Japan*. London: Routledge, 2007. doi.org/10.4324/9780203180389.

Inkster, Ian. *The Clever City: Japan, Australia and the Multifunction Polis*. Sydney: Sydney University Press, 1991.

Jackson, Steven J. and Stephen Haigh. 'Between and beyond Politics: Sport and Foreign Policy in a Globalizing World'. *Sport in Society* 11, no. 4 (2008): 349–58. doi.org/10.1080/17430430802019169.

Jones, Paul and Vera Mackie, eds. *Relationships: Australia and Japan: 1880s to 1950*. University of Melbourne History Monograph 28. Melbourne: University of Melbourne, 2001.

Keys-Statham, Christine. 'Australia's International Cultural Diplomacy'. *Australian Policy and History*, 13 November 2017. aph.org.au/2017/11/australias-international-cultural-diplomacy/, accessed 6 December 2020.

Lawler, Sir Peter. 'Sir Allen Brown: An Exemplary Public Servant'. In *The Seven Dwarfs and the Age of the Mandarins: Australian Government Administration in the Post-War Era*, edited by Samuel Furphy, 183–89. Canberra: ANU Press, 2015. doi.org/10.22459/SDAM.07.2015.09.

Lee, David. 'Australia's Embargo of the Export of Iron Ore: A Reconsideration'. *Journal of Australasian Mining History* 18, no. 1 (2020): 96–112.

Lee, David. *The Second Rush: Mining and the Transformation of Australia*. Redland Bay: Connor Court, 2016.

Lee, David. 'Sir John Latham and the League of Nations'. In *League of Nations: Histories, Legacy and Impact*, edited by Joy Damousi and Patricia O'Brien, 83–99. Carlton: Melbourne University Publishing, 2018.

Lo Bianco, Joseph. 'Asian Languages in Australian Schools: Policy Options'. Melbourne Asia Policy Papers 7, May 2005.

Lottuz, Pascal. 'Violent Conflicts and Neutral Legations: A Case Study of the Spanish and Swiss legations in Wartime Japan'. *New Global Studies* 11, no. 2 (2017): 85–100. doi.org/10.1515/ngs-2017-0018.

Malone, David A. 'The Modern Diplomatic Mission'. In *The Oxford Handbook of Modern Diplomacy*, edited by Andrew F. Cooper, Jorge Heine and Ramesh Thakur, 122–41. Oxford: Oxford University Press, 2013.

Martin, Alexander. 'The 1964 Tokyo Olympics: A Turning Point for Japan'. *Wall Street Journal*, 5 September 2013.

McCormack, Gavan, ed. *Bonsai Australia Banzai: Multifunction Polis and the Making of a Special Relationship with Japan*. Sydney: Pluto Press, 1991.

Megaw, Ruth. 'The Australian Goodwill Mission to the Far East in 1934: Its Significance in the Evolution of Australian Foreign Policy'. *Journal of the Royal Australian Historical Society* 59, no. 4 (1973): 247–63.

Melbourne, A.C.V. *Report on Australian Intercourse with Japan and China*. Brisbane: University of Queensland Press, 1932.

Menadue, John. *Things You Learn along the Way*. Melbourne: David Lovell Publishing, 1999.

Miller, Geoff. 'Diplomatic Reflections: An Australian View from Tokyo'. *Japanese Studies* 24, no. 2 (2004): 169–75. doi.org/10.1080/1037139042000302474.

Miller, Rachel. *Wife and Baggage to Follow*. Canberra: Halstead Press, 2013.

Murray, Stuart. 'Sports Diplomacy in the Australian Context: A Case Study of the Department of Foreign Affairs and Trade'. *Sports Law eJournal* 1, no. 1 (2013): 1–15. doi.org/10.53300/001c.6399.

Murray, Stuart and Geoffrey Allen Pigman. 'Mapping the Relationship Between International Sport and Diplomacy'. *Sport in Society* 17, no. 9 (2014): 1098–118.

Neale, Margo, ed. *Utopia: The Genius of Emily Kame Kngwarreye*. Canberra: National Museum of Australia Press, 2008.

Parry, Mayumi. 'Lessons from Japanese Family Homestays'. *New Voices in Japanese Studies* 1 (2006): 62–74. doi.org/10.21159/nv.01.07.

Pietsch, Juliet and Haydn Aarons. 'Australian Engagement with Asia: Towards Closer Political, Economic and Cultural Ties'. In *Australia: Identity, Fear and Governance in the 21st Century*, edited by Juliet Pietsch and Haydn Aarons, 33–46. Canberra: ANU Press, 2012. doi.org/10.22459/AIFG.11.2012.03.

Reynolds, Wayne. 'Australia's Quest to Enrich Uranium and the Whitlam Government's Loans Affair'. *Australian Journal of Politics and History* 54, no. 4 (2008): 562–78, doi.org/10.1111/j.1467-8497.2008.00516.x.

Rikki, Kersten. 'Australia and Japan: Mobilising the Bilateral Relationship'. In *Middle Power Dreaming: Australia in World Affairs, 2006–2010*, edited by James Cotton and John Ravenhill, 93–100. South Melbourne: Oxford University Press, in association with the Australian Institute of International Affairs, 2011.

Rix, Alan. 'Australia and Japan'. In *Seeking Asian Engagement: Australia in World Affairs, 1991–95*, edited by James Cotton and John Ravenhill, 134–48. Oxford University Press, Melbourne, in conjunction with the Australian Institute of International Affairs, 1997.

Rix, Alan. *The Australia–Japan Political Alignment: 1952 to the Present*. Routledge: London, 1999.

Rix, Alan. *Coming to Terms: The Politics of Australia's Trade with Japan, 1945–1957*. Sydney: Allen & Unwin, 1986.

Rix, Alan, ed. *Intermittent Diplomat: The Japan and Batavia Diaries of W. Macmahon Ball*. Carlton: Melbourne University Press, 1988.

Rudd, Kevin. *Asian Languages and Australia's Economic Future*. Brisbane: Queensland Government Printer, Brisbane, 1994.

Seidensticker, Edward. *Low City, High City: Tokyo from Edo to the Earthquake: How the Shoguns' Ancient Capital Became a Great Modern City, 1867–1923*. New York: Alfred A. Knopf, 1986.

Shimazu, Naoko. *Japan, Race and Equality: The Racial Equality Proposal of 1919*. London: Routledge, 2009.

Sissons, D.C.S. 'Japan'. In *Australia in World Affairs 1971–1975*, edited by W.J. Hudson, 231–70. Sydney: George Allen & Unwin, 1980.

Sissons, D.C.S. 'Manchester v. Japan: The Imperial Background of the Australia Trade Diversion Dispute with Japan'. *Australian Outlook* 30, no. 3 (1972): 480–502. doi.org/10.1080/10357717608444583.

Sudjic, Deyan. *Australian Embassy, Tokyo: Architects Denton Corker Marshall*. Blueprint Extra 02. London: Wordsearch, 1991.

Tamai, Sachiko, ed. *Reflections: Australian Artists Living in Tokyo*. Bloomington, Indiana: Balboa Press, 2019.

Walker, David. *Anxious Nation: Australia and the Rise of Asia 1850–1939*. St Lucia: University of Queensland Press, 1999.

Walker, David. *Stranded Nation: White Australia in an Asian Region*. Crawley: University of Western Australia Publishing, 2019.

Walker, David and Agnieszka Sobocinska, eds. *Australia's Asia: From Yellow Peril to Asia Century*. Crawley: University of Western Australia Publishing, 2012.

Walton, David. 'Australia and Japan'. In *Trading on Alliance Security: Australia in World Affairs, 2002–2005*, edited by James Cotton and John Ravenhill, 72–88. Melbourne: Oxford University Press, 2007.

Walton David, ed. 'The NARA Treaty: 30 Years On'. Special issue, *Australian Journal of International Affairs* 60, no. 4 (December 2006).

Watt, Alan. *Australian Diplomat: Memoirs of Sir Alan Watt*. Melbourne: Angus and Robertson in association with the Australian Institute of International Affairs, 1972.

Notes on Contributors

Alison Broinowski AM

Alison Broinowski AM is a writer, journalist and former diplomat, and is vice-president of Australians for War Powers Reform. Among other appointments overseas, she worked in Japan as a freelance journalist in the mid-1960s and was cultural counsellor at the Australian embassy in Tokyo in the mid-1980s. She has been a visiting fellow at the Australian Defence Force Academy, University of Canberra and The Australian National University. Alison has written and edited 11 books, including *The Yellow Lady: Australian Impressions of Asia* (Oxford University Press, 1992) and *About Face: Asian Accounts of Australia* (Scribe, 2003).

Richard Broinowski AO

Richard Broinowski AO is a former diplomat. His formative years were spent at the Australian embassy in Tokyo, but he also worked on Australian policies towards Japan in Canberra. He was later Australian ambassador to Vietnam; to the Republic of Korea; and to Mexico, the Central American Republics and Cuba. In retirement Richard has been an adjunct professor at the University of Canberra and the University of Sydney. He has written six books with historical narratives and is planning a seventh.

David Carter

David Carter is an emeritus professor at the University of Queensland and a fellow of the Australian Academy of the Humanities. His area of research is Australian literature and publishing history, cultural history, periodical studies, studies in modernity, and cultural diplomacy. His books include *Australian Books and Authors in the Australian Marketplace 1840s–1940s* (Sydney University Press, 2018) and *Always Almost Modern: Australian Print Cultures and Modernity* (Australian Scholarly Publications, 2013).

He held the position of Visiting Professor in Australian Studies at the Center for Pacific and American Studies, University of Tokyo, in 2007–8 and again in 2016–17.

Kate Darian-Smith

Professor Kate Darian-Smith is a historian of Australia, with numerous grants and publications on histories of Australia at war, migration, education and the professions, commemoration and heritage. Recent books are *The First World War, the Universities and the Professions in Australia 1914–1939* (Melbourne University Publishing, 2019) and *Remembering Migration: Oral History and Heritage in Australia* (Palgrave Macmillan, 2019). She is executive dean and pro-vice-chancellor, College of Arts, Law and Education, University of Tasmania, and was previously at the University of Melbourne. Kate has a long association with Japan through Australian studies networks. She was on the board of the Australia–Japan Foundation (2010–16), is a former president of the International Australian Studies Association and currently sits on the executive of the Academy of Social Sciences in Australia.

Philip Goad

Philip Goad is chair of architecture, co-director of ACAHUCH (Australian Centre for Architectural History, Urban and Cultural Heritage) and Redmond Barry Distinguished Professor at the University of Melbourne. He is co-editor of *The Encyclopaedia of Australian Architecture* (Cambridge University Press, 2012) and *Australia Modern: Architecture, Landscape and Design 1925–1975* (Thames & Hudson, 2019). Recent co-authored books include *Architecture and the Modern Hospital: Nosokomeion to Hygeia* (Routledge, 2019) and *Bauhaus Diaspora and Beyond: Transforming Education through Art, Architecture and Design* (Miegunyah Press, 2019). He is a fellow of the Australian Academy of the Humanities. In 2019–20, he was Gough Whitlam and Malcolm Fraser Chair of Australian Studies at Harvard University.

David Lee

Dr David Lee, associate professor in the School of Humanities and Social Sciences, University of New South Wales, Canberra, researches Australia's relations with the countries of the Asia-Pacific. He has edited volumes of official documents on Australia's relations with Indonesia and the People's

Republic of China. He has also authored or co-authored monographs on Australian foreign and international economic policy, Australia's relations with the United States and the resources trade with East Asian countries after 1960. He is collaborating on a biography of Sir John Crawford, working on a history of Australian independence and researching the development of Australian economic relationships with Japan and China.

David Lowe

Professor David Lowe is chair in contemporary history in Deakin University's School of Humanities and Social Sciences. David is a co-founder of the Australian Policy and History network. His research centres on cultural aspects of the history of international relations, including Australia's role in the world, and on remembering the legacies of modern wars and empires in comparative contexts. He is currently researching the history of postwar foreign aid, including the Colombo Plan and Australia's foreign aid program. He was Visiting Professor in Australian Studies at the Center for Pacific and American Studies, University of Tokyo, in 2019–20.

Murray McLean AO

Mr McLean AO served as a career officer with the Department of Foreign Affairs and Trade from 1970 until 2012. Fluent in Mandarin Chinese, McLean had early postings to Hong Kong and Beijing, later serving as political counsellor in Beijing and in Washington. Appointed Australian consul-general in Shanghai, he was awarded a Medal of the Order of Australia (OAM) in 1991. Senior appointments as head of East Asia Branch (1992–96), Australian high commissioner to Singapore (1997–2001), head of North Asia Division (2001–03), and as deputy secretary (2004) followed, before serving as Australian ambassador to Japan (2004–11). He was chair of the board of the Australia–Japan Foundation (2012–20), and ex officio on the board of the Australia Japan Business Co-operation Committee (2012–20). He continues as chair of the Foundation of Australia–Japan Studies. He was appointed an Officer of the Order of Australia (AO) in the 2013 Australia Day list, and in 2014, the Japanese Emperor Akihito honoured Mr McLean with the Grand Cordon of the Order of the Rising Sun.

Bruce Miller AO

Bruce Miller AO was Australian ambassador to Japan from 2011 until 2017, and has had over 40 years' association with Japan. He holds a bachelor of arts and a bachelor of laws from the University of Sydney. He spent most of his 32-year public service career handling Australia's relations with East Asia. In Australia, he occupied senior positions in the Department of Foreign Affairs and Trade and the Office of National Assessments, including as director-general. He left government in 2018 to take up board and advisory roles in the private sector and academia. He became chair of the Australia–Japan Foundation in August 2020. He was appointed an Officer of the Order of Australia in the 2018 Queen's Birthday Honours and awarded the Order of the Rising Sun, Gold and Silver Star by the Japanese government in November 2020.

Rachel Miller

Rachel Miller, with Diana Hall, drew on interviews and other materials to publish an account of wives, secretaries and women diplomats working for the Australian Department of Foreign Affairs, *Wife and Baggage to Follow* (Halstead Press, 2013). She accompanied her husband Geoff Miller on seven overseas postings, including when he was ambassador to Japan from 1986 to 1989.

David Walton

Dr David Walton is an adjunct fellow in the School of Humanities and Communication Arts, Western Sydney University. His research interests are at the intersection of international relations and diplomatic history. David is particularly focused on postwar Australian foreign policy towards the Asia-Pacific and specifically postwar Australia–Japan political and security relations. He has been a visiting professor at several universities in the Asia-Pacific, including the University of Tokyo (Japan Foundation Fellow), Meiji University, Beijing Foreign Studies University and the University of Seoul.

Index

as emblematic of Australia–Japan
  relationship, 43
as emblematic of relationship,
  77–78
impact of, 13, 230
Boxtel, Leonie, 174
Broinowski, Alison, 196
Brown, Allen, 54–55, 99, 129

Cairns, Jim, 111
Calvert, Ashton, 67–68, 70, 172,
  246, 255
Casey, Richard (R.G.), 44, 50, 83, 88
Changi prison, 14
cherry tree blossoms, 245, 248, 251
Chifley, Joseph Benedict (J.B.), 47
China
  Australian embassy in Beijing,
    145, 159, 162
  Chinese Civil War, 48
  growth of, 43–44, 258
  military presence, 69
  recognised by the United States,
    55
  relationship with Australia,
    242–243
  relationship with Indonesia, 92
  relationship with Japan, 50, 82
  seat on United Nations Security
    Council, 54
  as trading partner with Australia,
    43, 72
Cold War, 43, 48, 80, 240
Colombo Plan, 99, 187
  New Colombo Plan, 192, 258
Comprehensive Economic
  Partnership, 71
Consultative Committee on Relations
  with Japan (CCRJ), 232–233
Coombs, H.C., 117
Court, Richard, 72
Crawford, John, 8–9, 11, 51, 56, 62
  academic study of Australia–Japan
    relations, 105–111

Agreement on Commerce
  between Australia and Japan
  (1957), 102–105
Australia–Japan Foundation
  (AJF), 117–118
impact on Australia–Japan
  relations, 45, 98
managing Australia–Japan
  relationship, 109–111, 119
*Raw Materials and Pacific
  Integration*, 107
relationship with Whitlam,
  111–116
report, 59, 107, 118
and Saburō Ōkita, 106–107, 118
trade relationship reforms,
  98–102
vice-chancellor of ANU, 105
Critchley, Thomas, 79, 83
cultural councils. *See* Australia–Japan
  Foundation (AJF)
cultural diplomacy, 3, 194–202,
  206–207, 210–211, 212–213.
  See also soft power
Cumes, J.W.C., 112
Currie, Neil, 61–63, 123, 130, 131,
  196
Curtin, John, 7, 46–47

Dalrymple, Rawdon, 65–67, 135,
  238–239
Darian-Smith, Kate, 219, 224
defence cooperation, 15, 71–72,
  172, 252, 256–257, 258. *See also*
  strategic cooperation
Australia–Japan Joint Declaration
  on Security Cooperation
  (JDSC), 71, 72–73
East Timor, 69
Japan–Australia Reciprocal Access
  Agreement, 74
Japanese peacekeeping, 66–67,
  68, 240

www.ingramcontent.com/pod-product-compliance
Lightning Source LLC
Chambersburg PA
CBHW040152270326
41928CB00040B/3303